Speaking Power to Truth

Cultural Dialectics

Series editor: Raphael Foshay

> *The difference between subject and object slices through*
> *subject as well as through object.*
> —Theodor W. Adorno

Cultural Dialectics provides an open arena in which to debate questions of culture and dialectic—their practices, their theoretical forms, and their relations to one another and to other spheres and modes of inquiry. Approaches that draw on any of the following are especially encouraged: continental philosophy, psychoanalysis, the Frankfurt and Birmingham schools of cultural theory, deconstruction, gender theory, postcoloniality, and interdisciplinarity.

Series Titles

Northern Love: An Exploration of Canadian Masculinity
Paul Nonnekes

Making Game: An Essay on Hunting, Familiar Things,
and the Strangeness of Being Who One Is
Peter L. Atkinson

Valences of Interdisciplinarity: Theory, Practice, Pedagogy
Edited by Raphael Foshay

Imperfection
Patrick Grant

The Undiscovered Country: Essays in Canadian Intellectual Culture
Ian Angus

The Letters of Vincent van Gogh: A Critical Study
Patrick Grant

"My Own Portrait in Writing": Self-Fashioning in the Letters of
Vincent van Gogh
Patrick Grant

Speaking Power to Truth: Digital Discourse and the Public Intellectual
Edited by Michael Keren and Richard Hawkins

Speaking
Power
to Truth

Digital
Discourse
and the Public
Intellectual

EDITED BY MICHAEL KEREN AND RICHARD HAWKINS

AU PRESS

Published by AU Press, Athabasca University
1200, 10011 – 109 Street, Edmonton, AB T5J 3S8

ISBN 978-1-77199-033-2 (print)   978-1-77199-034-9 (PDF)
978-1-77199-035-6 (epub)   doi: 10.15215/aupress/9781771990332.01

A volume in Cultural Dialectics series:
ISSN 1915-836X (print)   1915-8378 (digital)

Cover design by Marvin Harder
Interior design by Sergiy Kozakov
Printed and bound in Canada by Friesens

Library and Archives Canada Cataloguing in Publication
    Speaking power to truth : digital discourse and the public intellectual /
edited by Michael Keren and Richard Hawkins.

(Cultural dialectics)
Includes bibliographical references and index.
Issued in print and electronic formats.

    1. Intellectuals. 2. Intellectuals—Case studies. 3. Intellectual·life.
4. Digital media—Social aspects. 5. Communication—Social aspects.
I. Hawkins, Richard, author, editor II. Keren, Michael, author, editor
III. Series: Cultural dialectics

HM728.S64 2015   305.5'52   C2015-900477-2
                                                  C2015-900478-0

We acknowledge the financial support of the Government of Canada through the
Canada Book Fund (CBF) for our publishing activities.

This book has been published with the help of a grant from the Federation for
the Humanities and Social Sciences, through the Awards to Scholarly Publications
Program, using funds provided by the Social Sciences and Humanities Research
Council of Canada.

Assistance provided by the Government of Alberta, Alberta Media Fund.

 Canada Council Conseil des Arts **Government** Canadian Patrimoine
for the Arts du Canada **of Alberta** ■ Heritage canadien

Contents

Acknowledgements

This volume is the product of long conversations we held at the University of Calgary about the fate of knowledge, scholarship, and intellect in the emerging digital age. We are grateful to the University of Calgary and the Canada Research Chairs Program which allowed us to spend very fruitful years in this inspiring environment. We would also like to thank the Social Sciences and Humanities Research Council for a workshop grant that enabled us to invite the contributors to the volume for a two day workshop in which we all crystallized our ideas on digital discourse and the public intellectual. Andrea Matishak, Naor Cohen, Kerry McArthur, and Nycole Wetmore were helpful in organizing the workshop and preparing the book for publication. We are particularly thankful to the wonderful staff at Athabasca University Press for turning what began as corridor conversations into a meaningful work of scholarship: acting director Megan Hall, former acting director Kathy Killoh, interior book designer Sergiy Kozakov, cover designer Marvin Harder, and our highly professional and conscientious editor Pamela MacFarland Holway.

Introduction
New Challenges to Knowledge in the Public Sphere

RICHARD HAWKINS AND MICHAEL KEREN

The ability to imagine and to reason logically toward an outcome is an attribute that defines humanity and shapes human civilization. In every society, however, the social function and value of some individuals is defined primarily or exclusively in terms of thinking—of being able to perform intellectual work. The outcomes are learning and knowledge, but also the possibility for action. Almost by definition, once something new is known, the potential exists to do something new or to do it differently. Thus, human civilizations have generally accommodated the idea that the pursuit of knowledge is not an idle pursuit—that it has consequences, which, depending upon many circumstances, may be perceived in a positive or negative way by the power structures that govern these civilizations.

Perhaps because scholars, writers, scientists, and artists can be seen to perform a social function as intellectuals, they have often been characterized as a distinct community or even as a social class. Certainly throughout its history as a proper noun, "intellectual" has typically imbued its nominee not only with knowledge, insight, and expertise but also with social, political, and ethical responsibilities to intervene in issues of the day on behalf of the public good. There is, of course, no necessary connection between intellect and virtue, especially public virtue. Nevertheless, for as long as there have been intellectuals, there is evidence that they have been involved in public life, sometimes from within the political system, as advisors, experts, or administrators, but also from without, as critics, activists, and advocates.

It is this external and nominally independent role that has long held the closest association with the figure of the "public intellectual," whom, in various ways, the authors in this volume define or describe broadly as a person concerned with symbols and ideas who comments publicly on the social condition with the objective of influencing or guiding its future. In practice, however, it is actually very difficult to place public intellectuals within social role categories, partly because they typically place themselves in the position of attributing social roles to others. The sociological literature has mostly followed the notion proposed by Edward Shils (1970) of the public intellectual as having some contact with the transcendental. Public intellectuals were seen as burdened with a mission: to introduce society to a universal set of norms sanctioned by a higher authority, like the biblical prophet who speaks divine truth to earthly powers. This prototype lies at the core of works by Mannheim ([1936] 1968), Parsons (1970), and others who considered intellectuals to be located in a given society yet versed in a universal culture, nurturing it and feeding its values back to that society.

This somewhat romanticized notion finds its apogee in "speaking truth to power," which has become a cliché for the social function of the public intellectual. However, this aphorism can be challenged in that it is hardly as if "truth" in this idealized form is any stranger to power. Intellectuals can also seek and obtain formal positions of power after the manner of a Disraeli, Wilson, Paderewski, or Havel. Others can decline such positions and, after the manner of Zola or Gandhi, become more powerful than the powers to which they speak. Indeed, one could argue that it is precisely by confusing power and truth in the public mind that totalitarianism can flourish—a process in which, historically, many intellectuals have also been complicit (Arendt 1978).

Knowledge in Contemporary Political Discourse

Power also speaks to truth to the extent that truth is associated with knowledge as established through investigation, experimentation, evaluation, and documentation. The production and dissemination of knowledge is subject to powerful internal forces of governance and oversight. This fact tends more easily to be perceived negatively in terms of abuses like suppression or censorship. But much the same set of forces also serve the positive function of establishing standards of practice by which knowledge is pursued systematically and new contributions to knowledge are assessed and classified. What historically have been accepted as "truths," in the sense of distinguishing knowledge from opinion or fact from fiction, are themselves products of complex negotiations, often over long periods of time, between progressive and repressive forces that coexist within the inherently disputatious governance structures of knowledge production (Ziman 1978; Gibbons 1999; Latour and Woolgar 1979; Mulkay 1991).

This is particularly noteworthy when we construe a public voice for academics, whose work, unlike that of journalists, novelists, or advocates, is largely conducted and debated well out of the public gaze but whose intellectual credibility has a long historical association with independent evaluation and validation through peer review. Polanyi (1962) proposed that the internal dynamics of the scientific enterprise constitute a "republic," subject to its own enforced norms of behaviour, whose primary responsibilities are confined mainly to the practice of systematic inquiry, as opposed to the utility or social relevance of its outcomes. However, to the extent that such a republic exists, it is an easy target for subversion. For example, Canadian scientists employed by government laboratories are now faced with a dictate from the government in power that prohibits them from disclosing and discussing their scientific findings in media interviews even though they are allowed to present these findings to other scientists at academic conferences that are nominally public. In other words, talking to other scientists is allowed because the public generally does not participate in this discourse anyway. Talking directly to the public at large is not allowed. Thus, the internal dynamics of the scientific community are manipulated for purposes of political message management while avoiding charges of outright censorship.

Powerful internal and external forces shape the process by which knowledge is defined and produced, and not always to the good. The issues are compounded as regards the utilization of knowledge, which can depend on how closely that knowledge conforms to dominant political narratives (Connolly 1983; MacRae 1976; Majone 1989). These narratives are now most strongly inflected by economic imperatives. Already by the 1960s,

Heilbroner (1962) could detect this inflection in the terms of political discourse, in that the perception of the nation-state had evolved from that of a "community" or "society," implying a need to govern, to that of an "economy," implying a need to manage. In such a regime, knowledge becomes valued not as a pathway to social or civic enlightenment but according to its demonstrated ability to add to the national bottom line.

More than at any previous time, the social value of knowledge is becoming harnessed to the ideological construct of "market forces." Over the past thirty or so years, for example, it has become the norm for governments who fund academic research to justify this expenditure by stressing its economic utility (Mowery et al. 2004). The exact nature of this utility is usually crudely or dubiously defined, as the aim is more to bring science into line with dominant liberal or neoliberal social values than to realize any economic value from science. The result is that universities are pressured to demonstrate specific and often short-term economic returns on public investments in education and research and to participate directly in turning knowledge into money (Feller 1990). In the face of such pressures, the public space of intellectual life can appear less the domain of appeals to transcendental notions of ethics, morality, and justice and more that of hard-nosed economics, which its proponents would assume to embody social virtues (Keren 1993).

Substantiating the Intellectual Foundations of Public Speech

Apart from the problem of defining a social role or category for the public intellectual, attributing this role to individuals is also problematic. As with Kenneth Clarke's iconic description of civilization as something you can define only when you see it, it may seem that these figures are much easier to identify than to typify. The situation is further complicated by the fact that not everyone who is engaged in intellectual pursuits seeks or accepts opportunities to become a public figure. Thus, it can be difficult to discuss public intellectuals as a social and political institution apart from specific personalities whose points of view happen to achieve public prominence.

It is even more difficult to link what an individual might say in the putative role of public intellectual with any actual substance, other than position and reputation—in other words, to link public pronouncements with the fruits of systematic thought and investigation, whether in the form of facts and evidence or genuine insight. The question of evidence is important because, arguably, a unique quality of intellectually inspired contributions to public life, as opposed to the mere adoption and promotion of an opinion, is a sense that the contribution is rooted not just in awareness, which to a superficial extent anyone can acquire quite easily, but also in an epistemology. This assumption of epistemological rigour links contributions to debates of the day with an understanding of what knowledge is with respect to a particular subject, how to recognize it, how to differentiate it from ignorance, and how to define its relevance in different contexts.

It is precisely this issue of substantiation that forms the primary focus of this volume and that distinguishes its arguments and conclusions from most of the literature on this subject. Previous explorations of public intellectuals tend to be biographical, focusing on specific individuals who have assumed this role, or sociological, focusing on public intellectuals collectively as a social institution, or political, focusing on interest groups and movements associated with particular intellectual positions or ideologies. Our focus in this volume is squarely upon the question of intellectual substance. We are concerned to investigate the evolution of intellectual substance per se in the interaction between public life, as embodied in the issues and debates of the day, and intellectual life, as embodied in the production and dissemination of knowledge. In particular, our concerns lie with how the question of substantiation is faring in a public sphere increasingly dominated by an ever-expanding array of electronic media that are increasingly bereft of indications as to the source, credibility, or epistemological framework of the content they carry.

In the sense explored here, the public sphere refers generally to the milieu in which the institutions and practices of social and political governance interact with the general population engaged in everyday life. In the broad tradition of the Frankfurt School, extending from Horkheimer and Marcuse in the 1930s and 1940s to Habermas in the present day, critical theorists have explored various versions of the theme that the public sphere has become defined by communication media. The purveyors of media are seen to acquire great political power, both as gatekeepers and as shapers of the public consciousness. In this regime, who speaks is determined by who grants access to the media, with the content and nature of the speech itself being forged by this power relationship.

Certainly public intellectuals require access to the public via a communication platform of some description, whether it be the speaker's stump, the book, the editorial column, or, increasingly, the sound bite, the blog, or the Tweet. Historically, the access of individuals to communication media has been restricted, whether by political power, by commercial considerations, or simply by production and distribution costs. The basic political economy of what conventionally has been referred to as mass media—books, periodicals, and broadcast media—spawned a copious literature on elites that has strongly inflected most views of the public intellectual as a social institution. In this environment, achieving the social status of public intellectual might seem like the product of a Faustian bargain between the purveyor of ideas and the purveyors of media. Inevitably, the influence of the media also raises questions about the credibility, or reliability, of intellectuals in the public eye and about how the role of the public intellectual is constructed, particularly in relation to concerns regarding the criteria by which the interests that own and control these media select individuals for public exposure in this role.

Departing from this tradition, the present collection of essays ponders the future of intellectuals in a technologically mediated public sphere that is no longer characterized by scarcity but instead by abundance. Ours is an era defined by an expanding diversity of open and interactive communication media to which a majority of the world's population now has access. Apparently in stark contrast to the rise of the traditional mass media, which first fascinated critical theorists in the 1930s, never before has the potential been greater for more individuals to communicate more directly with others in a greater variety of ways and, superficially at least, with fewer, and lower, entry barriers and less restriction and oversight.

This change has spawned multitudes of claims and counterclaims to the effect that democratic processes and the conduct of public affairs are being transformed in this new milieu. The authors represented here take issue with these claims. From a variety of perspectives and in several different contexts, they question assumptions that have crept, whether intentionally or surreptitiously, into recent discussions of media and politics to the effect that truth is a simple function of the amount of speech. This quantitative approach to truth implies that, as technology enables the number of speakers to grow, power relationships will accordingly be transformed, such that democratic principles and goals are promoted and nurtured. This tendency is a particularly insidious new form of technological determinism, in which social and political dynamics are confused with technological characteristics. Because access to the Internet appears to be "open," the tendency is to argue either that this openness is a product of democratic social forces—a dubious historical assumption—or, worse, that public affairs as conducted in this sphere will adopt similarly open characteristics—a dubious technological as well as political assumption.

In terms of our central concern with substantiation—with what underpins the credibility of those who appear in nominally public intellectual roles, as well as the validity of their statements and the quality of their insights—this new abundance of access to the public sphere raises many intriguing issues. One is that entirely obscure or even anonymous individuals and groups can now have access to the means of communicating with a mass audience on much the same basis as identifiable individuals and established institutions. Another is that the kind of wisdom and sagacity once attributed only to identifiable individuals and institutions is now commonly attributed to crowds or conferred upon disembodied bloggers.

While the authors in this volume do comment upon the social role of the public intellectual, their main concern is with fundamental questions about the basic concepts of truth, knowledge, and power in the contemporary public sphere. Technology is not regarded merely as an enabler of communication but as yet another embodiment of powers that seek to shape and mobilize public opinion to various ends. Much as intellectual life is no guarantor of virtue, neither is access to the public sphere through new technology a guarantor of independence or objectivity, much less veracity. Thus, the authors are concerned less with what public intellectuals are or what they say than with what underpins the credibility of interveners in the public sphere who seek to influence issues of the day with appeals to symbols and ideas.

Such concerns are overtly political and not contingent upon any particular interpretation or resolution of broader philosophical debates about the definition of knowledge or the objectivity of science, questions that have entertained the human mind for millennia and, barring catastrophe, are likely to persist for millennia more. Unavoidably, the reflections presented in this volume must engage with various aspects of sometimes long-standing debates about both public intellectuals and evolving media. However, the aim is to go beyond these debates and to explore their implications for the future in terms of how the fruits of intellectual work will be incorporated into the public sphere in a world where access to the agora of ideas is puta-tively unrestricted. Will the intellectual as a community or class be rede-fined? Will intellectual activity thrive or lose relevance? Will it matter? Or how will it matter?

Synopsis

The following chapters represent a wide range of perspectives on the issues raised above and take several approaches to exploring different aspects of the role, function, and future of the intellectual in the public sphere. These essays are divided into two parts. The first part applies perspectives ranging from the empirical to the philosophical to general questions and issues per-taining to the nature of knowledge, the dynamics of knowledge production, and the place of intellectuals in public life. The second part focuses in on some of the real-life challenges that confront public intellectuals who oper-ate in the new technological milieu. These case histories have a pronounced existential dimension. Three of them are rooted in the concrete experience of their authors, who have embraced and/or been thrust into public intel-lectual roles. These chapters illuminate how this crucial issue of substantia-tion plays out in contemporary practice in today's media environment and demonstrate the many pitfalls that may await intellectuals in the evolving public sphere when they challenge the substance of prevailing views and popular opinions.

In opening part 1, Richard Hawkins goes to the heart of the knowledge production process by exploring the often uneasy historical relationship between science and scientists and the public sphere, and, more generally, the challenges that arise when knowledge producers in universities assume the role of public intellectuals. He argues that, in a political sense, this rela-tionship goes far beyond the public communication of science or the public debate over scientific issues. As he observes, the fruits of academic investi-gation must now compete in a new information "ether" in which many of the traditional knowledge hierarchies have become confused. This makes it more difficult to substantiate not only the legitimacy of statements and opinions that claim a basis in science but in fact the very relevance of claims to scientific validation. Hawkins discusses how this situation can weaken the status of science and scientists in the public sphere and also how the internal dynamics of science as a profession and a career can sometimes subvert attempts to shape social outcomes with appeals to evidence and rigorous analysis.

In chapter 2, Eleanor Townsley argues that, despite the encroachment of new media, long-standing, and traditionally elite, formats for the expression of ideas continue to exert significant force in the shaping of public opinion. Through an empirical comparison of the opinion columns in the *New York Times* and the *Globe and Mail*, Townsley explores the ways that cultural forces (including the media industry itself) work to influence who has the opportunity to speak in the "space of opinion," as well as defining the terms of the debate—observing, for example, that the debate among the purveyors of opinion in the United States reflects partisan polarization to a greater extent than in Canada. While acknowledging that digital formats have contributed to a certain fragmentation of opinion, Townsley suggests that the impact of new media lies more with their ability to multiply the former powers of syndication. Not only do digital formats enable the views of an opinion columnist to reach far beyond the readers of printed newspapers, but the increasing interconnectedness of the landscape of opinion allows for more rapid dissemination and commentary. As Townsley points out, insofar as this broader landscape conditions the shape of opinionated speech, we would do well to focus attention on the implications of the transformation of public intellectuals into media intellectuals.

In chapter 3, Jacob Foster carries the discussion into the new media environment, which is putatively oriented away from an elite media class. Specifically, he casts a critical eye upon the prospect that "epistemic collectivism," or the construction of a collective intelligence from many individual contributions, might, in an age of interactive electronic media, supplant the single, autonomous intellect, thus undermining any future place for individuals in traditional public intellectual roles. He proposes that such a construction fundamentally misunderstands the nature of intelligence, collective or otherwise, and suggests that it is unsubstantiated faith in the inherent superiority of collective intelligence that presents potentially the most significant problem for political discourse. For Foster, the role of public intellectuals in a world of social media is to constitute a "representative meritocracy" capable of mediating between different degrees of collective intelligence on the basis of the recognition of expertise. Far from undermining democracy, he argues, the creation of a "digital republic empowered by devotion to individual creativity and the critical sense" would rescue collective epistemologies from descending into the mentality of the mob.

Chapter 4 turns to a very different dimension of collectivism, one in which public activism is undertaken anonymously by online communities. Drawing on Kierkegaard's "The Present Age," with its image of a passive "phantom public," and on the work of Internet theorists such as Clay Shirky, Charles Leadbeater, and Geert Lovink, Liz Pirnie explores the topical phenomenon of "hacktivism" and probes the potential of organized online communities to engage the public in political debate. In place of autonomous public intellectuals, who are increasingly swayed by motives of self-promotion, she suggests that we need to look to decentralized networks of individuals who work collectively to translate social critique into real-world expressions of dissent. Through her investigation of the online community Anonymous and its efforts to expose social wrongs, she proposes that this form of action may emerge to fill a vacuum caused by the detachment of conventional political and social institutions from the publics they are intended to serve.

In chapter 5, Boaz Miller sets the stage for part 2 of the volume by situating the discussion of the epistemological role of public intellectuals—their function in setting out knowledge frameworks for the pursuit of social and political outcomes—within the context of calls for action on the part of specific public intellectuals on an issue of growing concern, namely, anthropogenic climate change. Focusing on the arguments advanced by two very high-profile Canadian public intellectuals, one with a scientific background, the other a novelist and social critic, he examines how the two construct very different epistemologies concerning exactly the same issue. In so doing, Miller also reengages the question of scientific evidence and the challenges of deploying it in an effort to sway public opinion. As he demonstrates, both David Suzuki and Margaret Atwood base their pleas for action on the claim that global warming is an incontrovertible scientific fact, and yet neither of the social epistemic frameworks they employ is entirely capable of supporting this claim.

Chapter 6 steps directly into the lived experience of public intellectuals. In 2003, Karim-Aly Kassam was named one of Alberta's fifty most influential people. His contributions to public life draw in part upon his applied research in human ecology conducted in the circumpolar Arctic and the mountains of Central Asia, two regions that furnish illustrations used in his chapter. By inverting the "speaking truth to power" aphorism, the title of this volume draws attention to the ways in which truth can be usurped by the powerful, not always in the public interest. Kassam nevertheless makes a compelling case that this need not be so—that it is not impossible for truth to usurp power. But he is also very clear about the personal preparation and humility, as well as the institutional integrity, that are required before the public intellectual can muster truth to these ends. Kassam accordingly emphasizes the manner in which individuals become prepared, especially through academic training, to assume roles as public intellectuals. University professors should, he argues, serve as exemplars for students by making a habit of public scholarship—an activity that arises out of a sense of civic responsibility and is in fact fundamental to intellectual life in a democracy. Moreover, rather than continuing to view teaching as separate from research, we must integrate applied research into pedagogical practices so as to encourage students to pursue new insights founded on the direct experience of life and on a commitment to bettering the human condition in ways that recognize and respect the environments and the web of relationships on which people depend for their survival.

In chapter 7, Barry Cooper reflects on his own encounter with public notoriety as a university professor cast into the role of public intellectual. He begins by reflecting on the modern figure of the public intellectual in the light of classical Greek conceptions of the role of the poet-philosopher in political life, as someone who opposed the rule of tyranny through reasoned philosophical critique. Cooper argues that this role gave way, in the twentieth century, to what he calls "the philotyranny of the intellectuals," who, while short on philosophical insights, are long on obscurantist jargon and ideological fealty. He goes on to put flesh on the bone by illustrating, from his own experience, the issues that come into play for academic governance when academic freedom is exercised to take positions that are polarizing or otherwise unpopular among substantial portions of the population. Somewhat ruefully, Cooper concludes that, aside from common sense and the ability to write reasonably clearly, public intellectuals in Canada today must be equipped with a keen sense of irony.

In chapter 8, Michael Keren concludes the discussion by exploring a similar experience, one pertaining not to the academic milieu but to new media and new forms of political discussion. The issue revolves around how those who offer commentary in the digital public sphere react to criticism of themselves. In this case, the criticism took the form of comments made by the author about the degree of influence that unsubstantiated opinion, of the sort that appears frequently on blogs, will have on political discussion—comments that, from the standpoint of bloggers, represented a dissenting position. Surveying the online response to these comments, Keren argues that public discourse in the new media cannot be compared to the Greek agora, as some scholars suggest, without considering warnings, such as those issued in 1930 by José Ortega y Gasset in *The Revolt of the Masses*, on the dangers of political discourse that lacks inner inhibitions or constitutional constraints. Online discourse engages more individuals in the public conversation than ever before and also broadens that conversation to include private concerns hitherto excluded from the public sphere. All too often, however, the disinhibition associated with online behaviour produces anything but the civil, reasoned discourse demanded of intellectual activity.

Taken together, the authors in this volume show that the most significant issues for the future of the public intellectual as a social institution go well beyond the technological or social evolution of communication media. Intellectuals face many new challenges, generated by a multitude of factors—by public attitudes toward learning and knowledge, by practical needs that require knowledge to be applied to solving problems, and, increasingly, by often new and different commercial imperatives. There are also challenges from within as many of the criteria that have historically defined the objectivity and credibility of intellectuals, in particular concerning science, come under scrutiny, and even attack, from intellectuals themselves.

In reality, power also speaks to truth, sometimes elevating it, often suppressing it. In today's media, opportunities have never been greater for the exploitation of ideas and symbols in countless causes and by increasingly faceless interests seemingly devoid of Ortega y Gasset's inhibitions and constraints. Nevertheless, in the face of these observations, it is by no means clear that any fundamental balance between power and truth in the new media environment is shifting. What is spoken continues to be powerful to the extent that it conforms to prevailing political narratives, which continue to be embodied in media of information and communication. That these media are evolving is beyond question, but this likewise has always been so.

As the essays in this volume suggest, while media may evolve, power still speaks to truth much in the same ways as ever. The substantiation of knowledge claims, as embodied in ideas and symbols, is not increased merely by disseminating them, or by sharing them, or by broadening the definitions of knowledge, but in some way by transcending the media of communication, as indeed has always been the lot of the public intellectual.

References

Arendt, Hannah. 1978. *A Life of the Mind*. New York: Harcourt Brace Jovanovich.

Connolly, William E. 1983. *The Terms of Political Discourse*, 2nd ed. Princeton: Princeton University Press.

Feller, Irwin. 1990. "Universities as Engines of R&D-Based Economic Growth: They Think They Can." *Research Policy* 19 (4): 335–48.

Gibbons, Michael. 1999. "Science's New Social Contract with Society." *Nature* 402, supplement (2 December): C81–C84.

Heilbroner, Robert L. 1962. *The Making of Economic Society*. Englewood Cliffs, NJ: Prentice-Hall.

Keren, Michael. 1993. "Economists and Economic Policy Making in Israel: The Politics of Expertise in the Stabilization Program." *Policy Sciences* 26: 331–46.

Latour, Bruno, and Steve Woolgar. 1979. *Laboratory Life: The Social Construction of Scientific Facts*. London: Sage.

MacRae, Duncan. 1976. *The Social Function of Social Science*. New Haven: Yale University Press.

Majone, Giandomenico. 1989. *Evidence, Argument, and Persuasion in the Policy Process*. New Haven: Yale University Press.

Mannheim, Karl. (1936) 1968. *Ideology and Utopia: An Introduction to the Sociology of Knowledge*. Translated by Louis Wirth and Edward Shils. New York: Harcourt, Brace and World. Originally published as *Ideologie und Utopie* (1929).

Mowery, David C., Richard R. Nelson, Bhaven N. Sampat, and Arvids A. Ziedonis. 2004. *Ivory Tower and Industrial Innovation: University-Industry Technology Transfer Before and After the Bayh-Dole Act*. Stanford, CA: Stanford University Press.

Mulkay, Michael J. 1991. *Sociology of Science: A Sociological Pilgrimage*. Milton Keynes, UK: Open University Press.

Parsons, Talcott. 1970. "'The Intellectual': A Social Role Category." In *On Intellectuals*, edited by Philip Rieff, 3–26. Garden City, NY: Anchor.

Polanyi, Michael. 1962. "The Republic of Science: Its Political and Economic Theory." *Minerva* 1 (1): 54–74.

Shils, Edward. 1970. "The Intellectuals and the Powers." In *On Intellectuals*, edited by Philip Rieff, 27–56. Garden City, NY: Anchor.

Ziman, John M. 1978. *Reliable Knowledge: An Exploration of the Grounds for Belief in Science*. Cambridge: Cambridge University Press.

PART I

Perspectives

1   Establishing the Public Legitimacy and Value of Scientific Knowledge in an Information Ether

RICHARD HAWKINS

We now live, so we are told, in a knowledge economy, one in which the produce of our intellect is replacing the produce of the land and our own hands as the engine of prosperity. Although hardly a new idea, its contemporary statement is unique to the extent that it associates the characteristics and dynamics of knowledge explicitly with information technologies and the communication capabilities they support. The instrumental association between intellectual work, technological infrastructure, and public welfare inevitably raises questions about what knowledge is, how it interacts in human affairs, and how technical change might intervene in this process.

In this regard, it is impossible to avoid discussion of the public role of academic professions, whose primary function is not merely to produce and disseminate knowledge but also to evaluate its quality and significance and to act as the organizers and caretakers of various fields of knowledge and expertise. Historically, this function has been regarded to be in the public interest, at least for the most part. However, the contemporary knowledge economy-society construct assigns significantly new public responsibilities to the academy that complicate its status as a producer and arbiter of knowledge.

My aim here is to contemplate evolution in the function specifically of scientific knowledge in public life and to speculate on the future of the academic scientist in the role of public intellectual. This aim will be pursued in the context of evolution in the media through which scientists communicate with each other and with the public. For the sake of clarity, I will adopt a somewhat Popperian description of science as the practice of observing natural, human, and social phenomena systematically through the logically rigorous exploration of theories and hypotheses (Popper 1958). For my purposes here, a scientist is someone who is engaged professionally in such pursuits, and scientific knowledge is the result.

Science never unfolds so neatly, of course. As Watson (1968) observed, even if science is objective, scientists most certainly are not, or at least not all of the time. Moreover, not all knowledge comes from science, and not all academics are scientists. Academics produce knowledge in many forms that do not involve science as defined above. (These academics face their own challenges in the public sphere, but I will leave this discussion to others.) Also, the academy has no monopoly on intellectuals, who can emerge from any walk of life. We would do well to recall that Thomas Paine, whose revolutionary political tract *The Rights of Man* (1776) not only fuelled at least two major political revolutions but was also the very first international blockbuster bestseller, was by trade a tobacconist, tax inspector, and erstwhile inventor (Foner 1976).

In the contemporary knowledge economy framework, however, science is explicitly defined *also* as a wellspring of "intellectual raw materials," which, it is presumed, will enhance public welfare in the form of new technology. This presumption casts science in a particularly narrow, instrumental role. Pragmatist philosophers have always argued that the evidence of whether genuinely new knowledge has been produced is that something genuinely different can be *done* as a result—in principle, a perfectly valid test (Pierce 1878; Dewey and Bentley 1949). The problems begin when questions about the utility of knowledge encounter the social dynamics of science as an institution and a political environment in which the legitimacy or reliability of scientific knowledge and evidence can, and often is, called publicly into question.

The contemporary imperative that science be useful generates a much broader group of direct stakeholders, each of whom may assess the value of science on the basis of different objectives, be they technological, political, or social. When this expanded group of stakeholders is coupled with the now seemingly limitless technologically mediated possibilities for public engagement and with an expanding array of knowledge sources, it becomes a serious question whether academics still enjoy any edge at all in the public forum.

In this essay, I will pursue three related arguments. The first concerns the new media themselves. I will argue that it is now impossible to consider various forms of media in isolation, as standing apart from one another. The current media environment is more appropriately viewed as the product of a consistent historical pattern of development, in which each new feature is but punctuation in a much longer trajectory that always has been driven by many of the same forces. The second argument concerns the role of science and scientists in public life. Here my basic premise is that an essential tension exists between science and scientists that can be very difficult to reconcile in the public sphere. As I will argue, by nature, and somewhat counterintuitively, science fits rather uncomfortably into the space typically occupied by public intellectuals, and always has, even though the scientist may at times fare quite well in this role. My third argument, which pertains specifically to the context created by new media, is that issues surrounding the public role of scientific knowledge are much deeper than the simple question of how science is projected onto the public stage or communicated to the public. I will propose that in order to understand how scientists may fare as public intellectuals from this point forward, it is important to comprehend how media, old or new, are incorporated into the practice of science.

The Information Ether and the Public Function of Science

It is often claimed that the epistemological landscape of public life—what counts as knowledge and who counts as a knowledge producer or "knower"—is being transformed by the vastly more extensive capabilities of interactive media to engage individuals in various forms of discourse and to provide instant access to vastly greater resources of information and knowledge. I will introduce arguments that tend to cast doubt on this hypothesis, but I am more concerned to address the obvious corollary, namely, that the credibility of science and scientists in the public forum may somehow be compromised by the so-called democratization of knowledge through electronic media.

For one thing, this notion overlooks the fact that scientists, too, are intensively engaged with these media, as is the practice of science. Indeed, the core technologies of contemporary public media—the Internet and the World Wide Web—began life as vehicles for collaboration between scientists and technologists. That they are no longer exclusive to science is, however, neither an indication that the public has become more scientific nor that science has become more public. My other objection, however, is that it is simply too convenient to lay this challenge at the feet of technology. Instead, I will lay it at the feet of science itself, where it has always belonged.

Eco (2005) noted perceptively that our age is characterized by a preference for technology *over* science—that technology has come to fill a deep-seated human need for magic, which, now as always, succeeds by short-circuiting cause and effect. As a method, magic is the antithesis of science, but I would propose that Eco's observation is valid for scientists too, because so much of science is and always has been dependent upon technology (Petroski 2011). Moreover, as Borgmann (1984) observed, it is often those who are most engaged with technology who fail most completely to comprehend its role in their lives. Thus, we must avoid disassociating the fundamental dynamics of science as a community from the debate over the origins and evolution of electronic media.

In technological terms at least, the new media provide enormous potential for scientists to gain greater and more direct access to the public and also for the public to gain greater access to scientific knowledge. A marriage made in heaven? Perhaps. But a marriage made in Las Vegas to be sure, which, fittingly, is where most new electronic gadgets are introduced to the world. We should be under no illusions that the commercial goals of the new media are symmetrical with the loftier goals of a knowledge society or that the political economy of media has any necessary association with that of science or of public affairs.

The developers of new media have imposed a constant stream of innovation in the way that content can be generated, stored, and distributed by and among an ever more heterogeneous population of producers, intermediaries, and consumers. Today, we are catching a glimpse of the outcome: a media environment that is utterly pervasive but also indiscriminate—one whose internal logic is to become insidious in every aspect of human life.

The "cloud" has become the newest metaphor for this milieu, but in practice the term refers mainly to a technical architecture for the storage and distribution of data. To the user, it may signify subliminally the increasingly ephemeral nature of the network environment. But to the technologist, it describes only an engineering problem: how to make the links between any type or source of data and any type or source of medium completely transparent. Its motives are commercial and strategic, not visionary or philosophical, and certainly not scientific.

For these reasons, I prefer to describe the social functionality of this system in terms of an "ether," which in my meaning incorporates both the archaic scientific concept of an invisible, featureless medium filling the space between particles of matter and the more poetic concept of something existing above and beyond the clouds—of something *ethereal*. The restoration of these concepts seems a rhetorically apt way to reconceptualize the current media environment as it relates to contemporary social and economic issues.

Since the 1930s, the political economy of media has been conceptualized mainly around infrastructure, with the problems defined in terms of how to create more "democratic," or at least more equitable, access (see Mansell 2010; Ruggles 2005; Garnham 2000; Smythe 1981). More recent events, however, whether in the nature of the Arab Spring or the London riots, have forcefully demonstrated that the most pressing social issues have moved well beyond access as such. Rather, they now concern *potentialities*—opportunities to identify, configure, and deploy various "particles" of both data and media that hang in this ubiquitous yet amorphous ether such that the configuration can yield some kind of envisioned result. This is social action, not technological application.

Basically, I am referring here to the dynamic organization of networks, not just around the fixed capabilities of a technological medium but in the service of some human purpose, whether frivolous or profound. The problem with dynamic systems is that they teeter unpredictably between conditions of stability and chaos (Bak and Paczuski 1995; Agar 2004; Perrow 1986). The traditional industrial solution to this problem in the various media sectors has been to impose an artificial stability through a mixture of market concentration, proprietary technical platforms, and sympathetic public regulation (Melody 1987; Mansell 1993; Ballon and Hawkins 2009). In truth, however, this strategy is itself unstable, and we can track the outcomes of significant perturbations in a succession of iconic, archetypal, and to a large extent conflicting corporate cultures—from IBM "machine" culture, to Microsoft "control" culture, to Google "search" culture, to YouTube "producer" culture, and now perhaps to Facebook "clan" culture.

The point is that all of these perturbations are the product of the same forces. In the ether, one culture does not disappear with the appearance of another, and each tends to recede to the characteristics of previous cultures—for example, all tend eventually toward monopolization. Moreover, these cultures have been primarily defined not by changes in technology but by innovations in how technology, content, and the consumer are configured (Napoli 2010; Hawkins and Vickery 2008). A glimpse into the ultimate logic of network building is provided by user-generated content. Consumers produce content, at their own expense, that is distributed by a commercial intermediary for consumption by other consumers. Commercial value is created for the intermediary—YouTube or Facebook, for example—but not for the producer, who works for free.

Such developments continue an historical process by which more and more forms of human communication become commodities, dependent upon a commercial intermediary in order to be realized in their social context (Smythe 1981; Jhally and Livant 1986; Cohen 2008). For, indeed, although much of the content in the ether is "free," the ether itself is not. The ether is a commercial environment within a gigantic global machine that has been building for nearly two centuries and that embodies the most massive single financial investment in any industry in human history. To be sure, it is also a public space, but only in the way that a shopping mall or sports stadium is a public space.

A critical question for what follows is whether what we might call the emerging "ethos-of-the-ether"—its evolving social conventions and practices—bodes well or ill for the role of science and scientists in the public arena. The roots of the problem were illustrated well by *New York Times* columnist Randall Stross (2008) in his exploration of the origins of Google as a company. Unlike IBM or Microsoft, which were built up, respectively, by engineers and hackers, Google was founded by a couple of academic scientists whose motivations were only partly commercial or even technological. Rather, they were normative, aimed at realizing a presumed imperative to exploit the full capabilities of digital technology in order to make all information available to everybody.

This is very much an activist's imperative, and it forms a kind of post-Cartesian dictum: *If something is possible technically, then it must be.* However, it may also represent a new form of tyranny—one that *imposes* information on the public rather than restricting it. With respect to any putative public role for scientists in creating, organizing, and validating systems of knowledge, this is no idle point. Information theorists have long noted that no linear relationship exists between information (data) and knowledge. Not only does an increase in information not yield a corresponding increase in knowledge, it may, in some situations, actually function to reduce knowledge (see Bialek and Tishby 1999). A much used metaphor is the narrative of infinite length. As a narrative gets longer by introducing more information, it accumulates meaning, until it arrives at a critical length, at which point adding yet more information will cause the entire narrative to deform, until at some point all of its meaning is lost. The implication would seem to be that if all of the information in the world were to be imposed upon us, nobody would know anything at all. Epistemological apocalypse!

All of this is, of course, highly theoretical. In practice, the information ether does not relate every particle to every other particle such that one potentially infinite and meaningless narrative would ever emerge—this is precisely why the ether metaphor is apt. The point that information theorists are trying to make is that knowledge emerges not from information as such but from the boundaries that are placed around it. Boundaries change as knowledge increases, and these changes constitute evidence of learning.

Traditionally, many of these boundaries have been defined by academic science in ways that have given science a significant role in public life, if not always an overtly activist role. The significance of the ether is not merely that information becomes available to more people. Rather, it is that the ether itself becomes not only the primary public interface with information but also the cauldron within which information producers and consumers can construct a potentially infinite number of boundaries that might reinforce or undermine the boundaries defined by academic science. Although in many respects the ether is an outcome of organized science, it functions as a naïve analogue of the social arena in which humans constructed knowledge before science and from which science emerged. Most of the questions about the future public role of science revolve around much deeper questions concerning the continuance of this cycle.

Science and Scientists in the Public Sphere

Currently it is fashionable to promote linking science more closely with political and economic life. For example, the doctrine of "evidence-based policy" would seem to compel decision makers to act in accordance with the findings of rigorous, systematic, and independent investigation. This can appear very attractive to scientists, but also dangerous (Pawson 2002). The obvious corollary is that if there is no evidence, or if the evidence is incomplete or ambiguous, which in science it often is, then an easy excuse is generated for taking no action at all. Or, worse, the evidence provider becomes a convenient scapegoat should the action fail.

In practice, evidence-based policy may be just another example of how science can be neutralized by co-opting it into politics (Jasanoff 1995; Leiss and Chociolko 1994; Majone 1989; Salter 1988). In the present context, however, it well illustrates how injecting science into the public debate has always presented special problems, owing to the many intrinsic limitations imposed by the conventions of science itself. Ironically, these may weaken the power of science to affect public opinion, often for the simple reason that the conventions of academic science are unfamiliar outside the academy and often do not conform to what non-scientists perceive scientists to be and to be doing.

Science as a "Problem" in Public Life

Regrettably, the only lasting outcome of the Copenhagen Earth Summit may be the debacle created by the infamous Earth Summit e-mails. These appeared to show that environmental scientists were being picky about the findings they chose to publicize in order to support only one side of the global warming debate. Political professionals skilfully transformed the disclosure of these messages into a general impression that all climate science was suspect or bogus. However, regardless of the motives in this particular case, it is actually quite typical for scientists to be strategic about what is and is not disclosed and where and when. In preparing critical editions of the lab journals of seminal figures in twentieth-century physics, Holton (1986)—himself an eminent physicist—concluded that, in choosing which findings to publish first, scientists normally privilege those that tend to support the theories in which they have the greatest confidence and to suppress those that do not. Holton suggests that it could not be other—that unlike most of us, who either choose to "believe" or "disbelieve," scientists must often "suspend disbelief," which is not a deception but a challenge to others to come up with better explanations.

The point is, however, that these climate scientists were not undone by the ether, which they could exploit as adeptly or ineptly as anyone, but by the persistent reluctance of science as a community of practice to deal with criticism and controversy that come from outside science and by a chronic failure to tell the public exactly what science is and how it works (Feyerabend 1993; Smolin 2007; Latour and Woogar 1979). If, indeed, the public face of science is being transformed by the new media, the cause lies not in the imposition of new media on science but in the *internal* relationship between the scientific community and these media.

But if the practices of science itself can be twisted so easily in the ether in order to discredit it in the public eye, how can scientists possibly construct or maintain any credibility in the same space? One obvious strategy is to humanize science by associating it publicly with the personalities of selected scientists, thereby disassociating it from the practice of science itself. This may or may not lead scientists into the role of public intellectuals, but it does create celebrities, who, by definition, are famous simply for being famous. Arguably, however, neither status reflects the actual nature of science as a profession or practice. Smolin (2007) observes that the most characteristic thing about doing science is its absolute tedium—the Eureka! moments coming rarely, if ever, and always in the wake of what in most professions would be considered a mind-numbingly impossible number of mistakes, blind alleys, and failed attempts. Whether it be Dr. Frankenstein, Louis Pasteur, or Sheldon Cooper, the popular image of the scientist through history has been far from the realities of science as a vocation and as a career.

Moreover, in public affairs, it is doubtful whether scientific celebrity enhances the stature of science *as knowledge*. It certainly has not provoked any new fervour to engage with science at a professional level. Enrolment in science degree programs has fallen dramatically in most OECD countries since the 1970s. Not that long ago, the *Los Angeles Times* reported that some California schools were displacing science altogether in order to make more room for instruction aimed at raising basic math scores (Watanabe 2011).

Nevertheless, the celebrity scientist phenomenon has flourished, and it provides a useful illustration of the major questions inherent in any process whereby scientists become established in the role of public intellectual. Do they assume these roles by dint of their scientific credibility? Or by extra-scientific criteria, where their credibility claim is not as clear-cut? In today's media-rich and celebrity-obsessed culture, what is known appears to count for much less than who appears to know it and who, or what, brings it to public attention.

The Role of Public Intellectual as a "Problem" for the Academic Scientist
In one banal sense, all professional academics are "intellectuals" by definition in that their job description is to engage in intellectual pursuits like teaching, research, and writing. Most are also "public" intellectuals in the sense that in most countries (the United States being the only significant exception) they are also typically public employees. In almost all cases, much of the knowledge they produce is supported by public finance and is nominally public property. Nevertheless, few academic scientists ever become public intellectuals in the sense that they acquire an identifiable personal voice that they then exercise in a public forum in order to advocate certain positions, including some that may go beyond the specific content of their scientific work, with the intent of influencing events and public opinion.

When Albert Einstein, still the most iconic of all scientific personalities, arrived in the United States just before World War II, he was already a public *figure* because of the notoriety of his theory of relativity, which, although understood scientifically by only a few dozen academic physicists world-wide, had already become the first "celebrity" theory of twentieth-century science. Everybody knew who Einstein was, even though almost nobody understood anything about what he had done. However, the Einstein of the 1920s and 1930s was not yet a public *intellectual*, at least not in the sense that he used his scientific reputation to engage and influence public opinion in any great cause. Arguably, this role came about in the first instance not because of his radical thinking about the universe, although ultimately that sustained him in this role, but because of his warnings about Nazism and the possibility of weapons of mass destruction. The former may have won him a Nobel Prize and the status of public figure, but, arguably, the latter won him the front page of the *New York Times* and the status of public intellectual. Einstein also knew the dangers of taking this step. That he understood the physics of nuclear weapons was beyond question, but he could claim no equivalent understanding of international affairs. As he later famously remarked, "politics is more difficult than physics."[1]

The waters are made murkier still in that, within the paradigm of a knowledge economy, economists and politicians argue that science and scientists are now also agents of economic growth, or anyway that they ought to be. This adds a completely new dimension to the public role of science, one that seriously complicates the question of how to establish the quality, objectivity, and significance of scientific knowledge and how to organize and govern science as an institution (Ziman 1991; Feller 1990; Mowery et al. 2004; Sampat et al. 2003).

The traditional equivalent of both "property" and "profit" in science has always rested in the *reputation* scientists achieve by contributing insights that can be uniquely attributed to them as individuals (Dasgupta and David 1994). Replacing reputational with economic criteria, even indirectly, has many implications and creates additional moral hazards for the conduct of science and the integrity of the peer-review process upon which its credibility depends. For example, stories have emerged in the media about the apparently common practice whereby pharmaceutical companies hire ghost writers to prepare papers for publication in reputable scientific journals such that the papers spin their findings in commercially useful directions. Medical researchers and practitioners are then induced to lend their names as authors in order to obfuscate the corporate origin of the paper and its commercial agenda.

However, corruption is hardly unique to commercial motives. Creating and enhancing scientific reputations is every bit as open to abuse (see Smith 2006). Anyone who takes on the eccentric task of trying to assess the demography or impact of science by looking at publication patterns is immediately bedevilled by self-citation, citation pooling, editorial-board stacking, and countless other reputation-enhancing devices that are as old as science itself. Again, however, such conceits are not products of the publication media as such, even though they may be facilitated by them.

More critically, there are serious questions as to how much credibility or influence even an uncompromised scientific reputation actually has in a public sphere dominated by the forced chatter of 24-hour news or the opinion mills of the blogosphere. It would be fairly safe to say that very few individuals owning a smart phone would know that contained within these gadgets are theoretical advances in physics that have won at least two

Nobel prizes. The actual prize winners are largely unknown to the public, and, for the most part, they have derived very modest commercial proceeds from these ideas, if any at all. Should they become concerned enough about an issue of the day that they feel compelled to use their Laureate status to attract an audience for their views, the question is whether their reputation would be built upon public comprehension that they have won the ultimate scientific accolade or upon some distant association with a rather mundane electronic gadget that can be mastered easily by any six-year-old. More to the point, if competing for public attention on any issue, how would these scientists fare against a Bill Gates, a Steve Jobs, or a Mark Zuckerberg, who would be associated much more personally with the same gadgetry by the same public constituency?

Today, it is very easy to forget that, even up to the 1950s, the prospect that science might have economic value was quite a radical new idea. Although Bernal (1939) first proposed this idea in the 1930s, it took another couple of decades to catch on. Even Schumpeter (1934, 1942), now revered (mostly wrongly) as the prophet of the modern high-tech economy, was initially dismissive of the idea that science or technology had any intrinsic economic value, a view he never really abandoned. The organization of experimentally based science in the research university as we know it today, along with links to industry, came about only in the mid-nineteenth century (Freeman and Soete 1997). It was not until the post–World War II period of economic reconstruction and conversion that massive and completely unprecedented public investments were made in basic science, most with the intention of weaving closer and more intricate linkages between science and the industrial fabric (Bush 1945; Ruttan 2006).

Interestingly, however, despite increasing political pressures to maximize the economic return-on-investment from the university system, independent surveys of the interactions between academic and non-academic communities, whether in commercial or non-commercial contexts, suggest that such interactions remain confined to a relatively small, stable, and quite specialized segment of the faculty, with the notable exception of those in medicine and, to a lesser extent, information technology (Cohen, Nelson, and Walsh 2002; Fini, Lacetera, and Shane 2010). Again with the main exception of medical science (which is vertically integrated with the health industries), they also tend to indicate that academic institutions rank among the least significant sources of knowledge that industrialists consider to be important for creating new products and services (Cosh and Hughes 2010). The situation is, of course, complex, and such findings require much contextualization and explanation. All the same, they do not suggest the emergence of any particularly noteworthy "axis" of coordination and cooperation between academic science and industry, especially not one that is attracting academic scientists in significant new numbers.

The reasons are not difficult to fathom. For the individual scientist, public engagement carries many dangers and pitfalls of a purely professional nature. Undoubtedly, they conflict with long-established and institutionally powerful ideals about the purpose and practice of science. Moreover, this inertia is sustained by long-established processes of academic career building, which in the modern academy typically do not award much merit for public engagement. Quite the opposite: severe penalties can attend an academic who dares stray too far from the Ivory Tower, or for too long.

Once firmly established, however, some scholars succeed in gaining additional stature from public exposure. For example, Stephen Hawking's admirable career as the public face of cosmology as challenging and baffling a branch of science as ever entertained the human mind—does not appear to have harmed his credibility as a theoretical physicist. But then Hawking is remarkably careful not to stray very far from talking about science, even when speculating about sensationalist topics like alien invasions or the existence of God. Probably wisely, he leaves to others any discussion of the possible implications of cosmology for the public interest. Then again, Paul Krugman (1994) once noted that even though Hawking might be the most famous physicist since Einstein, he was not yet a serious contender for a Nobel Prize.[2] That, following a decades-long parallel career as a high-profile journalist, Krugman himself would eventually win the prize entails plenty of irony, but it does not seem to have affected his own credibility as an academic economist. Will the same happy fate await a Richard Dawkins or a Steve Jones? When they tire of going toe-to-toe with creationists and religionists, will anyone remember that they were also leading evolutionary biologists?

Quite clearly, factors affecting the public reputation of scientists may vary according to the characteristics of different scientific fields. They may also be affected by philosophical or ideological predilections in the populace and in the political elites. Quite clearly also, the forum in which a scientist pursues a parallel career as a public intellectual must be chosen with utmost care, as must the parameters placed around what he or she chooses to comment upon in this role. There are many dangers for scientists who venture outside of science as such, not least that they can become separated from the science that gave them a public forum in the first place.

The Practice and Public Functions of Science in the Information Ether

My concluding argument is that the future public role of science and scientists in the information ether will be determined first and foremost not by how the ether is mobilized in the interests of science—that is, in a public information role—but by how it is incorporated into the practice of science as a career.

A former university colleague, a brilliant scientist who was once the recipient of a prestigious MacArthur "Genius" Fellowship, is fond of quipping that when you receive this award, your IQ automatically goes up 100 points, but when the award runs out, it falls mysteriously back to its original level. Like all really good quips, this one is both amusing and dreadfully close to reality, certainly in terms of what it implies for a career as an intellectual, public or otherwise. Prestigious awards, fellowships, and prizes sit at the pinnacle of a formal system of academic knowledge management that originated in the eighteenth century as a way to organize and assess scientific output in order that scientists could learn from one another and monitor the emergence of new knowledge. It still serves this function, but it has also evolved into a system for the formal evaluation and ranking of science, mainly for the purpose of allocating physical and financial resources.

In the system as it exists today, not only do the reputations of scientists and the quality of scientific institutions come under scrutiny, but increasingly even the validity or utility of scientific disciplines are ranked and compared. It is now routine for governments who fund universities to consider research in the natural, medical, engineering, and management sciences to have greater socio-economic value than history or the fine arts, even though there is no evidence that this is the case, and plenty that it is not (Fini, Lacetera, and Shane 2010; Stoneman 2010). This is reflected everywhere in the distribution of resources. In Canada, for example, less than 4 percent of the entire national research and infrastructure budget is allocated to the social sciences, arts, and humanities. The reason has nothing to do with the social utility of these fields; it is entirely a product of the assumption that intellectual work acquires value mainly in the form of technology. The disciplines that seem to be most directly associated with this outcome are measured in this context, and the others are not.

Thus, what began as a system oriented toward the organization of learning has evolved into a system oriented mainly toward academic administration and the external assessment of the value of intellectual work. This evolution is significant because it signals a change in the reasons for making science nominally public and for how scientific reputations are built. This in turn has implications for how and why science is conducted, for the forms that scientific knowledge takes, and ultimately for its claims of value and validity in the public sphere.

This evolution was motivated by a real problem, first documented by de Solla Price (1961). Starting in the mid-1950s, public resources for science, which since the 1940s had escalated to unprecedented heights, had begun a steep decline, especially if compared to the corresponding increase in the production of PhDs. As de Solla Price predicted, these curves have never again moved in the same direction. Goldstein (1993) noted that, already by the 1990s, the likelihood that a new PhD would find a tenure track job in science had fallen from an average of about 10 in 15 in the mid-1960s to just 2 in 15 (fifteen PhD students being the average number supervised by the average US professor over a career). Likewise, the chances of being awarded significant research funding in a typical academic career had shrunk dramatically. Certainly when the increased costs of doing science are factored in, this resource decline has never been reversed.

Partly in response to these pressures, the ranking system has become extremely convoluted and complex. But it remains basically a grown-up version of a game played by children in any sandbox, namely, determining through various proxies—who works where, owns which car or lawn-mower, or plays which sport—just whose mom or dad is the biggest, the strongest, or, in this case, the smartest. In the academic sandbox, aside from awards and prizes, the smartest are identified mostly in terms of who is producing the ideas that are being incorporated into the work of other scientists, mainly as determined by the so-called impact factor of the journals in which they publish, reckoned in terms of average numbers of citations. In some fields, but to a much lesser extent, patent filings and company formation (the so-called translation factor) can also be taken into account.

The entire system is governed by an interlocking system of quality thresholds and hierarchies upon which the progress of a career in academic science is assessed. Thus, the system is more likely to regard the scientist who publishes regularly in *Science* or *Nature* to be figuratively "smarter" than the one who does not—to say nothing of the one who publishes trade books and in popular periodicals. Likewise, the professor from Harvard or Oxford must perforce be smarter than the one from Eastern Tennessee or Portsmouth.

The fallacy common to the academy and the sandbox lies in the association by proxy of variables that can be observed and counted, like publications, awards, or patents, with those that cannot, like the quality or influence of an idea or of an intellectual. Worse yet, these proxies, although highly sophisticated technically, are far more dependent on the availability of data than on robust theories as to how the variables are associated (Basberg 1987).

In terms of the public perception of science, the system is practically invisible. However, some of its implications can be very direct. DeMaria (2003) cites an example, drawn from medical science, in which the efficient dissemination of new findings can be literally a matter of life or death. He notes how new knowledge can easily bypass the most relevant clinical constituencies simply because, for career advancement reasons, its authors chose to publish in journals that have the highest prestige value rather than in those that are regularly read by specialists in the most relevant fields of application.

Arguably, there has always been a close relationship between the actual content of science (the nature of what is being explored and discovered) and the "exposure" of science, referring not so much to how scientific theories and findings are explained to and understood by the broader public but to how scientists make it known to their peers what is scientific and what is not, what are significant findings and what are not, who are leading scientists and who are not. This more than any other factor supports claims for the special credibility and objectivity of academic science. However, the practice of ranking the output of scientists on the basis of published output is actually quite recent, dating only from the 1970s. Its original purpose was to mitigate the burgeoning resource crisis by providing "objective" proxies explicitly for the purposes of making more efficient resource disbursements (Martin and Irvine 1983).

Nevertheless, a declining resource base and an increasing workforce never yields happy outcomes, and, in this case, it creates multiple moral hazards. The peer-review principle may be useful in enabling scientists to learn from each other, but it acquires a very different dynamic when more and more peers are competing for shares of a dwindling resource pool. Imagine, for example, a bidding process for a commercial contract in which each bid is evaluated by those who have submitted competing bids.

The system seems less transparently flawed in the academic context because it retains a certain intrinsic meritocratic logic and also because, despite its flaws, it appears to work at some level. Thus, it is true that not all scientists who publish in *Nature* are really top tier, but it is also true that few genuinely top-tier scientists have not published in *Nature*. In terms of public perceptions, however, given that *Nature* is read almost exclusively by scientists themselves, the public logic of the system entails likely a higher assumption of credibility for a Harvard professor than for a local community college instructor, even though both may have published in *Nature*.

Ranking Knowledge in the Ether

Probably the most obvious effect of the ether upon the knowledge system is that it provides an extraordinarily broad potential for the development of new proxies and also for the construction of new ranking systems. The public implications of this potential can be observed simply by plugging the same search term into the Google general site and the Google Scholar site. Some of the same materials will come up on the first page, but most likely in a very different order and from a much wider range of sources. Although the comparison would not be scientific, given the way Google assigns listing priorities, it would be nonetheless a fairly good demonstration that the knowledge goals evident on the public site would be very different from those on Google Scholar. Perhaps with Google we have, for the first time, a means of comparing the knowledge priorities of the public and academic spheres.

Another effect is public accessibility to rankings that academics cannot themselves control. For example, any ambitious prospective university student can now consult online a half dozen or so statistically rigorous assessments of the quality of thousands of universities and academic departments around the world based upon such indicators as the average number of faculty publications and citations in top-ranked journals, success in attracting research funds, student-faculty ratios, or even Nobel and Field Prizes. These determinations may or may not yet affect how students select which universities to attend, but they are already exercising university presidents to add yet another metric to the quality regime to which academic staff is expected to contribute.

Moreover, these "unofficial" rankings often prioritize indicators that are not prioritized in normal faculty assessments. For example, one of the leading university-ranking schemes evaluates the impact of university departments according to the numbers of downloads of working papers and other ephemera, including reports and briefings intended for public consumption, on the assumption (quite correct) that these are often closer to the leading edge of science, and of higher general impact, than publications in journals, which may lag the research by years and are mostly incomprehensible for purposes of public dissemination.

A potentially positive factor is that many scientists now use the ether to supplement, if not to bypass, the official ranking regime by communicating directly to the public. Look at virtually any web site of any department in any university and you would have to conclude that any member of that department for whom there was no link to a personal blog, web page, or the like was trying to hide something. In this respect, scientists have come out of the closet. Or have they? Many science blogs are published under pseudonyms, thus breaking the characteristic reputational bond between the science and the scientist. Moreover, publicizing your own work is clearly not the same thing as being, for want of a better term, "acclaimed" as a public intellectual by some external court of opinion.

Ultimately, one is left with doubts as to whether the new media offer a way out of some of the dilemmas faced by science and scientists in the public arena or whether they merely reinforce them by substituting different methods of surveillance and enforcement of professional norms within the scientific professions. For example, what would be the consequences should an anonymous blogging scientist be "outed," especially if what is published informally contradicts what has been published formally or draws out more direct and controversial public implications? Perhaps the more serious questions, though, concern the reasons that scientists might feel the need to circumvent or subvert the formal institution of science in the first place.

Knowledge Ranking and the Elevation of Scientists as Public Intellectuals

What seems sure is that Einstein's experience exemplifies a peculiar and perhaps obsolete process whereby scientific reputations can be transformed by opportunity and circumstance into reputations for general sagacity about issues of the day. Indeed, it is remarkable, and perhaps even salutary, that as Einstein's significance as an active contributor to science waned, the frequency of his public comments about a greater variety of other issues increased. However, it must be recognized that by the standards of the information ether, Einstein also had little competition for public recognition and did not really have to work at the task of becoming a public intellectual. He did not have to maintain a web site, or a blog, write a popular book, host a TV series, or even to climb the academic career ladder. In fact, throughout most of his career, he never held a mainstream academic position with normal duties and expectations. Moreover, he never had to contest his scientific credibility when making comments about matters outside of science. By today's standards, he had it easy.

Of course, scientists of Einstein's generation worked within a very different paradigm. How this evolved exemplifies the structural problem of how the knowledge-centered ethos of science can conflict with the information-centered ethos of the ether. Faced with the sheer volume of knowledge production in the past fifty years, scientists have inevitably become more specialized, and discoveries and insights have become more incremental. Accordingly, it has become more typical for scientists to cast the public issues of the day in narrower scientific contexts and to propose basically technical solutions. These may be valid solutions, but only in exceptional circumstances do they grab the public imagination and propel a scientist into a public role.

As Smolin (2007) notes, since the 1950s the theoretical sciences in particular have become largely a world of faceless expertise and arcane scholasticism rather than of expansive personalities and viscerally appealing theories like relativity or the Big Bang. Such observations are by no means unique to the natural sciences. In reflecting upon his tenure as editor-in-chief of the *American Economic Review*, one of the signature journals in economics, Clower (1989, 27) observed regarding new submissions: "What was remarkable was the absolute dullness, the lack of any kind of new idea. . . . Close to a thousand papers a year—and I swear that the profession would be better off if most of them hadn't been written, and certainly if most hadn't been published." Comments such as these raise questions as to whether science is somehow compromising its own credibility in the public mind by its own hand. The effect of new media in this endeavour may not even matter.

Jumping to such a conclusion, however, merely ignores the fact that knowledge can now be disseminated more efficiently than it can be produced and that scientists are under ever-increasing pressure to produce simply in order to advance their careers. Coupled with specialization, these pressures inevitably lead away from the radical conceptual breakthroughs characteristic of the early twentieth century and toward a dialectic of tiny increments.

Conclusion

Science will be a viable platform for the public intellectual not just to the extent that it can be made *intelligible* to the public—which is not always possible—but to the extent that its outcome or content has genuine social, economic and political significance that is *evident* to the public irrespective of how well they understand it as science.

This task will be easier in some fields than in others. The obvious utility of antibiotics can completely mask the much less obvious utility of high energy physics, even though it is actually not that difficult for any reasonably educated citizen to comprehend its utility, once explained. The real danger is that the dynamics of science as a profession may lead to a failure of explanation and of public engagement. This danger is the direct product of a disconnect between how knowledge is produced and how scientific careers are built. The ether already plays a huge role in reinforcing this disconnect. The question is whether the scientific professions can also mobilize it to thwart this result.

Notes

1 The remark was attributed to a conversation at Princeton University in 1946, later documented by Greenville Clark in the *New York Times* (22 April 1955).
2 Krugman also neglected to explain fully that, under the rules, Nobel Prizes in the natural sciences are not awarded for theory, which is

Hawking's strong suit, until and unless that theory has been demonstrated empirically in some way. Einstein's theory had to wait over a decade for the demonstration that secured him the prize. The Nobel Prize for economics, a recent addition, requires no such demonstration.

References

Agar, Michael. 2004. "We Have Met the Other and We're All Nonlinear: Ethnography as a Nonlinear Dynamic System." *Complexity* 10 (2): 16–24.

Bak, Per, and Maya Paczuski. 1995. "Complexity, Contingency and Criticality." *Proceedings of the National Academy of Sciences* (USA) 92: 6689–96.

Ballon, Pieter, and Richard Hawkins. 2009. "Standardization and Business Models for Platform Competition: The Case of Mobile Television." *International Journal of Information Technology Standards and Standardization Research* 7 (1): 1–12.

Basberg, Bjørn. 1987. "Patents and the Measurement of Technological Change: A Survey of the Literature." *Research Policy* 16: 131–41.

Bernal, John Desmond. 1939. *The Social Function of Science*. New York: Macmillan.

Bialek, William, and Naftali Tishby. 1999. *Predictive Information*. arXiv:cond-mat/9902341v1 [cond-mat.stat-mech].

Borgmann, Albert. 1984. *Technology and the Character of Contemporary Life*. Chicago: University of Chicago Press.

Bush, Vannevar. 1945. *Science—the Endless Frontier: A Report to the President on a Program for Postwar Scientific Research*. Washington, DC: US Government Printing Office.

Clower, Robert W. 1989. "The State of Economics: Hopeless but Not Serious?" In *The Spread of Economic Ideas*, edited by David C. Colander and A. W. Coats, 23–30. Cambridge: Cambridge University Press.

Cohen, Nicole S. 2008. "The Valorization of Surveillance: Towards a Political Economy of Facebook." *Democratic Communiqué* 22 (1): 5–22.

Cohen, Wesley, Richard Nelson, and John P. Walsh. 2002. "Links and Impacts: The Influence of Public Research on Industrial R&D." *Management Science* 48: 1–232.

Cosh, Andy, and Alan Hughes. 2010. "Never Mind the Quality Feel the Width: University-Industry Links and Government Financial Support for Innovation in Small High-Technology Businesses in the UK and the USA." *Journal of Technology Transfer* 35: 66–91.

Dasgupta, Partha, and Paul. A. David. 1994. "Toward a New Economics of
Science." *Research Policy* 23: 487–521.

de Solla Price, Derek J. 1961. *Science Since Babylon*. New Haven: Yale
University Press.

DeMaria, Anthony N. 2003. "Editors Page: A Report Card for Journals."
Journal of the American College of Cardiology 42 (5): 252–53.

Dewey, John, and Arthur Bentley. 1949. *Knowing and the Known*. Boston:
Beacon Press.

Eco, Umberto. 2005. "Science, Technology and Magic." In *Turning Back the
Clock: Hot Wars and Media Populism*, 103–12. New York: Harcourt.

Feller, Irwin. 1990. "Universities as Engines of R&D-Based Economic Growth:
They Think They Can." *Research Policy* 19 (4): 335–48.

Feyerabend, Paul. 1993. *Against Method*, 3rd ed. London: Verso.

Fini, Riccardo, Nicola Lacetera, and Scott Shane. 2010. "Inside or Outside the
IP System: Business Creation in Academia." *Research Policy* 39: 1060–69.

Foner, Eric. 2005 [1976]. *Tom Paine and Revolutionary America*. Oxford:
Oxford University Press.

Freeman, Christopher, and Luc Soete. 1997. *The Economics of Industrial
Innovation*. Cambridge, MA: MIT Press.

Garnham, Nicholas. 2000. *Emancipation, the Media, and Modernity:
Arguments About the Media and Social Theory*. Oxford: Oxford
University Press.

Goldstein, David. 1993. "Scientific PhD Problems." *American Scholar* 62 (2):
215–220.

Hawkins, Richard, and Graham Vickery. 2008. *Remaking the Movies: Digital
Content and the Evolution of the Film and Video Industries*. Paris: OECD.

Holton, Gerald James. 1986. *The Advancement of Science, and Its Burdens:
The Jefferson Lecture and Other Essays*. Cambridge: Cambridge University
Press.

Jasanoff, Sheila. 1995. *Science at the Bar*. Cambridge, MA: Harvard University
Press.

Jhally, Sut, and Bill Livant. 1986. "Watching as Working: The Valorization of
Audience Consciousness." *Journal of Communication* 36: 124–43.

Krugman, Paul. 1994. *Peddling Prosperity: Economic Sense and Nonsense in
the Age of Diminished Expectations*. New York: W. W. Norton.

Latour, Bruno, and Steve Woolgar. 1979. *Laboratory Life: The Social
Construction of Scientific Facts*. London: Sage.

Leiss, William, and Christina Chociolko. 1994. *Risk and Responsibility*.
Montréal and Kingston: McGill-Queen's University Press.

Majone, Giandomenico. 1989. *Evidence, Argument, and Persuasion in the Policy Process*. New Haven: Yale University Press.

Mansell. Robin. 1993. *The New Telecommunication: A Political Economy of Network Evolution*. London: Sage.

———. 2010. "The Life and Times of the Information Society." *Prometheus* 28 (2): 165–86.

Martin, Ben R., and John Irvine. 1983. "Assessing Basic Research: Some Partial Indicators of Scientific Progress in Radio Astronomy." *Research Policy* 12 (2): 61–90.

Melody, William H. 1987. "Information: An Emerging Dimension of Institutional Analysis." *Journal of Economic Issues* 21 (3): 1313–39.

Mowery, David, Richard Nelson, Bhaven Sampat, and Arvids A. Ziedonis. 2004. *Ivory Tower and Industrial Innovation: University-Industry Technology Transfer Before and After the Bayh-Dole Act*. Stanford, CA: Stanford University Press.

Napoli, Philip M. 2010. *Audience Evolution: New Technologies and the Transformation of Media Audiences*. New York: Columbia University Press.

Pawson, Ray. 2002. "Evidence-Based Policy: The Promise of 'Realist Synthesis.'" *Evaluation* 8 (3): 340–58.

Peirce, Charles S. 1878. "How to Make Our Ideas Clear." *Popular Science Monthly* 12 (January): 286–302.

Perrow, Charles. 1986. *Complex Organizations: A Critical Essay*, 3rd ed. New York: Random House.

Petroski, Henry. 2011. *The Essential Engineer: Why Science Alone Will Not Solve Our Global Problems*. New York: Vintage Books.

Popper, Karl. 1958. *The New Scientific Spirit*. Boston: Beacon Press.

Ruggles, Myles. 2005. *Automating Interaction: Formal and Informal Knowledge in the Digital Network Economy*. Creskill, NJ: Hampton Press.

Ruttan, Vernon. 2006. *Is War Necessary for Economic Growth?* Oxford: Oxford University Press.

Salter, Liora. 1988. *Mandated Science: Science and Scientists in the Making of Standards*. Dordrecht: Kluwer.

Sampat, Bhaven, David Mowery, and Arvids A. Ziedonis. 2003. "Changes in University Patent Quality After the Bayh–Dole Act: A Re-examination." *International Journal of Industrial Organization* 21: 1371–90.

Schumpeter, Joseph A. 1934. *The Theory of Economic Development: An Inquiry into Profits, Capital, Credit, Interest and the Business Cycle*. Translated by Redvers Opie. Cambridge, MA: Harvard University Press.

———. 1942. *Capitalism, Socialism and Democracy*. New York: Harper & Brothers.

Smith, Richard. 2006. *The Trouble with Medical Journals*. London: Royal Society of Medicine Press.

Smolin, Lee. 2007. *The Trouble with Physics*. New York: Houghton Mifflin Harcourt.

Smythe, Dallas W. 1981. *Dependency Road: Communications, Capitalism, Consciousness and Canada*. Norwood, NJ: Ablex.

Stoneman, Paul. 2010. *Soft Innovation: Economics, Design, and the Creative Industries*. Oxford: Oxford University Press.

Stross, Randall. 2008. *Planet Google: One Company's Audacious Plan to Organize Everything We Know*. New York: Free Press.

Watanabe, Teresa. 2011. "California Teachers Lack the Resources and Time to Teach Science." *Los Angeles Times*, 31 October.

Watson, James D. 1968. *The Double Helix: A Personal Account of the Discovery of the Structure of DNA*. New York: Atheneum.

Ziman, John. 1991. *Reliable Knowledge*. Cambridge: Cambridge University Press.

2 Public Intellectuals, Media Intellectuals, and Academic Intellectuals

Comparing the Space of Opinion in Canada and the United States

ELEANOR TOWNSLEY

What are the conditions under which intellectuals compete to narrate social life in the public sphere? In what follows, I examine this question through a comparative analysis of the opinion columns published in two elite newspapers, one in Canada and one in the United States. Drawing on insights from field analysis (Bourdieu and Passeron 1990; Bourdieu 1993, 1996, 1998, 2005), theories of the public sphere (Habermas 1989, 1996), and the growing number of empirical studies of civil societies and public spheres (Jacobs and Townsley 2011; Schudson 2011; Somers 2008; Alexander 2006, 2010; Wuthnow 2002; Putnam 2001; Jacobs 2000; Eliasoph 1998; Lichertman 1996), I ask several questions. To what extent are the elite spaces of opinion similar in the two countries? Do they possess a similar internal composition? And what does our understanding of the institutional landscape of public conversation suggest about strategies for public intellectuals in the early twenty-first century?

Public Intellectuals and the Space of Opinion

This chapter builds on two ongoing lines of research, one concerning public intellectuals and the other the space of opinion. Both attempt to map the institutional contexts in which intellectuals operate. Both are also concerned with developing an empirical approach that can illuminate how intellectual products circulate across different cultural fields over time. The goal is to understand the dynamics of the cultural traffic in intellectual tropes and traditions (Beilharz 1997; Smith 1998; Appadurai 1996; Kauffman and Patterson 2005).

In the first line of research, I analyze the use of the term "public intellectual" in the elite political public sphere of the United States. If the public sphere is that part of society where political and cultural elites discuss matters of common concern, then the term "public intellectual" is an important political trope that circulates in the public sphere and operates as a cultural shorthand to hold, contain, and organize moral tension about intellectuals and politics in the contemporary United States (Townsley 2006, 40). Since the adoption of the public intellectual trope in the elite public sphere of the United States in 1987, it has attracted authors and meanings, and has become fully normalized as a part of the public conversation about intellectual life.

As a practical point of departure, in this research I charted attributions of public intellectual status in elite news media (Townsley 2006). By dismissing the fraught question "Who truly is an intellectual?" in favor of asking, "Who attributes intellectual status to whom and why?" I was able to identify the intellectual stakes at issue in debates about public intellectuals that occurred in the last quarter of the twentieth century. This line of investigation was further developed in collaborative research on Canada with Neil McLaughlin (McLaughlin and Townsley 2011). Tracing every mention of the term "public intellectual" in twenty-five English-language newspapers in Canada between 1988 and 2005, we mapped the cultural diffusion of US debates about public intellectuals as they were adopted and adapted in the public sphere of English-speaking Canada. Throughout, we deliberately sought to ground our analysis in an extended comparison of the institutional geographies of cultural fields in Canada and the United States.

This comparison shows that despite institutional similarities between the countries, debates about public intellectuals in Canada and in the United States have been conducted in nationally specific terms. First, in English-speaking Canada, such debates are typically refracted through concerns about Canadian national identity, with issues of "Canadianness" and the role of the Canada Council occupying a prominent place. In the

United States, while the discussion is still concerned with national identity and domestic political issues, it is far more self-referential in the sense that it imagines the US to be at the center of every story and issue.[1] When other countries are mentioned in the US debates about public intellectuals, it is usually in the context of a universal narrative of human experience to which the US debate is heir in a long-standing Western tradition. Second, in the United States, the main issue is a conservative critique of the university and the liberal political agendas associated with the 1960s and, later, with multiculturalism. In Canada, by contrast, political criticism of academics is both less common and less bitter, and debates about public intellectuals are less subject to the ideological divisions of party politics that dominate political discourse in the United States.

A close historical analysis of how different speakers use the term public intellectual in Canada shows the influence of French and British traditions of intellectual and public discourse. The way that conservative intellectuals use the public intellectual trope in particular tends to be more ironic and British than is the case in the United States. Of course, the landscape of conservative cultural and media institutions in Canada has also changed over the last 30 to 40 years, and these changes may indicate a convergence in conservative intellectual styles. At this point, however, this is an open question.

Finally, research on the diffusion of debates concerning public intellectuals shows that in Canada, as elsewhere, the cultural fields of journalism, the academy, and politics are unevenly globalized. For example, Canadian academics, like their counterparts in other countries, are more likely than either politicians or journalists to define themselves and their work in terms that are more global.[2] In every cultural field, however, there are elite career paths from Canada to the United States and (sometimes) back again.

The second line of research on which the current analysis draws is a large collaborative project on intellectuals and the space of opinion in the United States that I undertook with Ron Jacobs (Jacobs and Townsley 2011). This work defines the space of opinion as an especially influential part of the elite political public sphere where intellectuals participate in a critical dialogue with political elites, sometimes on behalf of a citizen-audience. Such intellectuals are media intellectuals. Formally defined, the space of opinion is that part of the public communicative infrastructure in which the elites of our huge, complex societies debate matters of common concern. We follow Bourdieu (2005) in locating this space at the overlapping intersection of several institutional orders. These include the journalistic field, from which the space of opinion was born, as well as the media field more generally, including entertainment media. The space of opinion also intersects the traditional political field of democratic institutions and office holders and the relatively new, field-like space of think tanks, lobbies, and advocacy groups, which are increasingly oriented toward, and even embedded in, the media. In addition, the space of opinion overlaps with the academic field and other cultural fields, including trade publishing, small literary magazines, commercial and independent film, comedy formats, and so forth. Indeed, the "softer" sections of the newspaper—Arts, Sports, Lifestyle, Society, and so forth—all have their own opinion columnists, who are connected to the political columnists at the same time that they are connected to the cultural fields on which they provide commentary (Diamond 1993).

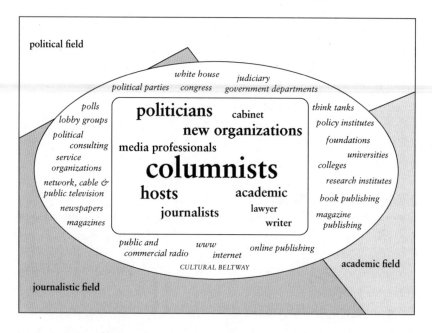

Figure 2.1. The social space of opinion in the United States

Figure 2.1 provides a schematic depiction of the space of opinion in the United States, using data from the US sample to scale the size of the type so that it is proportional to the number of opinion authors from various institutional backgrounds (Jacobs and Townsley 2011, 85). It shows that professional columnists occupy the most territory in the space of opinion, followed by politicians, while lawyers and writers (and, to a lesser degree, academics) have a much smaller share.

The prominent position of columnists reinforces a central finding of this research, namely, that traditional formats of opinion, such as the elite newspaper column, continue to play a central role in organizing large public conversations about matters of common concern. This continues to be true despite the decline in print readership and the proliferation of new media in recent decades. To be sure, there is evidence that readership has become more segmented and that readers consume fewer opinion texts (such as national newsmagazines) that are shared across broad audiences. Many have also observed heightened partisanship in the space of opinion too (Baum and Groeling 2008; Jamieson and Cappella 2008; Morris 2005; Kull 2003; Sunstein 2001). All of this is cause for concern if we are committed to an ideal of traditional democratic deliberation based on open, rational, evidence-based public discussion. Our joint research takes note of a different trend, however, that cuts across these findings about cultural frag mentation—the ever-increasing interconnection between opinion formats. In addition to the traditional authority associated with elite print outlets, elite print columnists, such as those who write for the *New York Times*, now enjoy a much wider celebrity through the syndication and republication of their opinions, especially in digital formats that circulate through ever expanding social media. In this increasingly interconnected landscape of opinion, the role of the elite newspaper columnist may be more important than ever.

Many new formats are also connected to one another through an emergent mode of media metacriticism. In this mode, opinion authors working in one format monitor and criticize news and opinion generated in other formats. There is evidence that even the most highly partisan outlets monitor opinion in the mainstream press such as the *New York Times* and engage in multiple levels of intertextual referencing (Jacobs and Townsley 2011). This intertextuality has been particularly important for conservative media outlets in the United States (Jacobs and Townsley 2014). It is not surprising to find figures such as Fox News Channel commentator Sean Hannity, as well as columnists and hosts on public television, quoting opinion in the *New York Times* to initiate a debate or open an interview. In fact, intertextual claims to authority have a long history in opinion formats, especially in the wider space of television, where hosts use opinion from a range of elite newspapers to ground interviews with prominent political figures as well as journalistic debates about politics and public policy.

In short, traditionally print-based (but evolving) media formats remain centrally important to the space of opinion, a space that is increasingly interconnected both technically and textually. The space of opinion is also the institutional setting in which sociologists, philosophers, scientists, and literary academics compete with journalists, politicians, and lobbyists to define social objects and to narrate social life. Most scientific findings are interpreted for the public "downstream" from the academy by journalistic gatekeepers such as science reporters and book review editors, who have ready access to mass media (Gieryn 1999). Similarly, much political life occurs in and through mass media (Townsley 2011): for example, Barack Obama accepted the US presidency on television in November 2008 in front of a celebrating world, well before his official inauguration in January 2009. Intellectual and political claims are of course made in a range of cultural fields—philosophy, the natural and social sciences, the humanities and the arts, as well as business and politics—but it is in the space of opinion that such claims are typically parsed as part of a (more or less) centralized social learning process enabled by the communicative institutions of the public sphere. The space of opinion can therefore serve as a strategic research site for examining how intellectuals proffering opinions compete to narrate the issues of the day to a broader public.

Intellectual Fields in Canada and the United States

Broad institutional similarities exist in the intellectual life of Canada and the United States. In both countries, the elite spaces of opinion are located at the complex intersection of journalism, the academy, and politics. Both countries are liberal democratic capitalist societies with overlapping political histories. This history includes a commitment to freedom of the press rooted in a common British tradition, which, in Canada, is further informed by the French tradition of the public intellectual. A dense network of ties also exists between Canadian and US institutions, as both people and texts circulate across and between cultural fields in the two countries over time (McLaughlin and Townsley 2011).

At the same time, Canadians frequently express concern about the asymmetry of the relationship between Canada and the United States, given that the latter is a much larger, more internationally dominant, wealthier, and more culturally self-referential society than their own. As a result, considerable ambivalence exists in Canada with regard to the influence of the United States in politics, journalism, and academia. This influence is real, and yet important differences exist between the two countries that are likely to affect the space of opinion.

Looking first at the journalistic field, although Canada's national newspaper, the *Globe and Mail*, has a lower circulation than the *New York Times*, the *Globe* plays a similar role in Canadian intellectual and political life: it is the paper of record that documents and centralizes the national conversation about political and cultural topics. Up to a point, this might also be said of some other newspapers, notably the *National Post* but also more regional papers like the *Ottawa Citizen* and, to a lesser extent, the *Montreal Gazette* and the *Toronto Star*. What is different, however, is that these papers, including the *Globe*, operate in an overall political landscape of newspaper publishing in Canada that is more partisan than in the United States. Although Canadian newspapers are not formal party organs, as in Europe, there are closer relationships between Canadian newspapers and organized political interests than we see in the Anglo-American tradition (Hallin and Mancini 2004; Hallin 2005). So, for example, Canada's *National Post* is a more overtly ideological paper of the political right than is the case for most papers with a national audience in the United States.

At the same time, in terms of its overall character, political debate in Canadian journalism is considerably less strident than in the United States. The partisan affiliations of individual newspapers notwithstanding, there is greater room for voices from the political left than one sees in mainstream publications in the United States (McLaughlin and Townsley 2011). Historically, Canadian journalistic styles tend to be slower and calmer than in the United States. This is even true of right-wing political talk radio in Canada, which is far more civil than its notoriously partisan and hyperbolic counterpart in the United States. For this reason, we might expect to find greater receptivity to a wider range of voices in the Canadian space of opinion.

The structural organization of the academic field also reveals differences between Canada and the United States. The modern research university was institutionalized earlier in the twentieth century in the United States than in Canada, and American universities are far more hierarchically arranged, institutionally diverse, and competitive with one another than has historically been the case in Canada (McLaughlin 2005). At the top of the institutional hierarchy in the United States are elite private universities such as Harvard, Yale, Princeton, and Columbia. These are organizations with endowments so enormous that they dwarf even the most prestigious Canadian universities. Compare Harvard's endowment of $32.3 billion, Yale with $20.8 billion, Princeton with $18.2 billion, and Columbia with $8.2 billion with the University of Toronto's endowment of $1.6 billion and McGill's of $1.1 billion (National Association of College and University Business Officers 2014; all numbers are in 2013 US dollars). Most Canadian colleges and universities receive some degree of public funding, with undergraduate tuition fees that are not only lower than those in the United States but also fairly standard across the country. In addition, admission to university in Canada does not rely on competitive SAT tests in the same way that it does in the United States (Davies and Hammack 2005). Partly because Canadian universities are perceived to differ less radically in terms of quality (and cost), Canadian students are less likely to travel out of province for higher education. The Canadian university system also does not have an elite, moneyed, and expansive sector of liberal art colleges, which is so important in the United States; there are really no counterparts to Amherst (with an endowment of $1.8 billion), Smith ($1.6 billion), Oberlin ($728 million), Mount Holyoke ($632 million), and Reed College ($485 million), for example (National Association of College and University Business Officers 2014). Finally, until relatively recently, Canadian research universities have not had the tradition of competing among themselves for the academic publishing "stars," which has long been the norm in the United States. Given the "flatter" landscape of Canadian higher education that McLaughlin (2005) describes, I would expect to find that academics who appear in the Canadian space of opinion are more diverse in their institutional origins than their counterparts in the United States.

The contemporary Canadian university system has, however, been undergoing a period of institutional transformation in recent decades, as government funding declines and administrators attempt to raise money from the private sector, including donations from alumni, and as academic capitalism reshapes the relationship between scholarship and profit in higher education. The Canadian federal government is also attempting to stem the brain drain to the United States by creating a culture of innovation, accountability, competition, and entrepreneurship through a range of economic and professional incentives such as the Canadian Research Chairs program, begun in 2000, and the Centres for Innovation grants announced in 2002 (Siler and McLaughlin 2008). These professionalizing tendencies on the US model may, however, work, as indeed they do in the US, against academics participating in the space of opinion.

In addition, the political field in Canada differs significantly from that in the United States. Canada has a parliamentary system, which retains ties to the British monarchy. In particular, the office of the Governor General—the formal head of state and the representative of the British Crown—has been an important focus of political debates (McLaughlin and Townsley 2011). Perhaps because the parliamentary system tends to diffuse power and subordinate individual personality to the party platform, as well as limiting both the period and the allowable cost of campaigning, politicians in Canada generally have a less visible public profile and tend to play a more limited role in space of public opinion. Some of the most prominent public intellectuals in the United States are politicians or former politicians, such as Al Gore or the late Daniel Patrick Moynihan. Sarah Palin's career from state governor to national political candidate to Fox News contributor suggests that the boundaries between the political and journalistic fields are relatively more porous in the United States. Moreover, think tanks are integral to political life in the United States, where intellectual debate is, to a substantial degree, shaped by various ideological and research-oriented institutes and foundations, as well as by advocacy organizations and lobby groups. Although the influence of think tanks has been on the rise north of the border in recent decades (Abelson 2000), these institutions remain less numerous and less powerful in Canada. For all these reasons, I would expect to find fewer political actors in the Canadian space of opinion than in the United States—fewer elected politicians, executive branch officials, or members of think tanks.

Finally, by means of subsidies, grants, and other incentives, the Canadian government plays a significant role in publishing and other cultural industries, which would not otherwise be financially viable. In the United States, the large market for commercial books and films creates many more opportunities for ex-politicians, journalists, and academics to engage in political commentary in the public sphere. In what are predominantly privatized systems of cultural production and distribution, books by writers such as Thomas Friedman, Edward Said, Noam Chomsky, Al Gore, and Cornel West all reach mass audiences, as do the documentaries of Michael Moore. There are, of course, Canadian equivalents to these media intellectuals, such as Naomi Klein, who also reaches her audience through books, films, and radio. But the Canadian market is comparatively tiny, with the result that Canadian authors often have their eye on the larger American market.

Indeed, as is well known, the production of books, movies, radio content and other cultural goods in Canada faces enormous competition from works produced in the United States. Although the cultural industries are a substantial proportion of gross domestic product in the Canada and the United States,[3] the absolute size of the economies and their cultural sectors are very different. In a report generated by the United Nations on the creative economy, data collected in 2002 revealed the total contribution of the creative industries to Canada's GDP to be CAD$37,465 million while the creative industries of the United States, for that same year, contributed USD$341,139 million. This difference helps to explain the widespread cultural concern in Canada about preserving forms of cultural production that are specifically Canadian. Government subsidies through agencies like the Canada Council represent a much larger piece of the pie for Canadian authors and filmmakers than government support does for their counterparts in the United States. This works to create an elite, publicly financed, and arguably more accountable literary culture in Canada. Similarly, the historically preeminent status of the Canadian Broadcasting Corporation (CBC) means that publicly funded television and radio still contribute heavily to political and cultural debate in Canada. I would thus expect to see a larger representation from the government-funded cultural sector in the Canadian space of opinion.

Who Speaks in the Space of Opinion?

To explore the above hypotheses, the following analysis compares opinion columns from the two newspapers of national record in Canada and the United States: the *Globe and Mail* and the *New York Times*. This method has obvious limits in that it does not capture the full range or variation in print media or opinion outlets in each national context. Nonetheless, there are compelling reasons to look at the opinion columns in each of these newspapers as a critical element in broader public conversations. As the papers of national record, each boasts substantial (albeit declining) reading audiences. Moreover, as I argued earlier, opinion pages serve as a central location for national conversations that engage elites across all sectors of society (Kowalchuk and McLaughlin 2009; Jacobs and Townsley 2011).

The US data consist of the *New York Times* subset (n = 632) from the larger samples of news commentary and opinion that Ron Jacobs and I collected for 1993–94 and 2001–02 (the first two years of the Clinton and Bush administrations, respectively) in connection with our project on media intellectuals.[4] In Canada, data from the *Globe and Mail* (n = 678) were collected as a replication of the American sample, as part of a larger project on public sociology and public intellectuals directed by Neil McLaughlin at McMaster University.[5] For each op-ed piece, we recorded information on the occupational background of the author, following a similar logic in the Canadian and American samples. Given that an opinion author's primary occupation is not always immediately apparent, and given that elite figures often change positions over time, moving from one institutional order to another, our policy was (1) to use the first author in the rare case that more than one author was listed, (2) to code the primary occupation cited in the byline, or, failing such information, (3) to identify the institutional location of the author at the time that he or she wrote the column.

The occupational background of opinion authors in the *Globe and Mail* and the *New York Times* is shown in table 2.1. As expected, the figures reveal a broadly similar institutional profile among authors of opinion columns in Canada and the United States, with the vast majority hailing from the fields of journalism, politics, and government. About two-thirds of all op-eds in both the *Globe and Mail* (55.6 + 7.4 + 1.5 = 64.5%) and the *New York Times* (61.1 + 5.5 + 1.6 = 68.2%) were written by opinion columnists, journalists, and professional media strategists, including media owners, pollsters, or other workers who make their living in the industry.[6] This dominance of authors from journalism is to be expected. If the products of the media industry form the material conditions for the circulation of opinion in mass publics, it makes sense that professional news broadcasters and those who deal in the business of public information will also be heavily represented among those who specialize in news commentary.

Table 2.1. Distribution of op-eds by occupation of author

	Globe and Mail	New York Times
Columnist	55.6	61.1
Journalist	7.4	5.5
Media strategist	1.5	1.6
Elected politician	2.1	4.3
Executive branch official	0.7	2.4
Representatives of civil society organization	8.6	4.4
Academic	10.9	13.1
Lawyer	2.1	1.1
Writer	7.7	3.8
Other[a]	3.5	2.7
	(N = 678)	(N = 632)

[a] Occupations represented by five or fewer individuals, including artists, musicians, comedians, counsellors, doctors, mothers, religious leaders, athletic coaches, and athletes.

Among these authors, opinion columnists are by far the most frequent contributors to the spaces of opinion in Canada and the United States. In both countries, there are small coteries of elite columnists, fifteen in Canada and ten in the United States (see table 2.2), each of whom appeared ten times or more in our sample; these columnists represent 5.6 percent of all authors in our Canadian sample (15/268) and 4.0 percent of all authors in our US sample (10/250). The ten opinion columnists writing in the United States together account for nearly half (47.4%) of all op-eds in the *New York Times*. In fact, the late William Safire alone accounts for 9.0 percent of the US sample. Similarly, in Canada, we find fifteen authors who appear ten times or more and who account for just over half (51.0%) of all op-eds published in the *Globe and Mail*, with Jeffrey Simpson and Robert Sheppard writing a total of nearly 20 percent of all the op-eds in the paper.

Although it is true that media insiders dominate the space of opinion in both Canada and the United States, they do not control it completely. In both countries, we also see academics, representatives from civil society organizations, politicians and executive branch officials, writers, lawyers, and a wide range of others who speak in the space of opinion. Moreover, while at first glance the distributions of media outsiders in Canada and the United States

Table 2.2. Frequent op-ed writers

	Author	Number of op-eds	Percentage of all op-eds
Globe and Mail	Jeffrey Simpson	67	9.9
	Robert Sheppard	54	8.0
	William Thorsell	28	4.1
	Margaret Wente	26	3.8
	Giles Gherson	21	3.1
	Lysiane Gagnon	20	2.9
	Edward Greenspon	18	2.7
	William Johnson	17	2.5
	Rex Murphy	16	2.4
	John Ibbitson	15	2.2
	Robertson Cochrane	14	2.1
	Hugh Winsor	14	2.1
	Jeff Sallot	12	1.8
	Rick Salutin	12	1.8
	Paul Sullivan	12	1.8
	Frequent authors combined	**346**	**51.0%**[a]
	(N = 678)		
New York Times	William Safire	57	9.0
	Bob Herbert	43	6.8
	Anthony Lewis	40	6.3
	Thomas L. Friedman	27	4.3
	Russell Baker	26	4.1
	A. M. Rosenthal	23	3.6
	Maureen Dowd	22	3.5
	Frank Rich	22	3.5
	Anna Quindlen	21	3.3
	Paul Krugman	19	3.0
	Frequent authors combined	**300**	**47.4**
	(N = 632)		

[a] Owing to rounding, the percentage figures in this column total 51.2.

Note: A "frequent" writer was defined as one who appeared ten or more times in the samples collected.

look roughly similar—that is, they hail from either the political or the academic field, they are mostly middle-aged and predominantly white, and the vast majority are men, with women accounting for only about 15 percent of opinion authors in each country (see table 2.A)[7]—if we compare the occupational distributions more closely, several important differences emerge.

Looking at the boundary between politics and journalism (see table 2.1), the pattern is, as expected, that elected politicians and executive branch officials are less likely to write opinion columns in Canada (2.1 + 0.7 = 2.8%) than in the United States (4.3 + 2.4 = 6.7%). Associated research in both countries further suggests that the greater representation of politicians in the US space of opinion is even more pronounced when the analysis is expanded to other news publications and television outlets (Jacobs and Townsley 2011; Kowalchuk and McLaughlin 2009). This undoubtedly reflects differences between the political systems of the two countries. In the American system, elected members of Congress have more autonomy to speak than do members of the Canadian Senate, who are political appointees, or even members of the House of Commons, who are subject to a much more confining party discipline than politicians in the United States. This pattern strongly suggests that the space of opinion in the United States is more closely tied to the political field than it is in Canada. Further research is needed to determine whether the tighter relationship observed in the US between the political field and the space of opinion is connected either to a heightened influence of the space of opinion on political outcomes and/or to lower autonomy for speakers in the US opinion space as compared to the Canadian opinion space.

Table 2.3. Frequent op-ed writers

	1993–94	2001–2	Total sample
Globe and Mail			
Male	89.3	82.0	85.1
Female	10.7	18.0	14.9
	(N = 289)	(N = 389)	(N = 678)
New York Times			
Male	87.3	81.6	83.9
Female	12.7	18.4	16.1
	(N = 251)	(N = 381)	(N = 632)

Outside of party politics proper, the occupational distribution in table 2.1 also shows that there are nearly twice as many representatives of civil society organizations in the space of opinion in Canada (8.6%) than in the United States (4.4%). As work by Thomas Medvetz (2012) has shown, think tanks occupy a new "fieldlike" space of influential cultural and political institutions and serve as a platform for a rising stratum of pundits, often conservative intellectuals, who compete with academics in the space of opinion to define social issues. In the United States, this sector grew dramatically over the last thirty to forty years, and this has been reflected in the space of opinion as an increase in both the absolute number and the relative proportion of opinion speakers from civil society organizations over time (Jacobs and Townsley 2011, 104). In our *New York Times* sample, the majority of these authors (71.4%) are from think tanks rather than lobbies (10.7%) or professional and advocacy groups (17.9%).[8] While a definitive comparison between the two countries must await in-depth analysis of the larger Canadian group of opinion authors from civil society organizations writing in the *Globe and Mail*, a cursory look at the data reveals fewer think tank intellectuals and a greater number of union representatives and members of advocacy organizations. To the extent that unions or, for example, consumer organizations speak more directly on behalf of mass publics than do lobbyists for political parties or business interests, this finding supports the claim that the Canadian space of opinion encompasses a wider diversity of voices from civil society than does the American one.

Another indicator of diversity among opinion authors in both countries is the substantial proportion of opinion authors from autonomous cultural fields such as academia, the legal profession, or the literary field (see table 2.1). In Canada, 20.7 percent of authors in the *Globe and Mail* are from these categories (10.9 + 2.1 + 7.7); in the United States the proportion is 18.0 percent (13.1 + 1.1 + 3.8). In fact, after professional opinion columnists, academics are the second largest group of opinion authors in both the *Globe and Mail* and the *New York Times* and appear in roughly comparable proportions (9% and 13.1%, respectively). One argument is that this is likely to enhance the autonomy of the space of opinion since academics, writers, and legal thinkers are like professional opinion columnists in their conditions of work and their ability to speak in their own voice when they enter the space of opinion. The logic is that because academics, writers, and legal thinkers generally enjoy high levels of autonomy in their professional work, they are not as subject to political and economic influence as other opinion authors. Politicians, publicists, pollsters, and lobbyists, by contrast, are more likely to represent a point of view on behalf of some other interest and therefore to present opinions that cleave more closely to existing conceptual frameworks and arguments in the political and journalistic fields.

Looking closely at academic opinion authors (see table 2.4), we find that they typically come from elite institutions. In the United States, the highest proportion of academic opinion authors comes from Ivy League schools and other "Research I" institutions.[9] There is also a definite bias toward the East Coast and to schools in Washington, DC. In Canada, Ontario institutions are heavily represented (the top three are all in that province, two of them in Toronto), but most of the major universities in other provinces also appear; these are for the most part medical-doctoral institutions, which can be thought of as the top tier in the Canadian system. This difference between the countries may be associated with the generally flatter landscape of Canadian institutions of higher education mentioned earlier (McLaughlin 2005; Siler and McLaughlin 2008). Canadian academic opinion authors are also more likely to come from foreign institutions than are those in the US, which again suggests a greater openness to diverse voices in the Canadian space of opinion.

Table 2.4. Institutional affiliation of academic opinion authors (by percent)

Globe and Mail		New York Times	
University of Toronto	13.4	Yale University	13.3
University of Western Ontario	11.5	Harvard University	9.6
York University	9.6	Stanford University	7.2
University of Calgary	5.8	Georgetown University	4.8
Carleton University	5.8	University of California, Berkeley	4.8
University of British Columbia	5.8	Boston College	3.6
Université de Montréal	3.8	Columbia University	3.6
McGill University	3.8	Cornell University	3.6
Simon Fraser University	3.8	MIT	3.6
University of Manitoba	3.8	Boston University	2.4
Université du Québec à Montréal	3.8	George Washington University	2.4
University of Victoria	3.8	New York University	2.4

Globe and Mail		New York Times	
University of Alberta	1.9	Northwestern University	2.4
Laval University	1.9	Princeton University	2.4
Royal Military College of Canada	1.9	University of Alabama	2.4
Mount Saint Vincent	1.9	University of Maryland	2.4
Institut national de la recherche scientifique	1.9	University of Pennsylvania	2.4
University of Regina	1.9	University of Texas at Austin	2.4
Ryerson	1.9	American University	1.2
Chesnut Hill College (Philadelphia)	1.9	Brandeis University	1.2
Tel Aviv University	1.9	Brown University	1.2
UCLA	1.9	Cooper Union	1.2
University of Berne	1.9	Emory University	1.2
California State University, Fresno	1.9	George Mason University	1.2
University of Minnesota	1.9	Indiana University	1.2
		Pepperdine University	1.2
		Sarah Lawrence College	1.2
		US Army War College	1.2
		University at Albany, SUNY	1.2
		University of California, Merced	1.2
		University of California, San Francisco	1.2
		University of Illinois at Chicago	1.2
		University of Louisville	1.2
		University of Southern California	1.2
		Williams College	1.2
		Woods Hole Oceanographic Institution	1.2
		Sorbonne	1.2
		Yeshiva University	1.2

Note: In the Globe and Mail sample (N = 678), 61 op-ed pieces (9.0%) were written by academic authors. In the New York Times sample (N = 632), the figure was 83 (13.1%).

As table 2.5 illustrates, academic opinion authors are also more likely to be from the social science disciplines than from professional, natural science, or humanities disciplines. In both countries, the social scientists in the space of opinion are typically economists, political scientists, and international relations experts, although the numbers become too small here to allow for statistically significant comparisons. Larger analyses of op-eds in Canada (Kowalchuk and McLaughlin 2009) and the United States (Jacobs and Townsley 2011) confirm, however, that, in the academic field, social scientists dominate the space of opinion but that sociologists are less well represented than economists or political scientists. The other similarity between the opinion spaces in Canada and the United States is the very low representation of natural scientists, a pattern that has been observed elsewhere for the United States (Townsley 2000, 2001, 2006).

Table 2.5. Percentage of academic op-eds by discipline of author

	Globe and Mail	*New York Times*
Humanities	32.8	18.1
Social sciences	39.3	41.0
Natural sciences	4.9	7.2
Professions	23.0	33.7

An examination of the humanities and professional disciplines tells a somewhat different story, however. In the United States, the professional disciplines are comparatively well represented among opinion authors, constituting a third of all academic opinion authors (33.7%). The proportion is substantially lower in Canada (23.0%). By contrast, opinion authors from humanities disciplines are a much stronger presence in Canada (32.8%) than in the United States (18.1%). In addition, in the United States, academics from the humanities are typically historians who write on popular themes, such as the national founders, the Constitution, or important historical events or figures, while in Canada they regularly include literary intellectuals and philosophers (although here, too, historians who write on national themes are well represented). This more literary trend in the Canadian space of opinion is also visible in the larger proportion of non–academically affiliated writers of all kinds in the Canadian sample. These are authors of fiction, non-fiction, or popular history and, as table 2.1 shows, they account for 7.7 percent of all opinion authors in the *Globe and Mail*. This is more than double the proportion of writers who publish op-eds in the *New York Times*.

Collectively, these findings suggest that the space of opinion in Canada is comparatively open to voices outside the journalistic field. The higher proportion of opinion authors from a range of civil society organizations, together with the comparatively smaller number of authors who are affiliated with formal political institutions, suggests the existence of a greater diversity of political voices in the Canadian space of opinion. There also appears to be higher representation of literary intellectuals among opinion authors in Canada, as well as a tilt toward humanities disciplines among academic authors. This may be an effect of the greater importance of the larger government-funded sector in the arts and cultural production in Canada, particularly in a context of concerns about national distinctiveness.

Despite their empirical limits, these findings suggest that future research might do well to take up questions about the critical capacity of the space of opinion in each country. Does a stronger boundary exist between the political and journalistic fields in the space of opinion in Canada, and if so, does this explain why we find that legitimate political opinion in Canada is more civil and runs a wider gamut than political opinion in the United States (McLaughlin and Townsley 2011)? Do opinion authors in Canada have more critical autonomy than their American counterparts? Does the greater representation of politicians in the US space of opinion mean that the *New York Times* or perhaps the US journalistic field in general is more closely connected to power, government, and empire than the space of opinion in Canada? And, finally, to the extent that the Canadian space of opinion is becoming more like that of the US, are we likely to see a convergence of political opinion styles and media formats? These are questions for future research.

Conclusion

From the perspective of public intellectuals or public sociology, there is an assumption that participation in the public sphere is important. What this participation should look like, however, has proved contentious. Should academics speak in the public sphere as experts on specific topics or as citizens? How much energy should academics expend in the quest to attract a public audience for their ideas? Is it reasonable to expect, or indeed to defend, a special public status for academics? Whatever the answers to these questions, it is clear that the mass media have come to play a pivotal, and indeed inescapable, role in organizing the conditions for public intellectual work. In this context, public intellectuals are increasingly called to be media intellectuals.

In one sense, of course, intellectuals have always been media intellectuals, in that they have relied on the communications media to teach, publish, and innovate. In our digital age of social media, this reliance seems even more obvious. For those academics who would be public intellectuals, then, it seems urgent that they develop a clear understanding of the constraints and opportunities of intellectual production in the mediated formats that organize the contemporary public sphere. Those scholars and scientists who decry public intellectual roles may also do well to consider the challenges of being a media intellectual, as the environments of intellectual life are increasingly mediated and interconnected with the public conversation. In other words, the choice *not* to participate may soon become a non-option for intellectuals and scholars of all stripes.

Moreover, while writing op-eds in a national newspaper is certainly not the only form of public action available to intellectuals, academics, and scientists, doing so does have an affinity with the academic vocation of research and writing. Writing such commentary has long been associated with a certain kind of intellectual prestige—and even the aspiration to influence changes in parliamentary power (see Habermas 1996, 373). Consider, too, that normative democratic theories stress the importance of critical discourse for rational deliberation (Habermas 1989, 1996; Said 1994), and one might argue that academic intellectuals, by virtue of training and institutional location, are especially well placed to offer critical input as well as specific expertise to broader public debates (Foucault 1980; Bender 1997; Swartz 2003; Fuller 2009).

If academic and other opinion intellectuals can exercise effective influence in this way, what light, if any, can a compositional analysis of the space of opinion like the one I have offered here shed on these issues? I suggest the contribution is in helping us to think about how academic intellectuals and other intellectuals navigate the space of opinion and, in particular, the format of the opinion column. One important issue is access. Media insiders, such as professional opinion columnists, write frequent columns and are able, over time, to establish themselves as personalities and to develop characteristic viewpoints and detailed arguments. Figures like Jeffrey Simpson and Margaret Wente, in Canada, and, in the United States, David Brooks and Maureen Dowd are well-known characters in the space of public opinion. This is likely to be less true for media outsiders, the vast bulk of whom appear only once in the opinion space in either Canada or the United States, as table 2.6 shows.

Table 2.6. Percentage of authors by number of appearances

	Globe and Mail	*New York Times*
1	79.5	78.5
2	8.2	12.0
3 to 10	6.7	5.6
More than 10	5.6	3.9

What does such limited access mean for the quality of opinion offered by academics and other media outsiders? One possibility is that academics will be prompted to offer a pithier, more succinct version of longer work, sharing their hard-won research or insight in a manner accessible to wider publics. This ability to articulate the essence of new ideas is in line with the dominant academic understanding of the public intellectual and also accords well with the understanding in the journalistic field that media outsiders are a source of alternative points of view and fresh perspectives (e.g., Rosenfeld 2000). An alternative hypothesis is that constricted access to the space of opinion may have perverse consequences for academic intellectuals and other media outsiders. Limited access and the short format of the opinion column may cause authors to present their opinions in reduced, partisan, or overly monolithic terms. If an author has only one chance to state a position, there may be pressure to present that position in the starkest possible formulation. This possibility suggests that those interested in public intellectuals and in the quality of discourse in the public sphere should concern themselves with the conditions (cultural, political, economic, and institutional) that affect opinionated speech more generally. Such an analysis can inform the question of how academic intellectuals should confront the challenge of being a media intellectual if they are to fulfill a public intellectual calling.

Notes

1 On the self-referentiality of English and Anglo-American intellectual fields, see, for example, Altbach (2006), Jacobs and Townsley (2008), and, especially, Platt (2006) on journals and Heilbron (1999) on the world system of translations.

2 For an Australian comparison, see Connell, Wood, and Crawford 2005.

3 "In 2007, the creative industries accounted for 6.4 per cent of the U.S. economy, generating foreign sales and exports in the order of $125.6 billion, one of the largest exporting sectors in the American economy. In Canada, the cultural sector provided 3.5 per cent of GDP and almost 6 per cent of the growth in value added" (United Nations 2010, 30).

4 The larger project (Jacobs and Townsley 2011) also collected opinion columns from USA Today, as well as television transcripts from NewsHour, Face the Nation, Crossfire, and Hannity and Colmes (n = 1819).

5 The sampling strategies were different in each country. In Canada, op-eds were sampled for every tenth day in the sample period, whereas the US sample used a random number generator to select a 10 percent sample of dates during each sample period (see Kowalchuk and McLaughlin (2009) for details). This yielded a slightly larger sample in Canada but otherwise reliably comparable data on op-ed authors.

6 The logic of the professional media strategists category is to include those people who are not journalists but whose careers and actions depend on expert knowledge of the journalistic field. In Bourdieuian terms, this would include those salaried workers in the journalistic field who derive their expertise from the "heteronomous" pole of journalistic distinction. Some owners are included, first, because their managerial positions allow them to pursue media strategies that affect the social space of opinion and, second, because they view themselves and are viewed by others as major players in the space of opinion. Political consultants and party strategists are included because of their expertise in public relations, which allows them easy access to media publicity. In other words, these are all people who are not professional journalists but whose livelihoods and identities depend on the news media. This is a sensible category in terms of most histories of professional journalism inasmuch as this range of competing positions in the journalistic field are precisely those against which high-end objective journalism defines itself (Schudson 1978; Abbott 1988).

7 Looking at the breakdown by sample period shows that the proportion of women among opinion authors in both countries increased dramatically between the early 1990s and the 2000s. These are impressive gains, but

they do not occur evenly across all occupational groupings. In fact, they are almost entirely accounted for by the introduction of one or two women into the ranks of elite opinion columnists. At the *Globe and Mail*, these were Lysiane Gagnon and Margaret Wente and, at the *New York Times*, Gail Collins and Maureen Dowd. These are doubtless real gains for women journalists, but they are not evidence of widespread changes in journalistic cultures or modes of recruitment.

8 The larger US sample reveals however that the balance shifts when a broader range of media formats and platforms are included. For example, on both *USA Today* and network television, lobbyists and authors from professional advocacy groups dominate.

9 This designation refers to a classification scheme developed in 1970 by the Carnegie Foundation for the Advancement of Teaching. Although the Carnegie Foundation has since retired the classification framework that designated particular institutions as "Research I" institutions, the term is still used by universities to indicate their commitment to research and doctoral programs (McCormick and Zhao 2005).

References

Abelson, Donald E. 2000. "Do Think Tanks Matter? Opportunities, Constraints and Incentives for Think Tanks in Canada and the United States." *Global Society* 14 (2): 213–36.

Abbott, Andrew. 1988. *The System of Professions: An Essay on the Division of Expert Labor*. Chicago: University of Chicago Press.

Altbach, Philip G. 2006. "The Tyranny of Citations." *Inside Higher Education* 43: 3–5.

Alexander, Jeffrey C. 2010. *The Performance of Politics: Obama's Victory and the Democratic Struggle for Power*. New York: Oxford University Press.

———. 2006. *The Civil Sphere*. Oxford and New York: Oxford University Press.

Appadurai, Arjun. 1996. *Modernity at Large: Cultural Dimensions of Globalization*. Minneapolis: University of Minnesota Press.

Baum, Matthew, and Tim Groeling. 2008. "New Media and the Polarization of American Political Discourse." *Political Communication* 25 (4): 345–65.

Beilharz, Peter 1997. *Imagining the Antipodes: Culture, Theory and the Visual in the Work of Bernard Smith*. Cambridge: Cambridge University Press.

Bender, Thomas. 1997. *Intellect and Public Life: Essays on the Social History of Academic Intellectuals in the United States*. Baltimore: Johns Hopkins University Press.

Bourdieu, Pierre. 2005. "The Political Field, the Social Science Field, and the Journalistic Field." In *Bourdieu and the Journalistic Field*, edited by Rodney Benson and Erik Neveu, 29–47. Malden, MA: Polity.

———. 1993. *The Field of Cultural Production*. Edited by Randal Johnson. New York: Columbia University Press.

———. 1996. *The Rules of Art*. Translated by Susan Emanuel. Stanford, CA: Stanford University Press.

———. 1998. *On Television*. Translated by Priscilla Parkhurst Ferguson. New York: New Press.

Bourdieu, Pierre, and Jean-Claude Passeron. 1990. *Reproduction in Education, Society and Culture*. Translated by Richard Nice. New York: Sage.

Connell, R. W., Julian Wood, and June Crawford. 2005. "The Global Connections of Intellectual Workers: An Australian Study." *International Sociology* 20 (1): 5–26.

Davies, Scott, and Floyd M. Hammack. 2005. "The Channeling of Student Competition in Higher Education: Comparing Canada and the U.S." *Journal of Higher Education* 76 (1): 89–106.

Diamond, Edwin. 1993. *Behind the Times: Inside the New New York Times*. New York: Villard Books.

Eliasoph, Nina. 1998. *Avoiding Politics: How Americans Produce Apathy in Everyday Life*. Cambridge: Cambridge University Press.

Fuller, Steve. 2009. *The Sociology of Intellectual Life*. London: Sage.

Gieryn, Thomas F. 1999. *Cultural Boundaries of Science: Credibility on the Line*. Chicago: University of Chicago Press.

Habermas, Jürgen. 1989. *The Structural Transformation of the Public Sphere: An Inquiry into a Category of Bourgeois Society*. Translated by Thomas Burger. Cambridge, MA: MIT Press.

———. 1996. *Between Facts and Norms: Contributions to a Discourse Theory of Law and Democracy*. Translated by William Rehg, Cambridge, MA: MIT Press

Foucault, Michel. 1980. *Power/Knowledge: Selected Interviews and Other Writings, 1972–1977*. Edited by Colin Gordon. New York: Pantheon.

Hallin, Daniel C. 2005. "Field Theory, Differentiation Theory, and Comparative Media Research." In *Bourdieu and the Journalistic Field*, edited by Rodney Benson and Erik Neveu, 224–43. Malden, MA: Polity.

Hallin, Daniel C., and Paola Mancini. 2004. *Comparing Media Systems: Three Models of Media and Politics*. New York: Cambridge University Press.

Heilbron, Johan. 1999. "Book Translations as a Cultural World System." *European Journal of Social Theory* 2 (4): 429–44.

Jacobs, Ronald N. 2000. *Race, Media, and the Crisis of Civil Society: From Watts to Rodney King*. Cambridge: Cambridge University Press.

Jacobs, Ronald N., and Eleanor Townsley. 2008. "On the Communicative Geography of Public Sociology." *Canadian Journal of Sociology* 33 (3): 1–20.

———. 2011. *The Space of Opinion: Media Intellectuals and the Public Sphere*. New York: Oxford University Press.

———. 2014. "The Hermeneutics of Hannity: Format Innovation in the Space of Opinion After September 11." *Cultural Sociology* 8 (3): 240–57.

Jamieson, Kathleen, and Joseph Cappella. 2008. *Echo Chamber: Rush Limbaugh and the Conservative Media Establishment*. New York and Oxford: Oxford University Press.

Kauffman, Jason, and Orlando Patterson. 2005. "Cross-National Cultural Diffusion: The Global Spread of Cricket." *American Sociological Review* 70 (1): 82–110.

Kowalchuk, Lisa, and Neil McLaughlin. 2009. "Mapping the Social Space of Opinion: Public Sociology and the Op-ed in Canada." *Canadian Journal of Sociology* 34 (3): 697–728.

Kull, Steve, Clay Ramsay, and Evan Lewis. 2003. "Misperceptions, the Media, and the Iraq War." *Political Science Quarterly* 118 (4): 569–98.

Lichterman, Paul. 1996. *The Search for Political Community: American Activists Re-inventing Commitment*. Cambridge: Cambridge University Press.

McCormick, Alexander C. and Chun-Mei Zhao. 2005. "Rethinking and Reframing the Carnegie Classification." *Change* 37(5):51–57.

McLaughlin, Neil. 2005. "Canada's Impossible Science: Historical and Institutional Origins of the Coming Crisis in Anglo-Canadian Sociology." *Canadian Journal of Sociology* 30 (1): 1–40.

McLaughlin, Neil, and Eleanor Townsley. 2011. "Contexts of Cultural Diffusion: A Case Study of Public Intellectual Debates in English Canada." *Canadian Review of Sociology / Revue canadienne de sociologie* 48 (4): 341–68.

Medvetz, Thomas. 2012. *The Rise of Think Tanks in America: Merchants of Policy and Power*. Chicago: University of Chicago Press.

Morris, Jonathan. 2005. "The Fox News Factor." *Harvard International Journal of Press/Politics* 10 (3): 56–79.

National Association of College and University Business Officers (NACUBO). 2014. U.S. and Canadian Institutions Listed by Fiscal Year 2013

Endowment Market Value and Change in Endowment Market Value from FY 2012 to FY 2013. Revised February 2014. Accessed June 15, 2015.

Platt, Jennifer. 2006. "Journals and Their Editorial Boards." Paper presented at the annual meeting of the American Sociological Association, Montréal, Québec, 11–14 August.

Putnam, Robert. 2001. *Bowling Alone: The Collapse and Revival of American Community*. New York: Simon and Schuster.

Rosenfeld, Stephen S. 2000. "The Op-Ed Page: A Step to a Better Democracy." *Harvard International Journal of Press/Politics* 5 (3): 7–11.

Said, Edward W. 1994. *Representations of the Intellectual: The 1993 Reith Lectures*. New York: Pantheon.

Schudson, Michael. 1978. *Discovering the News: A Social History of American Newspapers*. New York: Basic Books.

———. 2011. *The Good Citizen: A History of American Civic Life*. New York: Free Press.

Siler, Kyle, and Neil McLaughlin. 2008. "The Canada Research Chair Program and Social Science Reward Structures." *Canadian Review of Sociology / Revue canadienne de sociologie* 45 (1): 93–119.

Smith, Bernard. 1998. *Modernism's History: A Study in Twentieth-Century Art and Ideas*. New Haven: Yale University Press.

Somers, Margaret. 2008. *Genealogies of Citizenship: Markets, Statelessness and the Right to Have Rights*. Cambridge: Cambridge University Press.

Swartz, David L. 2003. "From Critical Sociology to Public Intellectual: Pierre Bourdieu and Politics." *Theory and Society* 32: 791–823.

Sunstein, Cass R. 2001. *Republic.com*. Princeton: Princeton University Press. http://press.princeton.edu/chatpers/s7014.pdf. Accessed June 22, 2015.

Townsley, Eleanor. 2000. "A History of Intellectuals and the Demise of the New Class: Academics and the U.S. Government in the 1960s." *Theory and Society* 29 (6): 739–84.

———. 2001. "'The Sixties' Trope." *Theory, Culture, and Society* 18 (6): 99–123.

———. 2006. "The Public Intellectual Trope in the United States." *American Sociologist* 37 (3); 39–66.

———. 2011. "Intellectuals, Media and the Public Sphere." In *The Oxford Handbook of Cultural Sociology*, edited by Jeffrey Alexander, Ronald Jacobs, and Phillip Smith, 284–317. New York: Oxford University Press.

United Nations. 2010. *Creative Economy Report 2010. A Feasible Development Option*. A joint publication of the United Nations

Conference on Trade and Development and United Nations Development Program. http://unctad.org/en/Docs/ditctab20103_en.pdf.

Wuthnow, Robert. 2002. *Loose Connections: Joining Together in America's Fragmented Communities*. Cambridge, MA: Harvard University Press.

3 The Eye of the Swarm
Collective Intelligence and the Public Intellectual

JACOB G. FOSTER

The recent proliferation of new social media technologies has radically increased the speed with which individuals can find, share, and generate content. As the key adjective "social" suggests, much of this activity is collective, relying on a dramatic increase in both interconnection and interaction. Without these social media we would have no Wikipedia, no lolcats, and perhaps no Arab Spring. Indeed, the success of projects like Wikipedia gives some credence to one of the key components of the Web 2.0 vision: collective intelligence. As Tim O'Reilly (2005, 3) put it, "an essential part of Web 2.0 is harnessing collective intelligence, turning the web into a kind of global brain." Indeed, the metaphor of the global brain is an old one; Marshall McLuhan (1994, xxiii) wrote eerily similar words almost fifty years ago: "We have extended our central nervous system in a global embrace."

The basic formula of collective intelligence is simple. When you pool together a large number of choices, votes, tags, edits, or posts, you end up with more than a mere jumble of individual actions; out of this swarm of activity emerge knowledge and information processing. Indeed, collective intelligence is not an imaginative flight of cyberpunk fancy; you use it every day. When you Google "collective intelligence," Google's PageRank algorithm leverages all those hyperlinks to prioritize your search results

(Langville and Meyer 2006). When you use Wikipedia to confirm that Wikipedia is indeed a form of social media, you rely on the fact that some individual edited the article on social media to include references to Wikipedia, and many other individuals chose to let those references stay.

The more excitable advocates of collective intelligence, however, claim that emergent information processing is often superior to the insights of well-informed experts. Under some circumstances, this is indeed the case. At first blush, then, this rapidly emerging collective brain might seem to threaten the job security of public intellectuals, who use their individual brains to help the public sort out thorny issues. Fear not, Paul Krugman and David Brooks: it turns out that collective intelligence is generally bad at the activities that public intellectuals typically perform. As Clay Shirky (2008, 137) noted when discussing the *Los Angeles Times*'s brief and disastrous experiment with letting the hive mind help pen its editorials, "An editorial is meant to be a timely utterance of a single opinionated voice—the opposite of the characteristics that make for good wiki content." More crucially, public intellectuals tend to intervene on matters (like politics) that are fraught with conflicting values. In order to reach its full potential, however, collective intelligence requires broad agreement on both fundamental values and a "body of knowledge and techniques"—what Michael Nielsen (2011, 75) calls "shared praxis." In the absence of shared praxis, it is hard to know how best to aggregate individual contributions.

So why raise the issue of collective intelligence in a book on public intellectuals? As I will argue, a careful exploration of when and why collective intelligence functions—and when and why it fails—indicates that the new social media represent not a threat but an opportunity for public intellectuals. By engaging with the products of collective intelligence—and, just as crucially, with their producers—public intellectuals can help collective intelligence become *more intelligent*. In understanding how this might work, however, we'll need to consider more than the nature of collective intelligence; we'll need to consider both the nature of intellectuals and the nature of human learning and culture.

What Is Collective Intelligence?

In thinking about collective intelligence, I find it useful to tack between two extreme characterizations: a weak form and a strong form. The weak form is, in essence, a fact about statistics, and one can state with some precision the conditions under which such a collective will be more intelligent, on average, than any individual. Weak form collective intelligence is good for answering questions with definitive, quantitative answers. The classic illustration, popularized by James Surowiecki in *The Wisdom of Crowds* (which in turn popularized the idea of collective intelligence), goes back to the early twentieth century. According to Surowiecki (2005, xi–xiii), renowned statistician and eugenicist Francis Galton found himself at a county fair. The fair was holding a competition to see who could come closest to guessing the weight of an ox. Eight hundred locals, of widely varying expertise, entered a guess. Now Galton had a rather dim view of democracy, due to his rather dim view of most human beings. In order to demonstrate the inherent fallibility of the masses, Galton gathered these guesses and analyzed them, evidently believing that guessing the weight of an ox was a reasonable proxy for the democratic process. To his astonishment, the crowd did well. In fact, the *average* of their guesses was as close to the actual weight of the ox as any individual guess—even guesses by experts like butchers and farmers. To his credit as a scientist, Galton (1907) wrote up this dramatic refutation of his hypothesis in *Nature*.[1]

Why did this work? The political scientist Scott Page (2007, 208) states it crisply in his diversity prediction theorem: *collective error* equals the *average individual error* minus the diversity of the predictions. In other words, the accuracy of a collective prediction depends not only on the accuracy of individual predictions, but also on the diversity of the crowd, that is, the degree to which individual predictions deviate from the average of all the predictions. The collective error can be small—the collective "intelligence" can be high—even with large individual errors. Consider, for example, collectives in which the individual errors are independent and lack systematic bias. In such cases, for each overestimate, there is a (roughly) countervailing underestimate.[2] This is more or less what happened in Galton's case[3], and this principle is often what underwrites the weak form of collective intelligence, in spirit if not always in detail.

There are many ways that weak-form collective intelligence can go wrong. But if your collective carefully obeys the requisite constraints, and you ask the right question, then weak-form collective intelligence does its magic. Strong-form claims brush past many of these constraints, relying on notions from the theory of complex adaptive systems to make rather mystical assertions about the emergence of collective intelligence under many (or most) conditions. When people talk seriously, rather than metaphorically, about giant brains, strong-form collective intelligence is afoot. Now most people who know what they're talking about don't take collective intelligence for granted in the way the strong form does. As Clay Shirky (2006) noted, responding to Jaron Lanier's "Digital Maoism"—an early and insightful critique of strong form collective intelligence—"the target of the piece, the hive mind, is just a catchphrase, used by people who don't understand how things like Wikipedia really work."

While I think Shirky is largely right, he underestimates the pervasiveness of "hive mind" thinking among many of the consumers and some of the producers of social media. Larry Sanger (2006), one of the founders of Wikipedia, discussed such invocations of the "hive mind" in his response to Lanier: "In late 2004 I publicly criticized Wikipedia for failing to respect expertise properly, to which a surprisingly large number of people replied that, essentially, Wikipedia's success has shown that 'experts' are no longer needed, that a wide-ranging description of everyone's opinions is more valuable than what some narrow-minded 'expert' thinks." This conviction is strong-form thinking, and it is still alive today, as revealed by a recent article in the *Chronicle of Higher Education* in which a historian, Timothy Messer-Kruse (2012), describes his struggle to correct the Wikipedia entry on the Haymarket riot on the basis of his recent scholarship on the subject. He was told, in essence, that from the perspective of Wikipedia his expert research on primary sources was less credible than the accumulated historical consensus, which he was contesting on the basis of new primary evidence. He quotes an editor: "Wikipedia is not 'truth,' Wikipedia is 'verifiability' of reliable sources. Hence, if most secondary sources which are taken as reliable happen to repeat a flawed account or description of something, Wikipedia will echo that"—a statement strikingly similar to the view that Sanger labels "epistemic collectivism" (to which we'll return below).

There are many instances of successful collective intelligence, however, that are neither as simple as guessing the weight of an ox nor as grandiose as the universally expert-displacing giant brain of the strong form. One of the most fascinating examples is offered by Michael Nielsen (2011) in *Reinventing Discovery*, in which a huge team of over fifty thousand people played Garry Kasparov in what Kasparov described as "the greatest game in the history of chess" (15). The "World Team" played so successfully because it combined social media technologies with good protocols for information sharing and deliberation—and, of course, lots of individual human intelligence and expertise. Nielsen uses this and similar examples to develop a fascinating theory of what one might call "middle-range" collective intelligence. Such collective intelligence is more sophisticated in its abilities and more complex in its foundation than the weak form, while being more realistic and realizable than the strong form. As we will see, like the weak form, this type of collective intelligence applies only in some situations (conditions of shared praxis) and exploits certain principles to function successfully. Like the strong form, however, this type of collective intelligence can perform complex tasks as well as or better than experts. In the Polymath Project, for example, a large team of mathematicians (including some amateurs) rapidly tackled a problem that had challenged even the strongest team members (Nielsen 2011, 1–2; 209–13).

As I will argue, public intellectuals can radically improve and expand the scope of both weak-form and middle-range collective intelligence. Similarly, I will propose that public intellectuals are in a position to communicate values that protect the crowd against the corrosive effects of epistemic collectivism and the strong-form ideology.

When Is the Collective Intelligent?

In order to show when and how public intellectuals can act to improve collective intelligence, I need to establish the parameters under which weak-form and middle-range collective intelligence can operate successfully. The basic requirements of the weak form are set out by Surowiecki in *The Wisdom of Crowds* (2005)[4]. Surowiecki's first two requirements are reflected in our discussion of Page's diversity prediction theorem. First, the members of the collective should be *diverse*. That is, their knowledge, beliefs, or assumptions shouldn't be *too* similar. This ensures that the errors in individual contributions will not share a systematic bias. Second, members of the collective should make their contributions *independently*. That is, they must not be unduly influenced by the opinions of others in making, say, their estimate of the weight of the ox. This ensures that the errors in individual contributions do not *become* correlated through some form of social interaction.

To these, Surowiecki adds a third requirement, namely, that the members of the collective must be appropriately *decentralized*. This requirement begins to extend beyond trivial weak-form cases (like guessing the weight of an ox) into the kind of collective intelligence that operates, at times, in more complex situations like the market. Decentralization can be thought of as another form of diversity, but one that allows a collective to bring together widely dispersed knowledge, as in von Hayek's (1945) classic account of the price mechanism. Finally, Surowiecki notes the absolute importance of an effective *aggregation mechanism*, such as averaging (in the case of Galton's ox) or prices (in the case of markets). Note that these four simple criteria already suffice to explain many dramatic failures of collective intelligence. Market bubbles, for example, are produced when the diversity and/or the independence assumptions are relaxed. Errors then become correlated (everyone starts to believe that housing prices will go up), and the collective stops being intelligent as it is consumed by a self-reinforcing process that magnifies both individual and collective error.

The principles for middle-range collective intelligence, as articulated by Nielsen in *Reinventing Discovery* (2011), build on many of these insights. Nielsen also emphasizes diversity and decentralization, although for slightly different reasons. His collectives tend to tackle more extensive or creative problems, with complex and interlocking or sequential subproblems. For him, diversity and decentralization increase the scope of available *expertise*. The middle-range collective operates not by a simple aggregation process but by what Nielsen (2011) calls an *architecture of attention*, which matches relevant expertise to appropriate subproblems. Consider the chess game mentioned earlier. Nielsen argues persuasively that the World Team, with its fifty thousand members, played so effectively in part because it was able to draw on players who were experts on many of the individual positions that emerged over the course of the game.

Indeed, decomposition into subproblems (what Nielsen calls *modularity*) is helpful for many reasons. Narrowing the scope of the problem makes it easier to find relevant expertise. It also makes it more likely that experts will be able to contribute: they have only a small subproblem to solve rather than a larger chunk (Nielsen calls this *microcontribution*). Decomposition can speed up the process, allowing parts of the overall problem to be solved in parallel. The collective is further enhanced in the presence of "a rich and well-structured information commons, so people can build on earlier work" (2011, 33). And, most fundamentally, the collective requires the *shared praxis* mentioned earlier, so that participants can come to an agreement about which forms of expertise are relevant to which subproblems and which microcontributions actually solve them.

Why Does Collective Intelligence Fail?

If the requirements of collective intelligence are so clearly stated—in either the weak form or the middle-range form—why does it so frequently fail? Humans, unfortunately, violate these basic requirements in many situations. We are subject to ancient cognitive biases and heuristics, and these biases often make it difficult to achieve the diversity and independence required for any form of collective intelligence to operate.

These biases, discovered in the pioneering work of psychologists Amos Tversky and Daniel Kahneman (1974), can be divided into individual biases (those we can put into play all by ourselves) and social biases (those that require others for activation). Individual biases include *anchoring*, in which numerical estimates tend to be extrapolated from an initial piece of numerical information and hence are unduly influenced by it; *availability*, in which information is given much greater weight than it merits if it comes easily to mind, like the grossly exaggerated fear of shark attacks (which I happen to share); and *confirmation*, in which information is given greater weight when it confirms our previously held beliefs. These individual mechanisms help to undermine diversity by pushing individual beliefs in similar directions.

Social biases are especially pernicious in social media contexts. One bias familiar to anyone who has ever been to high school (i.e., most of us) is *conformity*. The conformity bias causes us to prefer the belief held by the majority even when this belief directly contradicts our own experience. The most famous illustration of this bias is the Asch experiment, in which a group of "participants" (actually in league with the experimenter) was able to persuade a naïve subject that his perception of the length of a line was incorrect (Asch 1951). This bias obviously undermines independence, providing a powerful social mechanism for generating correlated errors. Equally disruptive is the *prestige* bias, in which the behaviours or beliefs of apparently successful and high-status individuals are copied, perhaps again contradicting individual experience (Henrich and McElreath 2003). Prestige bias undermines both diversity (in cases where similar prestigious individuals are used as models) and independence (as high-status individuals can introduce correlated errors into an entire population).

Individual and social biases are not always sources of error, however—one of the reasons for preferring the term *heuristic*. Indeed, they can often be adaptive, which explains, in part, why they have not been eliminated over our evolutionary history. This is especially true of the social biases, which are key mechanisms in the human propensity for social learning (Henrich and McElreath 2003). Our ability to learn from others, while requiring expensive investments in cognitive capacity, is essential to our species-unique capacity for cumulative culture. One of the great tensions in our evolutionary trajectory consequently pulls between the reliance on social learning and a disposition for individual learning. When information is costly to acquire, mechanisms for social learning will evolve; to use a common example, it is cheaper to learn not to eat poisonous mushrooms by conforming with a general practice of not eating them, rather than by trying one out (Henrich and McElreath 2003, 125). Similarly, it was probably quite advantageous to copy the behaviour of successful models when it came to foraging, hunting, and tool making, rather than working these things out on one's own.

At the same time, the conformity bias can generate errors through a process called an *information cascade* (Bikhchandani, Hirshleifer, and Welch 1992; Easley and Kleinberg 2010). Especially when the signal favoring one option over another is weak, early historical accidents can accumulate to send a strong social signal in support of the suboptimal option. Conformist individuals obey the social signal in preference to any private information they may have about the quality of various options. And prestige bias can fail because the behaviour or belief being copied from a high-status individual may not have anything to do with their status or success. Indeed, as it is often hard to tell how behaviours and beliefs map onto success, humans tend to copy these *en bloc*, which can transmit maladaptive behaviours (Henrich and McElreath 2003, 130).

These arcana about human social learning, while established in our evolutionary past, are relevant to our social media present and collectively intelligent future. The argument favouring social over individual learning in a context of costly information extends from poison mushrooms to the elaborate products of our cumulative culture, any *one* of which would be extraordinarily expensive to generate through individual learning and innovation. Some individual learning and tinkering is necessary if culture is to evolve, but, as biologist Mark Pagel recently argued, the number of innovators required may not scale as a function of population size. Technologies for communication, including language, writing, and eventually social media, allow a few innovators to share their insights with the vast multitudes, who can then take the easier route of social learning through copying (Pagel 2011). In fact, Pagel points out, the social media niches we are constructing may radically favour copying over innovation. Yet the collective intelligence stored in our cumulative culture—and more broadly available than ever, thanks to social media technologies—would grow more rapidly if more people leveraged their capacity for individual learning as well.

How Often Does Bias Distort Collective Intelligence? Three Brief Examples

To demonstrate that these cognitive biases actually have the advertised consequences for collective intelligence, I'll briefly review three examples from the scientific literature. First, what happens in practice when we relax the independence assumption? This question was recently explored by Dirk Helbing and collaborators, who showed that "even mild social influence can undermine the wisdom of crowd effect in simple estimation tasks" (Lorenz et al. 2011, 1). In these experiments, subjects were asked to perform a standard weak-form task, providing estimates of "geographical facts and crime statistics" (2). In some cases, the participants were allowed to revise their estimates over several rounds, on the basis of a "wisdom of the crowd" prompt (the averaged estimate of other participants) or a full-knowledge prompt, which showed the previous estimates of all other participants in that particular experiment.

These prompts introduce an element of social influence that obviously violates the conditions under which weak-form collective intelligence should work: independence is undermined by feeding participants aggregate or total information about other participants' guesses. Relaxing the independence condition, not surprisingly, decreases the diversity of estimates and also shrinks the range covered by the estimates—which is often centred not around the correct value but around some other value entirely. This experiment also uncovered an unsettling fact about the way that social learning works in such circumstances. Participants reported increasing confidence in their increasingly wrong estimates, perhaps through a combination of a conformist social heuristic (they were more confident as their estimate became more aligned with that of the group) and a confirmation-based individual heuristic (the convergence of others' estimates provides further "evidence" for the accuracy of the adjusted individual guess). It is easy to extrapolate from such simple situations to see how the social interaction allowed by social media, when pursued under a conformity and confirmation-heavy cognitive framework, destroys the underlying diversity and independence required for weak-form or middle-range collective intelligence.

Another experimental manipulation, particularly relevant for the online world, revealed how prestige bias and conformity bias conspire to undermine collective intelligence. In this case, Matt Salganik, Peter Dodds, and Duncan Watts (2006) created an artificial music market, in which participants could download real songs of varying quality. Exploiting the experimental possibilities offered by the Web, they actually created several replicates of the market. Each replicate was completely disconnected from the others, and its participants made their choices under different conditions. In the control case, no information was provided about other users' choices. In another case, information about others' choices was provided (i.e., the number of times each song had been downloaded) but this information was not made especially salient. In a third case, songs were actually *listed* in order of decreasing download count, which was also displayed. In this third case, others' choices became the primary principle of organization—rather like Google Scholar results, which display (and are often ranked by) citation counts. Unsurprisingly, sharing social information in either condition increased the inequality of outcomes. Giving greater emphasis to the prestige of particular options (equally, the strength of consensus around those options) increased inequality yet further. The unpredictability of the outcome—in other words, the variations in download share from replicate to replicate—similarly increased as social information was provided and made more prominent. The authors summarize the impact of social influence on collective intelligence quite pithily: "When individual decisions are subject to social influence, markets do not simply aggregate pre-existing individual preferences" (856).

But such effects are not limited to trivial cases (like weak-form estimation tasks) or to matters of taste (like music downloads). My collaborator James Evans (2008) explored how online availability of journals affected scholarly citation behaviour. The broad expectation, before Evans's study, was that online availability—particularly of a journal's back issues—would cause scholars to cite more deeply into the past, as search costs would plummet and apposite nuggets of prior work could be easily extracted from the literature. Likewise, conventional wisdom proposed that online availability would allow scholars to cite more broadly, liberating them from simple citation chasing and compensating for their limited acquaintance with journals outside their own discipline. Evans overturned these expectations almost entirely. As journals become available online, scholars cite with *less* historical depth than they would otherwise. While scholars do cite more broadly beyond their own discipline, their extramural citations narrow in focus, piling onto certain canonical sources and high-prestige journals. This is another manifestation of online technologies turbocharging ancient cognitive biases. Search tools like Google Scholar issue strong signals about the prestige of specific articles and arm researchers with information about others' choices, thereby activating conformity and prestige heuristics. Even the giant brains of academics—from whose ranks, I should add, many public intellectuals are drawn—seem to be subject to these social learning biases.

What Is the Online World Like?

These studies demonstrate the practical consequences of social learning biases for collective intelligence; the latter two do so in ways that are directly relevant to the social media niche. The online world is winner takes all, characterized by large and *increasing* inequality of user attention. This inequality is often reflected in fat-tailed distributions of links, page views, and so forth (Shirky 2008). The *architecture of attention* that rules the political blogosphere, for example, is not based on matching expertise to subproblems, but rather based on strong prestige and conformity biases. Unsurprisingly, when these heuristics are combined with economic forces, inequality is exacerbated, leading to a hollowing out of the online middle class (Lanier 2010) and an increasingly stark division into a small, high-prestige elite class and a vast, low-prestige mob. The elite class is capable of broadcasting its messages to huge audiences but is unable to leverage much interactivity with them, while the masses communicate quite interactively but only in small clusters (Shirky 2008). This rising inequality was noted by Matthew Hindman (2008) specifically with respect to the political sphere.

Those who hope that social media will transform the practice of democracy would do well to attend to this underlying tension. It is easier for the average person to produce and share information than ever before. Yet these new powers coexist with an architecture of attention that—in combination with current business models—produces profoundly anti-democratic consequences. There is a certain delicious irony in the fact that the behavioural dynamics of this futuristic social niche are dominated by ancient social heuristics like conformity and prestige.

The concentration of attention makes public intellectuals, or at least the celebrity ones, more powerful: they sit atop the hierarchy of attention created by conformity and prestige. At the same time, the latent collective intelligence surging through social media is not being leveraged as much as it could be. Only a few in the elite systematically draw on local, diverse informants; in most cases, information travels "up" only when occasional ideas, facts, or beliefs propagate virally through the swarm, generating a strong signal. There is also the possibility of algorithmically harvesting the latent collective intelligence—replacing a technologically mediated but nonetheless social mechanism for aggregating individual expertise with computational procedures, as in "mining" Google searches to identify emergent influenza epidemics (Ginsberg et al. 2009, though see Lazer et al. 2014). Ultimately, however, such practices only amplify the power of elite actors with access to the computational and algorithmic capacity to carry out such harvesting (Lanier 2010). Data-mining the crowd does little to enhance the participatory democratic potential of social media.

Can Public Intellectuals Enhance Collective Intelligence?

So what can those at the centre—public intellectuals—do to enhance the potential of collective intelligence for solving human problems? After all, broad democratic participation in collective intelligence could serve to connect esoteric expertise with profound local challenges, or to enhance the praxis of consensus formation around fundamental political questions. I suggest that we should first meditate on what, exactly, a public intellectual *is*. The great American psychologist and philosopher William James was the first to use the term *intellectual* "as a label of self-identification" in his 1907 speech "The Social Value of the College-Bred" (Taylor 2010, 26)[5]. James argued that the chief purpose of a college education was to create intellectuals, who were defined by a certain capacity for critical judgment: "The feeling for a good human job anywhere, the admiration of the really admirable, the disesteem of what is cheap and trashy and impermanent— this is what we call the critical sense, the sense for ideal values" (James 1987, 1244). He went on to claim that this critical sense was "the better part of what men know as wisdom" (1244) and was very clear about its origins: the broad critical sense possessed by true intellectuals was a generalization of a capacity for judgment developed more narrowly within academic or professional specialties. Note that this definition is more or less consistent with the reason we trust public intellectuals. They have developed and demonstrated their capacity for judgment within a narrow academic or professional specialty, and on the basis of this we give credence to their generalized judgment.

The content used when initially cultivating this capacity is irrelevant; what matters is what is trained ("the sifting of human creations," as James puts it) and how. Especially on the "how" question, James offers a corrective to the easy road of social learning through conformity or prestige. Training as an intellectual builds an individual's confidence in his or her capacity to make independent evaluations, rather than relying on the evaluation of others[6]. To be able to recognize "human excellence . . . only when ticketed and labeled and forced on us by others," James thunders, "this indeed should be accounted the very calamity and shipwreck of higher education" (1244).

In the spirit of William James, I propose a new social task for public intellectuals. It is to help make Jamesian intellectuals out of the myriad individual intelligences that together constitute the latent collective intelligence of the new social media. Many participants in these media already display some of these "intellectual" values. The stewards of Wikipedia, for example, sift and judge contributions in publicly accessible talk pages (Shirky 2008, 330–31).[7] I am calling, however, for a radical generalization of those values, such that the new social media are animated not by an ideology of epistemic collectivism or a heuristic of conformist and prestige-driven sharing but an explicit engagement with routine critical judgment and individual learning, curation, and creation.[8]

My two proposed maxims for public intellectuals are "Be an eye" and "Be an I."

Be an Eye (Not a Mouth)

Public intellectuals often benefit from the extreme skew in attention that characterizes the new social media. But they are also limited by it—unable to engage substantially with the millions to whom they speak on a daily basis (Shirky 2008). While they may not be able to meet their readers in dialogue, public intellectuals can serve as an eye for the swarm and, in so doing, teach by example the practical intellectual virtues advocated by William James.

First, public intellectuals can engage seriously with the products of the collective. James's warning about knowing excellence only when appropriately "ticketed and labeled" should caution those who hastily dismiss collective enterprises like Wikipedia or mock Twitter as endless chatter about what one had for lunch. Importantly—over and against the data-mining vision of "harvesting" the latent intelligence of the collective—their engagement must be humanistic if it is to teach the capacity for critical judgment. In that same speech, James (1987, 1243) remarked on the need for such humanistic approaches: "Geology, economics, mechanics are humanities when taught with reference to the successive achievements of the geniuses to which these sciences owe their being. Not taught thus, literature remains grammar, art a catalogue, history a list of dates, and natural science a sheet of formulas and weights and measures."[9] By calling attention—as Michael Nielsen does in *Reinventing Discovery*—to when, how, and why individuals, teams, or even mass groups have been able to produce human excellence, public intellectuals can extend a critical sense for the "really admirable" to the products of social media and, in so doing, cultivate that sense in the collective.

Data mining does, of course, play a role in this critical evaluation. It allows the when, how, and why questions asked by deep humanistic inquiry to be posed more broadly. Large-scale investigations of metaknowledge—that is, knowledge about knowledge (Evans and Foster 2011)—can provide some input on the still unsettled issue of what really counts as human excellence and what it really means to do a "good human job" in the intellectual domain. But such efforts to assess collective intelligence via algorithms—to "measure the swarm," so to speak—are a complement to, not a substitute for, the qualitative investigations and critical judgments described above, and should be animated by the same humanistic spirit.

Public intellectuals can also leverage their asymmetric resources and central position at the "eye" of the swarm to help develop new architectures of attention and new technologies of aggregation. In Nielsen's chess example, one of the heroes is a young chess master, Irina Krush, who served as the essential aggregator of suggestions from the thousands of participants on the World Team. She helped the team by developing technologies of aggregation (analysis trees) that served to centralize and coordinate the analysis and processing of the team's options. Her stature was earned by a brilliant early suggestion, and her recommendations were followed for the vast majority of the game—while a collapse in the architecture of attention she developed presaged the collapse of the World Team (Nielsen 2011). Public intellectuals can follow Krush's example for many of the difficult problems on which they intervene. Although these problems may lack the shared praxis of chess, the engagement and leadership of public intellectuals can help to develop, instill, or transmit such a shared basis for judgment.

Be an I

Like Mark Pagel a century later, William James emphasized the importance of individual learning and innovation in human history. In that same speech on the value of the "college-bred," he remarked that "individuals of genius show the way, and set the patterns, which common people then adopt and follow. The rivalry of the patterns is the history of the world" (James 1987, 1246). The critical sense is thus important not only in setting the patterns but in choosing the best ones to adopt, as the future will depend on these choices. In that spirit, public intellectuals can promote the critical sense through routinely and self-consciously practicing the faculty of judgment. They can demonstrate—and explicitly emphasize in their blogs, posts, and comments—the importance of non-social learning, of individual critical judgment, and of traditional scholarly values: drawing on diverse resources, examining independent and decentralized sources, and using effective, reflexive, and self-correcting mechanisms for aggregating these insights. In other words, and in many ways, the conditions under which individual intelligence operates best are *identical* to those under which collective intelligence operates best. When an individual is an "I"—when a person engages in significant individual learning and brings the best practices of traditional scholarship to bear on the vast collective commons made available and routinely updated by the Web and the new social media—he or she maximizes the likelihood of providing the individual insight or innovation, whether small or large, that enters most productively into collective intelligence of any sort.

Being an "I" in this way does more than make the collective more intelligent—it makes its members more human. Jaron Lanier is deeply concerned in *You Are Not a Gadget* by the way that many social media (most obviously ones like Facebook) "flatten" individuals by requiring them to conform to certain interfaces. Now, interfaces are always a necessity, but not all interfaces are good for all things. The Facebook interface, Lanier argues, is very good for clustering people to provide usable marketing information. But this isn't the same as real friendship. As he puts it (2010, 53), "A real friendship ought to introduce each person to the unexpected weirdness of the other." This undercurrent of humanism—and human interaction—is once again a useful tonic against the homogenizing forces of social learning. To the extent that we introduce each other to our unexpected weirdness, we are introducing each other to new, diverse, decentralized, and useful information—to the kind of provocative input that might stimulate individual or collective innovation and intelligence.

To What End?

I have argued that actions by public intellectuals along the lines I've described will promote a *generalization* of values that will ultimately make collective intelligence much more intelligent. The humanism, individuality, and critical judgment promoted by William James, and by the best of the new media participants, are precisely the values that enhance cognitive diversity, promote independence and decentralization, and cultivate good mechanisms for aggregating individual opinions, beliefs, and expertise. I believe that public intellectuals have an opportunity—indeed, a responsibility—to propagate these values: to restore the axiomatic foundations of collective intelligence, to promote the design of interfaces that encourage creativity and contribution rather than repetition, to imagine and even implement architectures of attention that draw focus to expertise rather than to prestige.

I hope that, in so doing, public intellectuals can help to rebuild the rapidly dying "middle" class of not-quite-public intellectuals—the local or narrow expert whose insights on a particular topic may in fact outstrip the insights of his or her far more prestigious and well-attended-to "betters" in the elite. Indeed, my hope is that the values I've outlined above will help to reunite the social media world into a continuous and integrated modular hierarchy of expertise and influence—a sort of "representative meritocracy." In such a world, at any particular level of geographic, social, or topical specificity, there would be a group of individuals in a position to speak up. To speak up not just figuratively, but to *literally* speak up the hierarchy of influence. Crucially, that group would *also* have the time, inclination, and local credibility to connect and engage with those less able to draw attention to their own ideas. This representative meritocracy would make the new social media vastly more democratic. Rather than a mob who can speak only through the occasional paroxysm of viral coordination or through involuntary algorithmic aggregation, we would have a digital republic—animated by devotion to individual creativity and the critical sense, able to draw effectively and efficiently on distributed expertise and knowledge. In such a world, we might speak of more than a collective intellect; we might truly speak of a collective intellectual.

Notes

1 This slightly compresses the story; in his original paper of March 7, 1907, Galton calculated the median, which was surprisingly close (1207 pounds, versus the reported true weight of 1198 pounds—though see Wallis (2014) for some mild inconsistencies in Galton's arithmetic and reporting). Galton later calculated the mean as well (1197 pounds), reporting this in *Nature's* letters to the editor ("The Ballot Box"). The mean was even closer. In fact, Wallis (2014) reads Galton's records to suggest that the ox really weighted 1197 pounds. This means that the crowd was spot on.

2 Mathematically, *collective error* is the square of the difference between the true value and the mean predicted value (that is, the average of all the individual predictions). *Individual error* is the square of the difference between an individual's prediction and the true value, and *average individual error* is simply the average of all the individual errors. *Diversity* is calculated based on how much individual predictions deviate from the mean predicted value (not from the true value). For each individual, compute the difference between that individual's prediction and the mean value; the average of the individual results represents the diversity of the

crowd. This relationship between collective error, average individual error, and diversity is, as Page notes, a mathematical fact. The diversity prediction theorem does *not* imply that increasing diversity is necessarily good (it may also increase average individual error), nor does it imply that decreasing individual error at the cost of decreasing diversity is necessarily bad: "If individual people predict perfectly, they cannot be diverse" (Page 207). Instead, it tells you what must be going on if a crowd with large individual errors nonetheless makes a good collective prediction: diversity in the crowd is compensating for large average individual error.

3 Galton's data display *some* signature of systematic error, with the negative errors being magnified and the positive errors "minified" (to use Galton's language). Displaying rather remarkable foresight, Galton speculates (1907) on the cause, using language Page would love: "the anomaly may be partly due to the use of a *small* variety of different methods, or formulae, so that the estimates are not homogeneous in that respect."

4 Both Surowiecki (2005) and Page (2007) consider many cases that fall somewhere between the weak-form and the middle-range, and Page provides compelling formal models of the way diversity contributes to collective intelligence across this spectrum. See, among many others, Hong and Page (2009) and Hong, Page, and Riolo (2012) for state-of-the-art formal models; Wooley et al. (2010) for experimental demonstrations; and Pentland (2014) for a popular overview of recent findings. The study of collective intelligence has made huge strides since I first drafted this paper in 2012; I am pleased to say that the overall argument remains compelling.

5 Strictly speaking, James uses the French term, *les intellectuels*, rehabilitating this anti-Dreyfusard term of abuse.

6 The importance of such confidence is beautifully expressed in Lindsay Waters's *The Enemies of Promise* (2004).

7 Such sifting doesn't always display the full panoply of Jamesian virtues. Messer-Kruse's experience with epistemic collectivism presents a challenging case. The excellence of his contribution was judged (and rejected) in part by appeal to scholarly consensus, i.e., the evaluation of others. Yet editors were *also* making the judgment that his contribution, though vouchsafed (i.e., "ticketed and labeled") by his expertise and professional standing, did not outweigh *their* reading of the balance of "reliable" secondary sources. Here multiple Jamesian values are in conflict. The most Jamesian resolution would have been evaluating Messer-Kruse's contribution and retaining it in the context of a larger debate, should it be found worthy. This seems to be what eventually happened: Messer-Kruse's analysis of the primary sources is

now reflected (and referenced) on the Haymarket Affair page (as of June 5, 2015). The current talk page displays admirable collective effort to sift and judge.

8 See Hanrahan (2013) for a concrete case of some of the tensions discussed in this essay. She contrasts professional music criticism with "technologically-mediated forms of cultural judgment" that prioritize consensus over aesthetic analysis, a tolerance for radical difference, and a cultivation of the listening public.

9 As a sociologist of science, I would downplay James's emphasis on "geniuses," but I embrace his broader point wholeheartedly.

References

Asch, Solomon E. 1951. "Effects of Group Pressure on the Modification and Distortion of Judgments." In *Groups, Leadership and Men*, edited by H. Guetzkow, 177–90. Pittsburgh: Carnegie Press.

Bikhchandani, Sushil David Hirshleifer, and Ivo Welch. 1992. "A Theory of Fads, Fashion, Custom, and Cultural Change as Informational Cascades." *Journal of Political Economy* 100: 992–1026.

Evans, James A. 2008. "Electronic Publication and the Narrowing of Science and Scholarship." *Science* 321 (18 July): 395–99.

Evans, James A., and Jacob G. Foster. 2011. "Metaknowledge." Science 331 (11 February): 721–25.

Galton, Francis. 1907. "Vox Populi." *Nature* 75 (7 March): 450–51.

———. 1907. "The Ballot-Box." *Nature* 75 (28 March): 509–10.

Ginsberg, Jeremy, Matthew H. Mohebbi, Rajan S. Patel, Lynnette Brammer, Mark S. Smolinski, and Larry Brilliant. 2009. "Detecting Influenza Epidemics Using Search Engine Query Data." *Nature* 457 (19 February): 1012–15.

Hanrahan, Nancy W. 2013. "If the People Like It, It Must Be Good: Criticism, Democracy, and the Culture of Consensus." *Cultural Sociology* 7 (1): 73–85.

Hayek, F. A. 1945. "The Use of Knowledge in Society." *American Economic Review* 35 (4): 519–30.

Henrich, Joseph, and Richard McElreath. 2003. "The Evolution of Cultural Evolution." *Evolutionary Anthropology* 12: 123–35.

Hindman, Matthew. 2008. *The Myth of Digital Democracy*. Princeton, NJ: Princeton University Press.

Hong, Lu, and Scott E. Page. 2009. "Generated and interpreted signals." *Journal of Economic Theory* 144 (5): 2174–96.

Hong, Lu, Scott E. Page, and Maria Riolo. 2012. "Incentives, Information, and Emergent Collective Accuracy." *Managerial and Decision Economics* 33: 323–34.

James, William. 1987. *William James: Writings, 1902–1910.* Edited by Bruce Kuklick. New York: Library of America.

Lanier, Jaron. 2010. *You Are Not a Gadget: A Manifesto.* New York: Alfred A. Knopf.

Langville, Amy N., and Carl D. Meyer. 2006. *Google's PageRank and Beyond: The Science of Search Engine Rankings.* Princeton, NJ: Princeton University Press.

Lazer, David, Ryan Kennedy, Gary King, and Alessandro Vespignani. 2014. "The Parable of Google Flu: Traps in Big Data Analysis." *Science* 343 (14 March): 1203–5.

Lorenz, Jan, Heiko Rauhut, Frank Schweitzer, and Dirk Helbing. 2011. "How Social Influence Can Undermine the Wisdom of Crowd Effect." *Proceedings of the National Academy of Sciences* 107 (9020): 1–6.

McLuhan, Marshall. 1994. *Understanding Media: The Extensions of Man.* Cambridge, MA: MIT Press.

Messer-Kruse, Timothy. 2012. "The Undue Weight of Truth on Wikipedia." *Chronicle of Higher Education*, 12 February. http://chronicle.com/article/The-Undue-Weight-of-Truth-on/130704/.

Nielsen, Michael. 2011. *Reinventing Discovery: The New Era of Networked Science.* Princeton NJ: Princeton University Press.

O'Reilly, Tim. 2005. "What Is Web 2.0: Design Patterns and Business Models for the Next Generation of Software." *O'Reilly*, 30 September, 1–5. http://oreilly.com/pub/a/web2/archive/what-is-web-20.html?page=1.

Page, Scott E. 2007. *The Difference: How the Power of Diversity Creates Better Groups, Firms, Schools, and Societies.* Princeton, NJ: Princeton University Press.

Pagel, Mark. 2011. "Infinite Stupidity: A Talk with Mark Pagel." *Edge: Conversations.* 15 December. http://edge.org/conversation/infinite-stupidity-edge-conversation-with-mark-pagel.

Pentland, Alex. 2014. *Social Physics: How Social Networks Can Make Us Smarter.* New York: Penguin Books.

Salganik, Matthew J., Peter Sheridan Dodds, and Duncan J. Watts. 2006. "Experimental Study of Inequality and Unpredictability in an Artificial Cultural Market." *Science* 311 (10 February): 854–56.

Sanger, Larry. 2006. Response. In "On 'Digital Maoism: The Hazards of the New Online Collectivism,' by Jaron Lanier." *Edge*: The Reality Club, 30 May. http://www.edge.org/discourse/digital_maoism.html.

Shirky, Clay. 2008. *Here Comes Everybody: The Power of Organizing Without Organizations*. New York: Penguin Books.

Surowiecki, James. 2005. *The Wisdom of Crowds*. New York: Anchor Books.

Taylor, Andrew. 2010. *Thinking America: New England Intellectuals and the Varieties of American Identity*. Lebanon: University of New Hampshire Press.

Tversky, Amos, and Daniel Kahneman. 1974. "Judgment Under Uncertainty: Heuristics and Biases." *Science* 185 (27 September): 1124–31.

Wallis, Kenneth F. 2014. "Revisiting Francis Galton's Forecasting Competition." *Statistical Science* 29 (3): 420–24.

Waters, Lindsay. 2004. *Enemies of Promise: Publishing, Perishing, and the Eclipse of Scholarship*. Chicago: Prickly Paradigm Press.

Woolley, Anita W., Christopher F. Chabris, Alex Pentland, Nada Hashmi, and Thomas W. Malone. "Evidence for a Collective Intelligence Factor in the Performance of Human Groups." *Science* 330 (29 October): 686–88.

4   Creating the Conditions for an Intellectually Active People

What Today's Public Intellectual Can Learn from Anonymous

LIZ PIRNIE

Since the emergence of the print revolution, public intellectuals have relied on books, newspapers, and periodicals in order to present their ideas to a broader public. Today, of course, the range of communication technologies deployed by public intellectuals can include not only radio and television but a variety of digital platforms. As a result, public intellectuals have, perhaps inevitably, developed into what some critics describe as "media" intellectuals—intellectuals concerned not merely with ideas but with commercial success, reputation building, and hence with public image. In the digital arena, public intellectuals seeking to market their ideas have become savvy creators and sharers of "sticky" content produced for consumption, discussion, and dissemination by the public at large, whether through the posting of comments or by linking, "liking," or Twittering. These "Public Intellectuals 2.1," as Daniel Drezner calls them, actively and strategically utilize the Internet and Web-based platforms, such as blogs, personal websites, or YouTube, to attract and engage their publics, thereby generating what he sees as a potential "renaissance" of the public intellectual (Drezner 2009, 49).

This "new dawn" of digital technology and communication has prompted some, such as media studies scholar Siva Vaidhyanathan, to declare that "there has never been a better time to be a public intellectual" (Vaidhyanathan 2006). While the array of tools available to the public intellectual has undeniably broadened, such declarations refer primarily to the logistical options available to the intellectual today, which have brought with them not only the potential for an increased output of ideas and opinion but also greater rewards for successful competition in the intellectual marketplace, in which ideas can be branded and commoditized. They speak little, however, to the cultural and political stakes entailed in the use of these new options or to the wants, needs, or character of the publics at whom these efforts are directed. As Alan Hudson (2003, 33) reminds us, "The debate about intellectuals, their worth and seriousness, only makes sense in so far as it distils and gives expression to a much more important subject: the state of public life."

Much has been written about the current state of public life. Many of those who constitute "the public": seem to have lost faith in both the moral legitimacy and the practical utility of traditional top-down models of institutional and political organization, which has generated an oppressive sense of powerlessness. This erosion of civic engagement is visible not merely in low voter turnouts but in the rise of a narrow, narcissistic preoccupation with self and self-interest. If the fundamental task of the public intellectual is to create the conditions for what John Stuart Mill ([1859] 2001, 33) called "an intellectually active people"—and if, as Edward Said (1994, xvii) argues, the nature of this task necessitates taking a position of "dissent against the status quo"—then two key questions for today's "Public Intellectual 2.1" can be articulated. First, what possibilities, and what impediments, do digital media present for a public intellectual's message of dissent? And, second, in an era of public passivity, how can public intellectuals work to foster the conditions for an "intellectually active" people? In what follows, I will argue that the social phenomenon of "hacktivism," exemplified in decentralized online communities such as Anonymous, offers some valuable insights for today's public intellectuals.

The Present Age

Especially in the wake of grassroots democratic movements in, for example, Iran and Tunisia, many critics have expressed concern about the political apathy that prevails in so many Western democratic countries. The degree to which these movements turned on the rapid dissemination of information has also served to focus international attention on efforts to restrict the free flow of information and on the implications of such practices for democracy. Although the Canadian political and economic context clearly differs quite radically from the circumstances that gave rise to these movements, it is still worth asking whether profound transformative social action is, in the words of Søren Kierkegaard ([1846] 1962, 42), "of all things, the most unthinkable."

In *Power and Betrayal in the Canadian Media*, political analyst David Taras argues that even at a time when current political events challenge the core of Canadian identity—a time when, arguably, the public most urgently requires a critical media—our national public media habitually fail to provide aggressive critical analysis or to "question the basic assumptions on which the political system rests" (2001, 58). As Taras (2001, 240) warns, a country that allows its media to abandon a commitment to fostering open debate and space for new and possibly controversial ideas creates the conditions for the atrophy of democracy. Writing nearly a century and a half earlier, Mill ([1859] 1986, 33) saw the degradation of the conditions that foster intellectual engagement as symptomatic of an atmosphere of "mental slavery," one characterized by a pervasive "dread of heterodox speculation" that prevents human beings from realizing their full intellectual capabilities. As he observed: "Where there is a tacit convention that principles are not to be disputed; where the discussion of the greatest questions which can occupy humanity is considered to be closed, we cannot hope to find that generally high scale of mental activity which has made some periods of history so remarkable" (33).

Mill's statement presaged the stakes at issue along today's new digital frontiers. Amnesty International's annual report for 2011 identifies freedom of expression, access to information, and tools of communication as critical to the ability of individuals to challenge repression and claim their human rights and potentials (Amnesty International 2011, xi–xix). As the report illustrates, the possibility of intellectual dissent and the conditions, both cultural and technical, of the public media are inextricably bound to one another. Where Taras, Mill, and Amnesty International converge is in the conviction not only that ideas create realities but that the suppression of ideas destroys the conditions under which it becomes possible to conceive ideas in the first place. Of course, individuals who recognize that their first duty is to follow the path of their intellect have not ceased to exist. Mill's concern, however, was that in a suffocating atmosphere of intellectual conformity, in which dissenting views are suppressed, the public intellect withers. What, then, must be done today to foster the conditions under which hegemonic views can be challenged and the public intellect is able to flourish?

For those who study communication and language, it is impossible to separate content ("What is being said?") from medium ("How is it being said?"). The efficacy of intellectuals' efforts to convey messages intended to spur social change thus depends in part on the specific technologies of communication they adopt. An early example of this recognition arrives in Søren Kierkegaard's essay "The Present Age" (1846), which mounts a scathing critique of "the Press" and its constitutive role in creating and sustaining an illusory "phantom," the public. In view of today's media-saturated landscape, it is not surprising that scholars such as philosopher (and webcaster) Hubert Dreyfus (2004) have returned to Kierkegaard's essay as a means of gaining insight into present-day concerns pertaining to the Internet and the public sphere.

"Ours is the age of advertisement and publicity," Kierkegaard declared: "Nothing ever happens but there is immediate publicity everywhere" ([1846] 1962, 35). For Kierkegaard, the daily papers of the mid-nineteenth century were instrumental in producing a degrading levelling of society to its lowest common denominator. As Steven Best and Douglas Kellner (1997, 43) note, the press was, for Kierkegaard, "a mass medium that addresses its audience as members of a crowd and that itself helps massify society," working to produce "a crowd devoid of individuality and independent judgment, their thought determined by the authority of printed words and editorial fiat." Kierkegaard's press posits as self-evident what he described as a "monstrous abstraction," a nothing known as "the public," made up of "unreal individuals who never are and never can be united in an actual situation or organization—and yet are held together as a whole" ([1846] 1962, 60). In so doing, the press weakens the connection between individuals and their concrete realities. "A generation, a people, an assembly of the people, a meeting or a man," Kierkegaard wrote, "are responsible for what they are and can be made ashamed if they are inconstant and unfaithful; but a public remains a public" (62). It is "everything and nothing," an entity that transforms individuals into a passive "third party" (64), reducing them from moral agents to the status of onlookers.

It is in the lack of connection to the concrete and the tendency to think purely in the abstract, Dreyfus (2004) argues, that Kierkegaard sees the error inherent to the Enlightenment's call to reason. In this world, despite lacking direct experience, people hold opinions on any and every public issue but are removed from any sense of personal responsibility or obligation to action. As Dreyfus (2004) puts it, "The public sphere thus promotes ubiquitous commentators who deliberately detach themselves from the local practices out of which specific issues grow and in terms of which these issues must be resolved through some sort of committed action." For Kierkegaard, it is not reflection itself that is evil but "a reflective condition and the deadlock which it involves, by transforming the capacity for action into a means of escape from action" ([1846] 1962, 68). Unlike a tumultuous and passionate revolutionary "age of action," which storms ahead, setting up new things and tearing down old, a "reflective age" is without passion, "hindering and stifling action as it transforms expressions of strength into a feat of dialectics: it leaves everything standing, but cunningly empties it of significance" (42). In this passive age, the ideals of revolution and the courage to revolt may be celebrated publicly through abstract calls to action ("Something must be done!"), but, when left to private reflection, individuals mock such decisive action as foolish or condemn it as too risky and find grounds to excuse themselves from the task. For this reason, profound transformative social action becomes "of all things, the most unthinkable" (42).

The Virtual Intellectual

In *Representations of the Intellectual* (1994), Edward Said argued that for each age and in each place, it is the defining task of public intellectuals to become "outsiders." He issued a reminder to public intellectuals that (like everyone else) they are deeply embedded in their cultural and historical circumstances. The question then becomes, "To what extent are intellectuals servants of these actualities, to what extent enemies?" (Said 1994, xv). To be servants rather than enemies, intellectuals must work to separate themselves from the ideological frameworks within which they are otherwise imprisoned. The intellectual vocation, Said wrote, consists in "maintaining a state of constant alertness, of a perpetual willingness not to let half-truths or received ideas steer one along" (23). In other words, liberation comes not from denying one's social embeddedness but from becoming fully and continually aware of it. For Said, intellectuals must constantly ask, "How does one speak the truth? What truth? For whom and where?" (88).

In a lecture delivered several years later, interactive media research Geert Lovink (1997) noted that missing from Said's view of the intellectual as moral agent, as someone who "speaks truth to power," was "an analysis of the dramatic changes of the public sphere itself." Recognizing the degree to which knowledge production and distribution had already become inseparably entwined with digital communication networks, Lovink noted that intellectuals could no longer live in a world of paper and hope to have any serious impact. At the same time, he cautioned that "the intellectual of the Media Age should not by definition be identical to the figure of the media personality"—the "intellectual as TV personality," who "seems to be part of the problem." The endless proffering of opinions, he argued, simply draws the public "deeper into a status of passive consumers." Lovick advocated instead for what he called, not a media intellectual, but a "Virtual Intellectual." Pointing out that *virtual* implies "ever changing, in constant contact with other e-writers (and readers)," he envisioned that "these new figures will be constituted through their specific mixture of local and global cultures, digitised and non-digitised source material, real and screen-only experiences" (Lovink 1997).

As Lovink (2004, 13) argued some years later, intellectuals working in the realm of the humanities were prone to view technology "from a quasi-outsider's perspective, assuming that technology and society can still be separated." But, he wrote, "the Internet is not a parallel world somewhere out there, it is an integral part of society," and its social networks should be understood as "osmotic interfaces between inside and outside" (9). Virtual intellectuals accordingly locate themselves *within* technology, adopting a reflexive understanding of their own situation as users of that technology. They recognize that in order to understand "from where" they speak, they must look to the architecture of the communication networks they use and how these technologies function as an inextricable part of social and economic systems. In an era in which "the state of public life" is not only expressed but actively shaped through digital media, the work of the public intellectual likewise cannot be separated from the technologies that dominate our day-to-day lives and mediate both our interactions with others and our process of self-fashioning.

Lovink (1997) suggests that "intellectuals who are only expressing opinions, in the belief that the media-industry (particularly television) still produces common sense content which shapes public opinion, should simply desist—they should boycott all talk shows and instead engage in fundamental research on the 'state of the media.'" Capable of fluidly traversing both online and "real-world" communications media, the virtual intellectual recognizes that to understand the state of the media is to understand the "state of self" (or selves). But negotiating the relationship of the self to digital media is not an easy task. As social media sites, banks, retailers, employers, and governments, among others, demand personal data that render individuals more visible and transparent, not only is privacy sacrificed but the line between private and public is blurred. As Eva Illouz notes, this blurring of boundaries makes it "virtually impossible to distinguish the rationalization and commodification of selfhood from the capacity of the self to shape and help itself and to engage in deliberation and communication with others" (quoted in Lovink 2011, 42). In other words, processes of self-definition and interpersonal exchange become entangled with the creation and marketing of a public persona. So how does the virtual intellectual escape the temptation to engage in self-promotion and image management?

Mainstream social media, such as Facebook, function by cultivating, stockpiling, and exploiting weak ties—that is, relatively loose links among more densely connected groups. The virtual intellectual seeks instead to escape the web of weak ties and, through participation in intensive network collaborations, to harness the Internet's potential to disrupt the status quo. These collaborations generally involve a limited number of members, who sometimes remain anonymous and whose goal is to exercise their intellectual freedom in the service of social and political critique—implicit in which is the right of access to information unfettered by censorship. Such networked communities offer an alternative to a collection of autonomous intellectuals struggling to create and maintain a public image.

Digital Dissent: Hacktivism and Organized Networks

In 2007, Canadian Policy Research Networks published its findings on low voter turnout among young people (aged 18 to 24) in a report titled *Lost in Translation*. The report, which aggregated the findings of six commissioned research papers on political participation among youth, concluded that although young people indeed had little interest in voting, there was strong evidence of "small 'p' political life." As the authors of the report noted, young people

> are quick to apply online tools and networks to mobilize socially and
> politically, but often do not identify their activities as being political.
> They are very impatient with traditional ways of political engage-
> ment—they are turned off by political parties and partisan politics,
> dislike hierarchical approaches to organization and mobilization,
> and don't think that formal politics is an effective route to affect
> change. . . . This generation is much more wired, getting more of its
> news and information online and from alternative sources, rather than
> mainstream media. These youth are more likely than older Canadians
> to participate in political demonstrations, to volunteer and to be a
> member of a group or organization. They volunteer for different activ-
> ities and are motivated by different reasons (e.g., reciprocal relation-
> ships, skills development, social purposes). They look for engagement
> that has personal meaning and delivers faster results than traditional
> routes. (MacKinnon, Pitre, and Watling 2007, vi)

"Youth are not disconnected from politics," the authors concluded; rather, "it is political institutions, practice and culture that are disconnected from youth" (vii). As they went on to say:

> Today's youth . . . are reinventing civic and political engagement.
> Unfortunately, their discourse is all too often either not understood
> or poorly captured by traditional surveys, academic research and
> their Baby Boomer parents. In this sense, their ideas and actions are
> misunderstood or misrepresented. They seem to get lost in translation
> between the new and the old—between their perspectives and trad-
> itional notions about political and civic engagement. (8)

Although the authors recognize that young people are legitimately participating in political action, what is absent from their list of alternative
political engagements is the act of abstaining from voting itself. Because
the primary objective of their research is to figure out how to increase voter
turnout among youth, the researchers approach this demographic with the

assumption that something is *already wrong* with young people—that they are not doing something they should and that what they *are* doing takes substandard forms ("small 'p' political life"). The authors seem reluctant to acknowledge that, if young people are "turned off by political parties and partisan politics," then perhaps it is the Canadian electoral process itself that creates the structural condition for what is perceived as their failure to vote. Through this lens, young people can be seen, not as individuals lost in translation, but rather as competent actors who have concluded that, although conventional institutions, including those of government, may still offer some absolute advantages, "the *relative* advantages of those institutions have disappeared—relative, that is, to the direct efforts of the people they represent" (Shirky 2008, 23).

It is in response to such frustrations that a particular form of "small 'p' political life" has assumed a pivotal position in today's social and political arena. With a healthy representation of young people, including some too young to vote, "hacktivism" has become one method of political resistance and protest. In *Hacktivism and Cyberwars. Rebels with a Cause?* Tim Jordan and Paul Taylor (2004, 172) describe hacktivism as "the first social movement of virtuality." Combining political dissent with the technical know-how needed to bypass computer network security systems and/ or overload web servers, the hacktivist stands at the intersection of what Jordan and Paul describe as "three divergent currents: hacking, informational societies and modern social protest and resistance" (2). As "activism gone electronic," hacktivism represents "the emergence of popular political action, of the self-activity of groups of people, in cyberspace" (1). Inspired in part by grassroots political movements, hacktivism exploits the potential of online community platforms to serve as vehicles for dissent, opposing itself to conventional models of organizing collective action that operate within the framework of mainstream institutions.

As Internet researcher Clay Shirky (2005) explains, traditional institutional structures are both inefficient and exclusionary, chiefly because the costs involved in coordinating individuals are generally high. As he puts it, institutional operational models, structured typically around centralized decision making, hierarchical power structures, a specialized professional class and capital intense operations; inherently goal oriented, inefficient, non-transparent, and exclusionary, are becoming "incoherent" entities due to cultural and power shifts engendered by the advent of new media, ICTs, e-mail, the Internet, and social networking platforms, based as they are in communicating, sharing, and above all, collaboration.

In contrast to institutions, which must develop an infrastructure capable of coordinating individuals, global communications technologies have made it possible, he argues, to create organizations that build collaboration into the infrastructure—"to design systems that coordinate the output of the group as a by-product of the operating of the system, without regard to institutional models." As not only users but developers of these technologies, hacktivists have the capacity to develop the communications infrastructure necessary to generate and sustain self-organizing communities. Moreover, as Shirky notes, conventional institutions are weighted toward those who make the largest contribution—toward the most productive employees—and so are incapable of capturing the value of a "distributed class" of individuals who contribute to the whole in only a small, but potentially significant, way. Inherent to the operation of these new social platforms and networks, however, are protocols that serve to enable individual contributions, no matter how limited, rather than acting as an obstacle to them (Shirky 2005).

This form of virtual community building, characterized by a diverse membership operating on a global scale for a wide range of purposes, is not, of course, unique to hacktivists. Numerous digitally based social networks and communities, such as Twitter, YouTube, Wikipedia, or Flickr, have similar attributes. The advantage of these communities, according to Charles Leadbeater (2008, 19), is that they function like "a vast bird's nest." Constructed by their users, these communities allow people to come and go, contributing something if they wish, with the value of their contributions judged quality rather than quantity. Contrary to the notion that hierarchal organizational structures ensure efficiency and order, Leadbeater suggests that the success of what he calls "We-Think" communities—those able to harness the energy and creativity of individuals en masse—lies precisely in their lack of any rigid, top-down structure of the sort in which "you look up to someone to tell you what to do."[1] As he explains (2008, 80): "We-Think succeeds by creating self-governing communities who make the most of their diverse knowledge without being overwhelmed by their differences. That is possible only if these communities are joined around a simple animating goal, if they develop legitimate ways to review and sort ideas and if they have the right kind of leadership." These communities do not lose their way or cease to function, devolving into chaos, provided they are able to establish the conditions that allow for "responsible self- governance" (79).

Although such networks have the virtue of enabling the construction of collaborative relations, one must be mindful of the technological architecture of these relationships. Writing of "the conjunction between software cultures and social desires," Geert Lovink and Ned Rossiter (2013, 10) point out that "crucial to this relation is the question of algorithmic architectures—something largely overlooked by many activist movements who adopt, in what seems a carefree manner, commercially motivated and politically compromised social media software such as Facebook, Twitter and Google+." Especially in light of revelations pertaining to the electronic surveillance activities of the US National Security Agency, sites such as Facebook have shown themselves to be far from transparent in terms of the architecture of their algorithms and the degree to which personal information is stored, used, shared, and sold. Indeed, as Lovink and Rossiter (2013, 10) note, commercial social media platforms have a number of drawbacks: "security of communication (infiltration, surveillance and a wilful disregard of privacy), logic or structure of communication (micro-chatting among friends coupled with broadcasting notices for the many subscribed to the cloud), and an economy of 'free labour' (user generated data, or 'the social production of value')."

The tendency of new and potentially subversive technologies to be co-opted by existing commercial and institutional structures is well recognized. Writing in 2004—the year that Facebook was founded—Lovink and Florian Schneider warned that "power responds to the pressure of increasing mobility and communications of the multitudes with attempts to regulate them in the framework of traditional regimes." As a result, networks lose their revolutionary capacity. "After an exciting first phase of introductions and debates," they write, "networks are put to the test: either they transform into a body that is capable to act, or they remain stable on a flatline of information exchange, with the occasional reply of an individual who dares to disagree." Far from harnessing the power of connection in the service of liberation, networking can instead produce "a rampant will to powerlessness that escapes the idea of collective progress" (Lovink and Schneider 2004).

Lovink and Rossiter (2013) accordingly draw a contrast between mainstream social media and what they call "organised networks." Rather than "exploiting the weak ties of the dominant social networking sites," such networks "emphasise intensive collaborations within a limited group of engaged users" (2013, 10). As they note, commercial social media foster a culture of monitoring, in which participants constantly keep tabs on one another's activities. In contrast, organized networks

> radically break with the updating and monitoring logic and shift atten-
> tion away from watching and following diffuse networks to getting
> things done, together. There is more in this world than self-improve-
> ment and empowerment. Network architectures need to move away
> from the user-centered approach and instead develop a *task-related*
> design undertaken in *protected mode*. (Lovink and Rossiter 2013, 11;
> emphasis added)

The hacktivist community collectively identified as "Anonymous" offers an especially useful illustration of a network architecture oriented not toward users but toward the task of "getting things done."

We Are Anonymous

It is perhaps most fruitful to begin with a discussion of what Anonymous is not.[2] Anonymous is not a cohesive group or club, with a clearly defined membership. Rather, it is best described as a loose and dynamic collection of online chat groups whose participants are able to move from one group to another, from one discussion to another, as they please. Anonymous is not a centralized entity but a distributed aggregate of individuals from around the globe. Nor, of course, is Anonymous a social media site on the Facebook model. Anonymous relies on Internet Relay Chat (IRC) channels—forums that allow for real-time Internet chatting—where anonymous participants ("anons") come together to suggest targets, debate strategies, and plan attacks, as well as simply to exchange ideas and joke around.

Anonymous is best known for its politically motivated hacking and ser-vice disruption activities, which have been directed against a wide array of specific targets. Depending on the issue and the target, the personal and political stakes involved for those participating may vary. As Leadbeater suggested, however, the success of groups like Anonymous depend in part on the fact that, despite their diversity, participants are unified around "a simple animating goal." In the case of Anonymous, namely, to combat efforts, whether on the part of governments or private organizations, to restrict access to information, to engage in online forms of surveillance, and to circumscribe political rights and freedoms. In accordance with the non-hierarchical structure of the "hive mind," or Leadbeater's "We-Think" communities, Anonymous has no recognized leaders. In fact, individuals who try to assume such a position within the community are quickly reminded of their place and can be removed from the IRC—a process that well illustrates democratic self-governance. Even *The Economist*, a publication not known for its subversive character, described Anonymous as "24-hour Athenian democracy" (*Economist* 2010).

Anonymous's signature strategy consists of a distributed denial-of-service (DDoS) attack, in which large numbers of personal computers tethered by software simultaneously send a high volume of traffic to a targeted website. These tsunami waves of site traffic overwhelm the web server, causing it to crash, thereby rendering the website non-operational for a period of minutes or hours. Perhaps not surprisingly, these attacks have been characterized in the media and by government and corporate representatives as crimes, even as acts of terrorism. In a more apt analogy, however, "DDoSing" might be thought of as an online sit-in meant to interrupt Web services, much like a physical sit-in can block traffic or prevent people from accessing a building.

Properly speaking, a DDoS attack is not hacktivism, as it does not actually involve hacking into computers. Nor, although characterized as a hacktivist group, does Anonymous consist solely or even primarily of computer hackers. Anyone, with or without hacking knowledge, can contribute to its operations.[3] Another misconception about Anonymous, often perpetuated in the mainstream media, is that the group is made up of nefarious youths, criminals, Internet thugs, and immature computer geeks who are more interested in causing trouble than in serious political action. But it is not clear that any evidence exists to support such characterizations. An unknown number of people participate in Anonymous, and, as Gabriella Coleman (2010b) notes, some of them "don't even bother to leave a trace of their thoughts, motivations, or reactions," while those that do express divergent opinions. Under such circumstances, it is simply not possible to generalize about their intentions, their motivations for participating, or their character as individuals. Contrasting Anonymous IRC chat with exchanges among Anonymous participants using Pirate Pad (a type of collaborative writing software), Coleman argues that "the documents and conversation on Pirate Pad reflect a calmer, more deliberate and deliberative side of Anonymous," indicating that at least "some of the participants are engaged in strategic and political thinking." Viewed from this perspective, participants certainly do not appear like adolescent troublemakers but "more like a group of seasoned political activists, debating the merits and demerits of actions and targets" (Coleman 2010b).

Anonymous began as a popular and anonymous image board called "4chan."[4] Initially, the group was not especially known for political actions but mainly for "trolling" (that is, invading and disrupting online discussions), DDoSing, and making public the personal information of targeted individuals. The motivation for such attacks was "lulz," a variant of the messaging abbreviation "LOL" ("laugh out loud") that refers specifically to laughter at another person's embarrassment or upset. Early in 2008, however, Anonymous turned its attention from trolling and pranking to the Church of Scientology, after the church threatened to take legal action against YouTube and other websites that had refused to take down a leaked video that featured actor Tom Cruise extolling the virtues of Scientology and was, the church claimed, intended for internal circulation only. In response to this attempt to interfere with the ideal of a free Internet, in January 2008, Anonymous led a series of "raids" against the Church of Scientology. In the wake of these raids, the Anonymous discussion boards took a reflective turn, with participants debating the meaning and purpose of their pranking. After much online debate, participants decided to organize a global day of action. On 10 February 2008, more than six thousand people took part in protests, many of them held in front of Scientology churches, in cities in North America, Europe, New Zealand, and Australia. According to Coleman (Goodman 2011), these early protests differed from the usual street protests in that the marchers seemed to focus less on articulating political messages and more on creating a carnivalesque atmosphere, with many protesters wearing Guy Fawkes masks. The masks, which have since become emblematic of Anonymous, are more than merely a disguise: they allude to the series of comics (and subsequent film) *V for Vendetta*, about an anarchist revolutionary, disguised behind a Guy Fawkes mask, who plans extreme and theatrical campaigns of violence against the police state in which he lives, hoping to issue a call to others to stand up and rule themselves.

Although its initial protests had a flavour of mischief making, Anonymous has evolved, changing tactics and strategies and collectively developing more efficient methods of mobilizing individuals and attracting media attention to its activities. In December 2010, Anonymous came to the awareness of the general public when it launched a massive protest, Operation Payback, against anti-piracy organizations and in defence of WikiLeaks. In response to WikiLeaks's publication of a cache of confidential diplomatic correspondence, the US government had called on PayPal, Bank of America, MasterCard, Visa, and Amazon to stop processing donations to WikiLeaks, despite the fact that WikiLeaks had not (and still has not) been charged with any legal infractions. Participation in the solidarity campaign marked a milestone in the history of Internet Relay Chat channels. Some seven thousand online anons succeeded for days in disabling the websites of some of the world's most powerful corporations, an accomplishment that speaks to Anonymous's organizational capacity to choose targets collectively, through polling, and to coordinate action by distributing collectively written documents indicating who is to be attacked, and who isn't, and issuing reminders about the importance of abiding by group decisions.

In the summer of 2011, Anonymous groups offered support to the Arab Spring uprising by hacking into and taking down government websites in both Tunisia and Egypt. Anonymous contingents were also instrumental in gathering support for the Occupy Wall Street (OWS) protest, initiated by the Canadian anti-consumerist magazine *Adbusters*, on 17 September 2011. Nathan Schneider (2011) describes OWS's decision-making body, the General Assembly, as "a horizontal, autonomous, leaderless, modified-consensus-based system with roots in anarchist thought," one that is "akin to the assemblies that have been driving recent social movements around the world." A similar approach to decision making is practiced on Anonymous's IRC channels. Of course, Anonymous cannot be credited for the success of the Tunisian revolution or the draw of thousands of participants to OWS and its offspring Occupy movements, although many anons—some wearing their trademark Guy Fawkes masks—took part in the occupations. However, the fact that recent social and political movements have relied heavily on digital modes of communication to develop and coordinate actions suggests the real-world, "away from keyboard" possibilities that exist when the weak ties created by social media platforms are animated by a commitment among users to ideas and shared desires.

According to Dreyfus (2004), "Kierkegaard would surely argue that, while the Internet, like the Press, allows unconditional commitments, far from encouraging them, it tends to turn all of life into a risk free game," one in which commitments are imagined more than enacted. Dreyfus goes on to suggest that "the test as to whether one had acquired an unconditional commitment would come if one had the incentive and courage to transfer what one had learned to the real world. Then one would confront what Kierkegaard calls 'the danger and the harsh judgment of existence.'" I would argue that, far from remaining safely enclosed within a virtual world of images and abstract ideas, Anonymous is very much grounded in the real world. In recent years, Anonymous groups have targeted numerous individuals, organizations, and government websites worldwide in an effort to stimulate commitment and prompt action on a broad range of issues, from centralized data storage and surveillance regimes, to censorship and the muffling of free speech, to anti-gay legislation and efforts of school authorities to cover up a case of gang rape, to political repression and struggles for democracy and human rights.

At the same time, campaigns like Operation Payback serve as a sobering reminder of the risks entailed in online acts of civil disobedience. On 6 October 2013, thirteen individuals were indicted for their part in Anonymous's DDoSing attacks on the Motion Picture Association of America, the Recording Industry Association of America, PayPal, Bank of America, MasterCard, Visa, and Amazon. The software used in DDoS attacks automatically encodes the sender's IP address, which means that senders must take steps to disguise their address prior to launching an attack. Evidently, these individuals neglected to do so, and, as a result, US federal authorities were able to trace the IP addresses and thus determine the identities of those involved. The lesson learned, if it was not already understood, is that anonymity must be actively pursued and protected. Anonymity does not dissolve identity and personal integrity, nor does it exempt individuals from responsibility and the need for commitment. The participation of anonymous individuals in collective protest is an act of resistance—one that should prompt people to ask not "What is the person wearing the mask hiding?" but "What is the masked performer trying to tell us?"

Conclusion

For Kierkegaard, the ultimate work of the enlightened individual was not to assume a position of authority and attempt to guide the lost masses toward wisdom. Although in revolutionary times, he argued, authoritative figures rose to lead the masses, in a passive age, characterized by the spirit of levelling, the role of the "man of distinction," the man who is "recognizable," is no longer to lead ([1846] 1962, 80). "From now on," he wrote, "the great man, the leader (according to his position) will be without authority . . . he will be *unrecognizable*" (80). Only by indirectly, anonymously, helping individuals as individuals—not as marginalized groups or unfortunate masses in need of liberation—and labouring to conceal their own efforts from those they help can these unrecognizable leaders assist in the awakening of others (82).

Recognizing the need for unrecognizability, Kierkegaard often chose to publish under pseudonyms. Especially in his so-called aesthetic writings, those aimed at a relatively popular audience, Kierkegaard sought to disguise his authorial voice—to give readers no clue to his identity—so as to prompt them to think for themselves. In Kierkegaard's view, individuals first had to be liberated from the suffocating abstraction of "the public" before they could come together as ethical citizens around a commitment, not to each other, but to the ideas they shared: "When individuals (each one individually) are essentially and passionately related to an idea and together are essentially related to the same idea, the relation is optimal and normative. Individually the relation separates them (each one has himself for himself), and ideally it unites them" (62). In contrast to the "phantom" public shaped by a dominating "Press," individuals who unite around a commitment to ideas do not vanish into the crowd; they continue to exist as distinct individuals, interacting with other individuals to form genuine, concrete communities.

Anonymous, I would argue, introduces the public intellectual not only to the power of network-coordinated activities but to "concrete" communities in a new form, one that is, ironically, virtual. If the role of the public intellectual as opinion leader and authoritative figure has indeed waned, and if the controlling interests of commerce and normative institutions compromise the legitimacy of autonomous intellectual work, then perhaps it is time for the public intellectual to collaborate, engaging with others in communities formed around a shared commitment, and, moreover, to do so anonymously—to remain *un*recognizable, rather than seeking a marketable public identity. In other words, perhaps public intellectuals should consider a shift from autonomy to anonymity. As Lovink (2011, 46) argues, this mode of engagement—anonymity in the online context—affords an opportunity for the virtual intellectual to "dismantle the performance of self and self-disclosure" and to "recoup an energy of metamorphosis."

In short, the lesson here is not that public intellectuals should become hacktivists or emulate the disruptive "shock" tactics of Anonymous or even necessarily participate in concrete political actions, though these remain avenues of participation. Rather, in a passive age, one distracted by the superficiality of images, they must seek ways to keep the spirit of dissent alive. As Lovink suggests, by choosing anonymity, the virtual intellectual also works to establish the conditions under which others can resist institutional demands for visibility and transparency. Perhaps for the present age, then, the most essential trait of a public intellectual is a commitment to understanding his or her own position in today's economy of identity management and consumption. To the extent that public intellectuals can forgo the temptation to be drawn into that economy and choose instead to exploit the collaborative potential of digital media, they may help to create the conditions from which an intellectually active people can emerge.

Notes

1 This phrase is from a lecture Leadbeater gave on decentralized models of organization. A videotape of the lecture, "Charles Leadbeater: Organizations and Democracy" (UsNowFilm, 2008) is available at http://www.youtube.com/watch?v=6v5FVNqhdNk. The phrase occurs 44 seconds into the talk.

2 I am indebted to the work of Gabriella Coleman, as well as to her comments during a *Democracy Now!* interview (Goodman 2011), for the snapshot of Anonymous that I present here. Coleman, a cultural anthropologist, has been following hackers, hacktivists, and online forums such as Anonymous since 2002.

3 Anonymous has created a video titled *How to Join Anonymous: A Beginner's Guide* (http://www.youtube.com/watch?v=XQk14FLDPZg), which begins by explaining that one can't join Anonymous, as it isn't an organization. It advises interested individuals that Anonymous has no

centralized infrastructure but instead uses existing Internet social networks and that, while this could change, the most active groups currently exist on Facebook, Twitter, and IRC and can be found by looking for key terms such as "Anonymous" or "AnonOps."

4 Image boards are similar to online bulletin boards, which are subdivided into various topics based on user interest. But, unlike text-based forums, image boards are centred around the posting of pictures and images.

References

Amnesty International. 2011. *Amnesty International Report 2011: The State of the World's Human Rights*. London: Amnesty International. http://files. amnesty.org/air11/air_2011_full_en.pdf.

Best, Steven, and Douglas Kellner. 1997. *The Postmodern Turn*. New York: Guilford Press.

Coleman, Gabriella. 2010a. "The Anthropology of Hackers." *The Atlantic*, 21 September. http://www.theatlantic.com/technology/archive/2010/09/the-anthropology-of-hackers/63308/

———. 2010b. "What It's Like to Participate in Anonymous' Actions." *The Atlantic*, 10 December. http://www.theatlantic.com/technology/ archive/2010/12/what-its-like-to-participate-in-anonymous-actions/67860/.

———. 2014. *Hacker, Hoaxer, Whistleblower, Spy: The Many Faces of Anonymous*. London: Verso.

Dreyfus, Hubert L. 2004. "Kierkegaard on the Internet: Anonymity vs. Commitment in the Present Age." *Kierkegaard Studies Yearbook, 1999*, edited by Heiko Schulz, Jon Stewart, and Karl Verstrynge (Berlin: De Gruyter, 1999), 96–109.

Drezner, Daniel W. 2009. "Public Intellectuals 2.1." *Society* 46 (1): 49–54.

Economist. 2010. "The 24-Hour Athenian Democracy." *Babbage*, 8 December. http://www.economist.com/blogs/babbage/2010/12/more_wikileaks.

Goodman, Amy. 2011. "Hacktivism's Global Reach, from Targeting Scientology to Backing WikiLeaks and the Arab Spring." Interview with Peter Fein and Gabriella Coleman. *Democracy Now!* 16 August. http:// www.democracynow.org/2011/8/16/hacktivisms_global_reach_from_ targeting_scientology.

Hudson, Alan. 2003. "Intellectuals for Our Times." *Critical Review of International Social and Political Philosophy* 6 (4): 33–50.

Jordan, Tim, and Paul Taylor. 2004. *Hacktivism and Cyberwars: Rebels with a Cause?* New York: Routledge.

Kierkegaard, Søren. [1846] 1962. *The Present Age and Of The Difference Between A Genius and An Apostle*. Translated by Alexander Dru. New York: Harper and Row.

Leadbeater, Charles. 2008. *We-Think: Mass Innovation, Not Mass Production*. London: Profile Books.

Lovink, Geert. 1997. "Portrait of the Virtual Intellectual: On the Design of the Public Cybersphere." 13 July. http://thing.desk.nl/bilwet/Geert/100.LEX.

———. 2004. *My First Recession: Critical Internet Culture in Transition*. Rotterdam: NAi Publishers/V2-Organization.

———. 2011. *Networks Without a Cause: A Critique of Social Media*. Cambridge: Polity Press.

Lovink, Geert, and Ned Rossiter. 2013. "Organized Networks: From Weak Ties to Strong Links." *Occupied Times of London* 23 (November), 10–11. http://theoccupiedtimes.org/?p=12547.

Lovink, Geert, and Florian Schneider. 2004. "Notes on the State of Networking: For Make World Paper #4." *Geert Lovink*. 26 February. http://geertlovink.org/texts/notes-on-the-state-of-networking/.

MacKinnon, Mary Pat, Sonia Pitre, and Judy Watling. 2007. *Lost in Translation: (Mis)Understanding Youth Engagement*. Ottawa: Canadian Policy Research Networks. http://cprn.org/documents/48800_EN.pdf.

Mill, John Stuart. [1859] 2001. *On Liberty*. Kitchener, ON: Batoche Books.

Said, Edward W. 1994. *Representations of the Intellectual*. New York: Pantheon Books.

Schneider, Nathan. 2011. "Occupy Wall Street: FAQ How It Came About, What It Means, How It Works and Everything Else You Need to Know About Occupy Wall Street." *The Nation*, 29 September. http://www.thenation.com/article/163719/occupy-wall-street-faq#.

Shirky, Clay. 2005. "Institutions vs. Collaboration." *TED Global*. https://www.ted.com/talks/clay_shirky_on_institutions_versus_collaboration?language=en

———. 2008. *Here Comes Everybody: The Power of Organizing Without Organizations*. New York: Penguin Books.

Taras, David. 2001. *Power and Betrayal in the Canadian Media*. Peterborough, ON: Broadview Press.

Vaidhyanathan, Siva. 2006. "The Lessons of Juan Cole," *The Chronical Review*. 28 July. http://chronicle.com/article/The-Lessons-of-Juan-Cole/31007

PART II
Case Studies

"Trust Me—I'm a Public Intellectual"

Margaret Atwood's and David Suzuki's Social Epistemologies of Climate Science

BOAZ MILLER

The debate about global warming and the science supporting it is one of the most heated discussions in international public life. The debate has been heavily politicized. In the United States, for example, Al Gore, who served as vice-president during the Clinton administration, continues to be a major spokesperson for the reliability of climate science, whereas conservative leaders strongly argue that the theory of human-caused global warming is not sufficiently supported by evidence. In this debate, public intellectuals play a special role, as they are perceived by the public as having special cognitive authority and trustworthiness.

In this chapter, I critically examine the views of two leading Canadian public intellectuals, David Suzuki and Margaret Atwood, on the science of global warming. I argue that the social epistemic models of science to which they are implicitly committed face difficulties in sustaining the positions they advocate.

"Politicians Who Reject Science Are Not Fit to Lead"

In 2006, CBC viewers ranked David Suzuki (born 1936) as fifth among the "top ten greatest Canadians," and, in 2011, he was voted "most trusted

Canadian" by *Reader's Digest Canada* for the third time in a row (Braganza 2011). Suzuki, now professor emeritus of genetics at the University of British Columbia, has authored more than fifty books. In 1974, he started the popular CBC Radio science program *Quirks & Quarks*, which he hosted until 1979. Since then, he has been the host of the popular television show *The Nature of Things*, which is aired in more than forty nations, and he has been involved in numerous other radio and television programs as well.

In recent years, Suzuki has been actively involved in issues surrounding global warning. In 1990, he co-founded the David Suzuki Foundation, one of the major aims of which is to fight global warning, both through public education and by sponsoring initiatives relating to carbon print reduction. His activism has also made him a controversial figure. Many Internet sites are devoted to debunking his image and refuting his claims.

When one reads the numerous pages about global warming on the David Suzuki Foundation website, the message is clear: the scientific evidence for the occurrence of anthropogenic global warming is overwhelming; more or less complete scientific consensus exists on the subject; major catastrophes will occur in the near future if we do not act to prevent global warming; it is still possible to act, but the window of opportunity is closing; the public is vastly misinformed about global warming thanks to a few fringe scientists, the media, various right-wing Internet sites that contain fringe science, conservative politicians, and industrialists; the public cannot distinguish reliable, that is, science-based, information from misinformation (Suzuki and Moola 2008; Suzuki and Moola 2011; David Suzuki Foundation n.d.).

Suzuki is very critical of climate skeptics, in particular politicians who refuse to accept the science and act on it, declaring that politicians who reject science are not fit to lead (Suzuki and Moola 2011). He has even called on students to try to find legal ways to jail politicians who ignore science, alluding to Canadian prime minister Stephen Harper, whose government backed away from the previous government's commitment to implementing the Kyoto protocol (Babbage 2008). He regards climate-change skepticism in the United States as part of an organized attack on science, which includes Republican politicians and religiously motivated creationists. He worries that Canada is going down the same path, but he finds some comfort in the fact that 80 percent of Canadians believe the science underlying the theory of climate change, as opposed to only 58 percent of Americans (Suzuki and Moola 2011).

What are the reasons, according to Suzuki, to trust current climate-change science? Suzuki stresses the existence of a wide agreement in the scientific community, which was been achieved by a process of peer review and critical dialogue among experts who abide by scientific method. Suzuki puts special emphasis on the fact that the scientific consensus is socially diverse and includes scientists from many countries:

> The overwhelming majority of scientists who study climate change agree that human activity is responsible for changing the climate. The United Nations Intergovernmental Panel on Climate Change (IPCC) is one of the largest bodies of international scientists ever assembled to study a scientific issue, involving more than 2,500 scientists from more than 130 countries. The IPCC has concluded that most of the warming observed during the past 50 years is attributable to human activities. Its findings have been publicly endorsed by the national academies of science of all G-8 nations, as well as those of China, India and Brazil. (David Suzuki Foundation n.d.)

While he acknowledges that science is not perfect, Suzuki believes that it is the best and most reliable means to gain knowledge of nature. He also regards consensus as the *aim* of scientific inquiry and views the social-epistemic process that results in a consensus as the best means for achieving knowledge:

> Science provides the best information about the world around us. Of course, it isn't a perfect system. Scientific conclusions are often tentative, and can only become more solid after more debate, more research, and more observation. The process can take years. And scientists, being human, also have their own biases and points of view that can influence the way they ask questions and interpret data. But in the arena of open scientific debate, over time, consensus can generally be achieved regarding the best possible understanding of an issue. Scientific consensus does not mean we will always get the right answer. But if I were to bet on an issue, I'd put my money on scientific consensus over an observer's hunch, a politician's opinion, or a business leader's tip. (Suzuki and Moola 2008)

What is the epistemic rationale underpinning Suzuki's view that such a process of consensus-forming critical deliberation in fact produces reliable knowledge? We can find an answer to this question in Helen Longino's critical contextual empiricism. Longino (1990, chap. 4; 2002, chap. 6) argues that the process of inquiry and its product, knowledge, are inherently social, in the sense of being inherently dependent on critical interaction between people. Longino regards objectivity as the ultimate aim of inquiry. She distinguishes between two meanings of objectivity—the veridical representation of reality and the lack of a subjective bias—and argues that the latter is required to achieve the former. Bias enters inquiry by filling the logical gap between theory and evidence. In cases where a theory is underdetermined by the existing evidence, inquirers make background assumptions that are neither logically necessary nor determined by the evidence and that typically reflect their biases and prejudice. Social norms of critical deliberation are therefore required to expose and eliminate such biases and thereby reach objectivity. Such norms grip on the individual inquirer in the sense that they require her to question and publicly defend her assumptions and claims to knowledge.

According to critical contextual empiricism, to count as knowledge, a consensus must be reached through a process of critical deliberation and scrutiny governed by four norms:

1. There are public venues of criticism, such as professional journals and conferences.
2. There is uptake of criticism: members of the community respond appropriately to the criticism and revise their views accordingly.
3. There are publicly recognized standards for the evaluation of theories.
4. There is tempered equality of intellectual authority: intellectual capacity and relevant expertise are the only criteria by which people are given the right to participate in the collective discussion, and all those who possess the needed intellectual capacity and relevant expertise can in fact realize their right to participate, regardless of gender, race, and so on.

The consensus-formation process used by the IPCC may be seen an attempt to implement the norms of critical contextual empiricism. In fact, the guiding principles of the IPCC process are similar to Longino's proposed norms. The IPCC also stresses the transparency of the process and the fact that scientists from both developed and developing nations are adequately represented in it:

> Three principles governing the review should be borne in mind. First, the best possible scientific and technical advice should be included so that the IPCC Reports represent the latest scientific, technical and socio-economic findings and are as comprehensive as possible. Secondly, a wide circulation process, ensuring representation of independent experts (i.e., experts not involved in the preparation of that particular chapter) from developing and developed countries and countries with economies in transition should aim to involve as many experts as possible in the IPCC process. Thirdly, the review process should be objective, open and transparent. (IPCC 2008, §4.2.4)

It follows, then, that criticism of the norms of critical contextual empiricism may apply to the IPCC epistemic principles as well. Indeed, such criticism exists. Critics argue that Longino's four norms are either too permissive or too restrictive and are neither sufficient nor necessary for knowledge. Goldman (2002) argues that these norms leave too much room for interpretive flexibility. Interpreted too permissively, a community of like-minded people that adopts such norms, such as a group of creationists with their own peer-reviewed journals, may be said to satisfy Longino's norms, although the agreement such a community reaches may not constitute knowledge. Interpreted too restrictively, a community of scientists who refuse to engage with far-fetched criticism, such as evolutionary biologists who do not engage with creationists, may be said to fail to meet Longino's norms.

Furthermore, these norms are neither necessary nor sufficient for knowledge. With respect to necessity, much of our current scientific knowledge has not been generated by critical scrutiny of this sort. Moreover, the standards of critical scrutiny that Longino requires may seem too high for ordinary human beings to meet. To what extent can scientists who are immersed in a particular program of research both in terms of conviction and in terms of their professional development, realistically be expected to engage in an impartial and equitable critical discussion while transcending their biases and prejudice? After all, a researcher must believe in her hypotheses in order to successfully defend them against criticism; and because scientists are rewarded for success, rather than effort, researchers' personal and collective success is strongly tied to the ultimate acceptance of their theories as the truth. This holds true especially in the climate science case, where scientists are under immense political pressure to present a unified front, given that every disagreement or uncertainty will be used by politicians to raise skepticism and argue that immediate action is not yet required.

As for sufficiency, Solomon and Richardson (2005) argue that openness to criticism and social diversity do not alone guarantee the existence of actual relevant criticism, hence wrong or unwarranted views may survive for a long time even in a community that is in principle open to criticism. They argue that the conditions for knowledge cannot be formulated solely in terms of the procedures that a community should follow. These formulations must also say something substantive about the conditions that the end product—the conclusions that the community reaches—must meet.

Another apparent difficulty with critical contextual empiricism is the problem of manufactured uncertainty. It seems that critical contextual empiricism faces difficulties in dealing with cases in which people seeking to prevent a certain view from being accepted cynically and deliberately insist on more and ever more critical scrutiny, no matter how strong the evidence in support of that view is. Because consensus is regarded as the aim of inquiry and a necessary condition for knowledge, bodies opposed to the existence of a particular piece of knowledge have a vested interest in inhibiting the formation of consensus or in creating the perception that a consensus does not exist. Indeed, Oreskes and Conway (2010) argue that the skeptical claims that global warming is not caused by human activity have not originated from within the scientific community but rather from politically motivated external actors who, consciously and cynically, have been manufacturing controversy on the subject.

Borgerson (2011, 445) argues that critical contextual empiricism can overcome the problem of manufactured uncertainty if we distinguish the level of certainty required for taking action from the level of certainty required for claiming knowledge. If these two issues are separated, interested parties will be less motivated to manufacture uncertainty. While I agree that such a separation is desirable, it does not help critical contextual empiricism, *qua* a theory of knowledge, to deal with the problem of manufactured uncertainty. Regardless of Borgerson's suggestion, critical contextual empiricism should be able to provide epistemic criteria for discerning between legitimate criticism and manufactured uncertainty, when it exists. Critical contextual empiricism should also be able to provide principles for defining the conditions under which closure in an epistemic community is warranted despite incessant criticism. It remains unclear how critical contextual empiricism can address these challenges.

By highlighting the importance of consensus, Suzuki may very well play into some of the skeptics' hands. Rather than discussing the evidence for global warming and the dangers that humanity faces as a result of it, the public debate centers on the question of whether a scientific consensus exists, when in fact there are good reasons to think that such a consensus is neither required for knowledge on the subject nor for the decision to take preventive action. That is, consensus is not a necessary condition for knowledge, and we do not need to wait to achieve the level of certainty that is required for legitimately claiming the possession of knowledge before we take preventive measures. Even a level of certainty that falls short of knowledge should suffice to prompt serious preventive actions against global warming, especially when the potential consequences of failing to do so are grave.

Suzuki also conveys a distorted image of science to the public, one that ignores the complex messy reality of research. Real scientific research is full of uncertainty, as well as academic politics and intrigue. In science, as in other human domains, power and authority are occasionally used to block certain views, but this should not licence sweeping skepticism and mistrust of science (Castel and Sismondo 2003). Encouraging public trust in scientific inquiry on the basis of a false idealized model of science as a disinterested enterprise of truth seeking is a hazardous tactic. Only under such circumstances can affairs such as the so-called Climate Gate occur (Ryghaug and Skjølsvold 2010). When, in the eyes of the public, scientists appear to fall short of meeting these unrealistic norms, climate skeptics have an effective weapon in their hands.

Finally, emphasizing consensus may actually inhibit scientific research and the growth of knowledge. Scientific pluralism and dissenting views are essential for successful inquiry. As Mill has famously argued (1993, 83–123), the existence of dissent is necessary for correcting our views when they are wrong and justifying them when they are right. But a public demand for a unified scientific front as a necessary condition for action may lead to the undesirable consequence of silencing dissenting voices within the scientific community (Beatty 2006).[1]

In sum, David Suzuki's argument for trusting current climate science puts too much weight on the existence of scientific consensus and relies on a noble, idealized model of science that, because unrealistic, is ultimately fragile and thus prone to backfire. Skeptics can all too easily subvert public trust in science by poking holes in this idealized model, thereby reinforcing their own claims. Suzuki's line of reasoning diverts public attention to less significant questions, such as whether a scientific consensus exists, and unnecessarily ties the climate-science debates to other politically charged debates, such as the evolutionism-creationism debate. Most importantly, his arguments sidestep the significant issues, namely, the actual quality of the scientific evidence and the risks that the international and global community should be willing to take even in the face of a degree—some would say a normal degree—of scientific uncertainty and less-than-perfect evidence.

"We Are Fine. There's Half a Tube of Food Left"

Margaret Atwood (born 1939) is among Canada's most prominent public intellectuals. A novelist, poet, literary critic, and essayist, she is considered one of the first distinctively Canadian authors, whose writing is both about Canada and for Canadians. Atwood is widely known around the world not only as an author but also as a feminist and environmentalist activist. Her writing and activism are closely intertwined.

Atwood is ambivalent about science. On the one hand, she values it. She comes from a family of scientists. Her father was an eminent zoologist who conducted field research in the backwoods of northern Québec, where she grew up, and her brother is a senior neurophysiologist. She is a passionate birdwatcher and the honorary president of the Rare Bird Club (Bird Studies Canada 2006). In her childhood, she was drawn to science, and she regards science and literature as two fields of human creativity:

> Human creativity is not confined to just a few areas of life. The techno-scientific world has some of the most creative people you'll ever meet.

When I was growing up, I never saw a division. For instance, my
brother and I both have the same marks in English and in the sciences.
My brother could have gone in the writing direction. And I could have
been a scientist. (Quoted in McCrum 2010)

Some of Atwood's novels, such as *Cat's Eye* (1989), feature scientists as
main characters and are informed by ideas from physics, which function as
metaphors for understanding women's experiences (Deery 1997).

On the other hand, Atwood is suspicious of science. Many of her novels
and stories depict a dystopian or post-apocalyptic world in which people
are confronted by the dreadful outcomes of current science and technology.
For example, in *Oryx and Crake* (2003) and *The Year of the Flood* (2005),
she tells the story of the survivors of an environmental catastrophe that led
to the collapse of civilization. She describes the society prior to this collapse
as segregated, dull, and violent, one in which animal abuse and child por-
nography are consumed as a form of entertainment and genetic engineering
has produced bizarre animals and human beings.

Atwood dislikes the characterization of her novels as science fiction.
She would rather characterize her work as "speculative fiction," namely,
"work that employs the means already to hand, such as DNA identifica-
tion and credit cards" and "can explore the consequences of new and proposed technologies in graphic ways, by showing them as fully operational"
(Atwood 2005). She deliberately avoids the word *progress*, preferring the
word *change*, as she does not believe that science and technology necessarily work to improve human life (Reach 2007).

Atwood also rejects the notion of objectivity as it is understood in mainstream Western philosophy and science. She denies the possibility of a neutral God-eye's representation of reality. While she was originally drawn in
her academic studies to philosophy in the analytic tradition, she turned to
English, she says, because she found it less restrictive: "Logic says A cannot
be A and non-A at the same time, but poetry says just the opposite" (quoted
in Reach 2007). Her novels reflect this attitude as well. As Cuder (2003, 4)
puts it: "In her writing, objectivity is always deceptive, a mere pretence. A
façade that may hide more obscure interests. . . . For Atwood, perspective
is all in the onlooker's eyes, and perceptions are necessarily subjective and
partial. No two accounts will ever be exactly the same, and therefore no
one can make a rightful claim to History." The perspectives that Atwood

represents in her novels are often those of women, often disempowered or abused, who are driven by the need to tell their stories to other women in an effort to make sense of their lives (Cuder 2003, 3).

Atwood's rejection of one objective representation of reality and the alternative she puts forward—a collage of necessarily partial, subjective, and incompatible views, in which those of disempowered women are privileged—echoes with feminist standpoint epistemology, associated inter alia with the work of Sandra Harding. According to Harding (1995), every view is inherently and inseparably connected to a specific agent's experience, identity, and position in society. There is no neutral point of view. Therefore, the presentation of certain scientific positions as neutral or objective is usually a political means to impose the views of the powerful on everybody else by claiming that these views simply represent things as they really are. If critical contextual empiricism requires social diversity in order to expose and eliminate the biases of specific agents and reach consensus, standpoint epistemology regards the attempt to detach a view from its subject as misguided. Diversity is required to bring different perspectives to light, especially those typically excluded from discourse, but the goal is not to merge them into one.

Standpoint epistemology should not be mistaken with simplistic relativism. For Harding, not all positions and views are on a par. Since views are tied to identity and experience, the views of agents whose experience and identity are relevant to the topic deserve more attention. For example, in society in which women are the primary caretakers, their views about child rearing deserve more consideration. Because for Harding, the epistemic and the political are inherently intertwined, marginalized standpoints that have a potential for liberating the oppressed should be privileged. Reflective views of the marginalized and oppressed about their own experience deserve special consideration and carry more weight than knowledge produced by the oppressors about the oppressed. Harding's and Atwood's ideas clearly resonate with each other.

Standpoint epistemology is controversial. The main criticism is that Harding's arguments rest on extreme and ultimately indefensible interpretations of Kuhn's ideas about scientific knowledge as historically situated and of Quine's thesis regarding the underdetermination of theory by evidence and are not sufficiently backed up by empirical data from the practice of science (Pinnick 2003). A detailed discussion of this criticism would exceed the scope of this chapter, but, in the present context, two considerations require mention. First, the model of science that standpoint epistemology advocates is *not* the one adopted by the IPCC. The IPCC has chosen to issue unified consensus statements that represent the collective view of the community of climate scientists. It has *not* chosen to bring forward a diverse array of perspectives, among which certain tensions between standpoints, including potential dissent, may exist, to privilege those of the disempowered. It is therefore difficult to justify the epistemic model of the IPCC reports on the basis of standpoint epistemology.[2]

Second, standpoint epistemology, which emphasizes the locality and partiality of perspectives, faces difficulties when it comes to offering epistemic support for causal claims of a global nature, such as the claim that greenhouse gas emissions cause an increase in atmospheric temperature. My point is not that it is impossible to find epistemic support for such claims on the basis of standpoint epistemology: I mean only that it is less suited to this task than other theories of knowledge and justification. How, then, are Atwood's writing and activism on climate change to be reconciled with her apparent allegiance to standpoint epistemology? To answer this question, let us look more closely at her statements on this issue.

Atwood has been very vocal in Canada and internationally about the need to take action to prevent the catastrophic consequences of global warming. For example, in 2007, she issued a message of support of the Green Party of Canada:

> Global warming—with the related environmental degradation, "natural" catastrophes, and accelerating species extinction—is surely the biggest issue facing, not just Canada, but the entire planet. Without oxygen to breathe, water to drink, and soil to grow food in, a cut to the GST is worth nothing. It won't matter if you're paying 1% less GST if you're dead. Nor will your survivors care much that they got a deal on your coffin—they'll be dead, too. Yet Stephen Harper's government has gone from outright denial of climate change to lukewarm attempts to cover up and paper over this issue, while all the time keeping Stephen Harper's pledge to "build a firewall around Alberta." Stephen Harper doesn't want us to develop alternate energy, he wants us to keep burning oil. That's why there was no significant money for green economic

development in his latest budget. The Green Party can be depended on to keep green issues front and centre. (Atwood 2007)

Atwood (2010) has contributed a short story to an edited collection of short stories on global warming, in an attempt to trigger an emotional response by readers that will motivate them to act. In interviews, she repeatedly refers to global warming as the most pressing problem facing humanity, one on which its survival depends. She also notes that her apocalyptic novels are inspired by the predicted global warming catastrophe.

Yet, as far as I can tell, in her public statements on global warming, Atwood, unlike Suzuki, has made no mention of the scientific consensus about it, and she rarely mentions the scientific evidence for it. This is not surprising, given that the theory of knowledge and justification to which she apparently subscribes does not recommend consensus formation as a reliable epistemic means. On the contrary, it regards such a process as detrimental to the aim of gaining knowledge because it eliminates the different standpoints from which different people argue, which are inherently part of the views they express.

Atwood's claims regarding global warming rest on a different line of reasoning. For her, global warming is a consequence of human overpopulation and overconsumption. Human beings, she argues, have been depleting all of the planet's life-sustaining resources, to a point that the planet cannot continue to sustain human life. To illustrate this point, she gives the following example, which is representative of her position:

> There's this test tube, and it's full of amoeba food. You put one amoeba in at 12 noon. The amoeba divides in two every minute. At 12 midnight the test tube is full of amoebas—and there's no food left. Question: at what moment in time is the tube half full? Answer: one minute to midnight. That's where we are apparently. That's when all the amoebas are saying: "We are fine. There's half a tube of food left." If you don't believe me, look at the proposed heat maps for 20, 30, 50 years from now, and see what's drying up. Quite a lot, actually, especially in the equatorial regions and the Middle East, which will be like a raisin. It's become a race against time and we are not doing well. (Quoted in McCrum 2010)

Atwood frames the scientific heat predictions within a neo-Malthusian apocalyptic vision of the death of humanity, not unlike her apocalyptic novels. She presents this apocalyptic vision as a fact of nature, with which it is impossible to argue. As she puts it: "Physics and chemistry are things you just can't negotiate with. These are the laws of the physical world" (quoted in McCrum 2010).

While Atwood and climate skeptics are in opposite camps with respect to accepting global warming, they have something in common. They both rely on theories that diverge, at least in emphasis, from the mainstream theories accepted by the climate science community. Atwood ties the dangers of global warming with an apocalyptic neo-Malthusian vision of humanity, while the IPCC refrains from connecting these two issues. Atwood's idiosyncratic advocacy may stem from her tacit subscription to standpoint epistemology, which does not approve of the methods and epistemic standards employed in current climate-change scientific research.

Conclusion

Public intellectuals are in an excellent position to shape the terms within which the public debate is conducted. Uncertainty is an inherent part of science, and science may not achieve certainty even when pressed by the public to do so. Certainty should therefore not be a condition for acting. Action may be required in the face of uncertainty and in light of theories that fall short of constituting irrefutable knowledge. When such knowledge is eventually gained, it may be too late to act on it, and the consequences may be too horrific to face.

Yet this is not the position that Margaret Atwood and David Suzuki are advocating. Although Atwood and Suzuki argue from two very different perspectives on science, they have something in common apart from pleading for action to prevent global warming. They both argue that the theory of anthropogenic global warming is an undeniable scientific fact, which the public and its leaders should unconditionally accept, and they both make their claims from within social epistemic frameworks that are incapable of supporting the alleged certainty of their claims. Thus, neither of them is making optimal use of their role as public intellectuals.

Acknowledgements

I thank the participants in the public intellectuals workshop at the University of Calgary for their useful comments. I am grateful to the Azrieli Foundation for the award of an Azrieli Fellowship.

Notes

1 I develop this line of argument more fully elsewhere. See Miller (2013) for the relations between knowledge and consensus, and Miller (2014) for the role of consensus in informing public decision-making.

2 The IPCC reports can be brought more into line with standpoint epistemology by considering the inductive risks that different people from different regions of the globe are willing to tolerate. Douglas (2009) identifies two types of inductive risks: wrongly accepting a false hypothesis and wrongly rejecting one that is true. She notes that there is an inherent trade-off between these two: the more we expose ourselves to the first, the less we expose ourselves to the second, and vice versa. She argues that social values determine the inductive risks that we are willing to take in a given context, and different social contexts may legitimately call for different balances between these two types of errors. When we think that the consequences of accepting a theory are not severe, we may lower the evidential threshold level required for accepting it. When we think that the risk is high, we may raise it. Since people in different regions of the globe face different predicted dangers and catastrophes resulting from global warming, it may be argued that they may legitimately weigh their risks differently and may therefore adopt different evidential standards for the acceptance or rejection of a theory. In this respect, the IPCC reports may, at least in principle, acknowledge differential standards for different researchers based on their standpoints.

References

Atwood, Margaret. 2005. "Aliens Have Taken the Place of Angels." *The Guardian*, 17 June. http://www.guardian.co.uk/film/2005/jun/17/sciencefictionfantasyandhorror.margaretatwood.

———. 2007. "Message of Support from Margaret Atwood." 9 November. http://greenparty.ca/node/3133.

————. 2010. "Time Capsule Found on the Dead Planet." In *I'm With the Bears: Short Stories from a Damaged Planet*, edited by Mark Martin, 191–94. London: Verso.

Babbage, Sarah. 2008. "Jail Politicians Who Ignore Science: Suzuki." *The McGill Daily*. 4 February.

Beatty, John. 2006. "Masking Disagreement among Experts." *Episteme* 3 (1): 52–67.

Bird Studies Canada. 2006. "Canadian Authors Named as Honorary Presidents." 28 April. http://www.bsc-eoc.org/organization/newsarchive/5-05-06.html.

Borgerson, Kirstin. 2011. "Amending and Defending Critical Contextual Empiricism." *European Journal for Philosophy of Science* 1 (3): 435–49.

Braganza, Chantal. 2011. "Most Trusted Canadians—3rd Annual Trust Poll Results." *Reader's Digest Canada*, 5 May. http://www.readersdigest.ca/magazine/most-trusted-canadians-3rd-annual-trust-poll-results.

Castel, Boris, and Sergio Sismondo. 2003. *The Art of Science*. Peterborough, ON: Broadview Press.

Cuder, Pilar. 2003. *Margaret Atwood: A Beginner's Guide*. London: Hodder and Stoughton.

David Suzuki Foundation. n.d. "Climate Change Deniers." http://www.davidsuzuki.org/issues/climate-change/science/climate-change-basics/climate-change-deniers/.

Deery, June. 1997. "Science for Feminists: Margaret Atwood's Body of Knowledge." *Twentieth Century Literature* 43 (4): 470–86.

Douglas, Heather. 2009. *Science, Policy, and the Value-Free Ideal*. Pittsburgh: University of Pittsburgh Press.

Goldman, Alvin I. 2002. "Knowledge and Social Norms." *Science* 296 (21 June): 2148–49.

Harding, Sandra G. 1995. "'Strong Objectivity': A Response to the New Objectivity Question." *Synthese* 104 (3): 331–49.

Intergovernmental Panel on Climate Change (IPCC). 2008. *Appendix A to the Principles Governing IPCC Work: Procedures for the Preparation, Review, Acceptance, Adoption, Approval and Publication of IPCC Reports*. Geneva: Intergovernmental Panel on Climate Change.

Longino, Helen. 1990. *Science as Social Knowledge: Values and Objectivity in Scientific Inquiry*. Princeton: Princeton University Press.

————. 2002. *The Fate of Knowledge*. Princeton: Princeton University Press.

McCrum, Robert. 2010. "Margaret Atwood Interview: 'Go Three Days Without Water and You Don't Have Any Human Rights. Why? Because You're Dead.'" *The Observer*, 28 November.

Mill, John Stuart. 1993. "On Liberty." In *Utilitarianism, on Liberty, Considerations on Representative Government*, edited by J. M. Dent, 69–187. London: Everyman.

Miller, Boaz. 2013. "When Is Consensus Knowledge Based? Distinguishing Shared Knowledge from Mere Agreement." *Synthese* 190 (7): 1293–316.

———. 2014. "Scientific Consensus and Expert Testimony in Courts: Lessons from the Bendectin Litigation." *Foundations of Science*, in press http://dx.doi.org/10.1007/s10699-014-9373-z.

Oreskes, Naomi, and Erik M. Conway. 2010. *Merchants of Doubt: How a Handful of Scientists Obscured the Truth on Issues from Tobacco Smoke to Global Warming*. New York: Bloomsbury Press.

Pinnick, Cassandra L. 2003. "Feminist Epistemology: Implications for the Philosophy of Science." In *Scrutinizing Feminist Epistemology: An Examination of Gender in Science*, edited by Cassandra L. Pinnick, Noretta Koertge, and Robert F. Almeder, 20–30. New Brunswick, NJ: Rutgers University Press.

Reach, Kirsten. 2007. "What Margaret Atwood Says About Writing." *Kenyon Review*, 7 December. http://www.kenyonreview.org/2007/12/you-can-pretend-you-were-here-with-us/.

Ryghaug, Marianne, and Tomas M. Skjølsvold. 2010. "The Global Warming of Climate Science: Climategate and the Construction of Scientific Facts." *International Studies in the Philosophy of Science* 24 (3): 287–307.

Solomon, Miriam, and Alan Richardson. 2005. "A Critical Context for Longino's Critical Contextual Empiricism." *Studies in History and Philosophy of Science* 36: 211–22.

Suzuki, David, and Faisal Moola. 2008. "Selective Information Overload." *Science Matters*, 23 March. http://www.davidsuzuki.org/blogs/science-matters/2008/03/selective-information-overload/.

———. 2011. "Politicians Who Reject Science Are Not Fit to Lead." *Science Matters*, 3 March. http://www.davidsuzuki.org/blogs/science-matters/2011/03/politicians-who-reject-science-are-not-fit-to-lead/.

6 Engendering a New Generation of Public Intellectuals

Speaking Truth to Power with Grace and Humility

KARIM-ALY KASSAM

"I die, I die!" the Mother said,
"My Children die for lack of Bread.
What more has the merciless Tyrant said?"
The Monk sat down on the Stony Bed.

The blood red ran from the Grey Monk's side,
His hands & feet were wounded wide,
His Body bent his arms & knees
Like to the roots of ancient trees.

His eye was dry; no tear could flow:
A hollow groan first spoke his woe.
He trembled & shudder'd upon the Bed;
At length with a feeble cry he said:

"When God commanded this hand to write
In the studious hours of deep midnight,
He told me the writing I wrote should prove
The Bane of all that on Earth I lov'd.

"My Brother starv'd between two Walls,
His Children's Cry my Soul appalls:
I mock'd at the wrack & griding chain,
My bent body mocks their torturing pain.

"Thy Father drew his sword in the North,
With his thousands strong he marched forth,
Thy Brother has armd himself in Steel,
To avenge the wrongs thy Children feel.

"But vain the Sword & vain the Bow,
They never can work War's overthrow.
The Hermit's Prayer & the Widow's tear
Alone can free the World from fear.

"For a Tear is an Intellectual Thing,
And a Sigh is the Sword of an Angel King,
And the bitter groan of the Martyr's woe
Is an Arrow from the Almightie's Bow.

"The hand of Vengeance found the Bed
To which the Purple Tyrant fled;
The iron hand crushd the Tyrant's head,
And became a Tyrant in his stead."

William Blake, "The Grey Monk"

What are the guiding principles that engender a new generation of public intellectuals among our undergraduate and graduate students? This is the question reflected upon herein. While public intellectuals emerge from a variety of professional backgrounds, including literature and the arts, the objective of this work is to reflect on the formation of public intellectuals in the realm of academic scholarship.

Historically, the word *intellectual* has been associated with social tensions arising from its range of meaning. This, in turn, has contributed to the term's significance and complex uses. *Intellectual* has been applied to people who use theory or organized knowledge to pronounce judgment on matters of public importance, as well as with a class of elites who engage in monopolies of knowledge that allow them to claim special understanding, and therefore privilege, because they are able to promote their own indispensability (Innis 1995). The word *intellectual* has also been used in an effort to transcend the dichotomy between the head and the heart, or between reason and emotion, in social and political discourse. An intellectual, in this sense, employs not only the faculty of reason but also the human capacities of empathy and imagination. Since the latter part of the eighteenth century, these individuals have been understood to act independently of established political, economic, or ecclesiastical institutions of power (Williams 1989). It is this particular use of the word *intellectual*, together with the subsequent action it inspires in young scholars, that is the subject of this essay.

William Blake's art and poetry are among the most effective examples of such independence from, and critical commentary on, institutions of power. In "The Grey Monk," written in the early nineteenth century, he eloquently challenges the hegemony of reason as the intellect's sole criterion of judgment, speaking of reason's limiting capacity when describing the Grey Monk, whose "eye was dry" when the mother cried, "My Children die for lack of Bread."[1] Blake illustrates the barrenness of the intellect if it encompasses only the faculty of reason and compellingly contends that "a Tear is an Intellectual Thing." Embracing the heart as part of the intellect frees not only the Grey Monk but the entire world from "fear." Although Blake's critical engagement lay with the deleterious effects of the Industrial Revolution and the hypocrisy of institutions such as the church and the English monarchy in the eighteenth and nineteenth centuries, his words have resonance for us today.

From the beginning of my academic career, I have been committed to public scholarship, but the events of 11 September 2001 were to permanently alter my scholarly life and simultaneously confirm my role in public discourse. As a Canadian of Muslim heritage, I felt compelled to understand the acts of terror in the context of the growing xenophobia and misunderstanding that threatened the foundations of pluralistic society, which is precisely what both the terrorists and their objective allies sought to achieve.[2] Urged by colleagues and friends, I responded immediately, writing an essay in the local newspaper as well as speaking and engaging in public discussions in church halls, corporate boardrooms, government offices, and school classrooms. I gained insight into the perspectives of Canadians from a wide variety of religious traditions as well as those who were atheists. These activities have resulted in two volumes of collective efforts to understand the short- and long-term implications of 11 September 2001 (Kassam, Melnyk, and Perras 2002; Kassam 2010b).

One of my most sobering realizations occurred moments before a television interview on an early morning talk show, hosted by a well-known comedian and news anchor, in the year following the events of 11 September 2001. In literature and the performing arts, the arc of tragedy is reflected in the arc of critical humour, which conveys truth by jest. The host commented that the political responses to these shocking events were providing ample material for such critical humour but expressed the fear of being censured by media bosses. Political decisions with massive implications for economic and human rights were thus evading critical scrutiny. It was at this moment that I fully understood the potentially transformative role that a tenured academic can play in democratic society, especially under conditions of stress—a role largely unavailable to individuals who must answer to their employer in the private or public sector. I would argue that this independence, this ability to contribute to public scholarship, is the raison d'être of tenure. Tenure is like a passport that affords protection by establishing one's citizenship in a community of inquirers. Similarly, rigorous and sustained scholarship provides the visa that enables ease of movement across boundaries. Together, they provide the freedom to enter and engage with a wide variety of sociocultural and political constituencies. This is how the public intellectual "speaks truth to power with grace and humility."

Armed with passport and visa, I have travelled to the circumpolar Arctic and to the Pamir Mountains of Afghanistan and Tajikistan, and my experiences there do not lead me to view terrorism as our major concern for the third millennium. Terrorism is only a symptom of something more fundamental—a reaction to the sociocultural and ecological changes that threaten the very foundations of the diversity of life on this planet and destabilize the plurality of cultures and intellectual traditions that this diversity of life supports. In the twenty-first century, humanity faces three simultaneous challenges: a global environmental, energy, and economic crisis. Humanity has no pre-established mathematical models that can provide us with formulaic or technocratic policy responses sufficient to untangle the riddle of our future.

This triumvirate of challenges and their implications for the life of the planet are indeed unprecedented in human history (Kassam and Avery

2013, 2). Scientists have proposed that humanity has entered a new geological epoch, the Anthropocene (the "age of humans"), characterized by humanity's mass impact on a planetary scale (Crutzen and Stoermer 2000). The term recognizes the capacity of human habitation to alter not only the ecological balance of the biosphere but the very physical nature of the planet. Rather than celebrating human achievement, however, the term is an admission of human culpability with regard to the mass extinction of life forms and alterations to climate. Beginning with industrial development in the eighteenth century, humanity has been altering its habitat at planetary scale that was hitherto not possible. It is not that anthropogenic influence on the planet is a new phenomenon (Cronon 1983; Mann 2005; Sayre 2012; Smith 1980). Human beings from their earliest beginnings interacted with and therefore influenced their habitat. What distinguishes the Anthropocene is the simultaneous compression of the dimensions of space and time on a global scale such that the magnitude and speed of human impact is staggering. Thus, we do not have enough time to critically consider the potential impact and ethical implications of our actions.

This new epoch is also characterized by myopia regarding the scope of human impact or what appears like willful blindness to the death of birth, in which extinction outstrips the pace at which new life forms evolve. The situation is worsened by the absence of a global consensus on an ethical code to guide humanity in its behaviour. The proposed new epoch is an acknowledgement that the planet is currently operating in a *no-analogue state* (Crutzen and Steffen 2003, 253). In other words, the conditions that now exist have no equivalent, no point of comparison, with the result that our past experiences may no longer be sufficient to allow us to form a response to what confronts us. Furthermore, the concept of the Anthropocene involves the recognition that the Earth's system includes human societies and that these humans are an integral component of the planet. Therefore, humanity can no longer sustain the illusion perpetuated by industrial society that two separate systems exist—one natural or geo-ecological and the other a human sociocultural and economic construct (Steffen et al. 2007; Kassam 2009a; Sayre 2012).

In much the same way, we can no longer cling to the idea that academic life and public life are two separate activities. University professors cannot regard public scholarship as an occasional activity; rather, it must be integrated into pedagogy and applied research, in order to illustrate to undergraduate and graduate students alike that public engagement is the cornerstone of intellectual life in a democratic society. Public scholarship arises out of an awareness of civic responsibility and sensitivity to the relationship between education and its real-world application. The academic distinction between research and teaching, while useful, is not a helpful means to stimulate young public intellectuals.

Drawing on ideas informed by human ecological research undertaken among indigenous communities in the circumpolar Arctic and in the Pamir Mountains of Afghanistan and Tajikistan, I offer below a number of pedagogical principles intended to create an enabling environment for young public intellectuals. These principles are biophilia, or love of life; intellectual pluralism; sociocultural and ecological relevance; the creation of an environment for insight; and phronesis, or practical wisdom. I will present three case studies that illustrate how these principles speak truth to power by challenging established metanarratives.

Principles That Engender Public Intellectuals

My teaching is framed by human ecological research, and this research, in turn, is inspired by a scholarly teaching environment. Human ecology describes the relationships between people and their environment—including other animals, plants, and their habitat. It is simultaneously a narrative about how human beings develop a sociocultural system on the foundation of their ecological habitat. Simply put, human ecology integrates human beings into the ecological system they inhabit and thus avoids the facile dichotomy between nature and culture. Both my research and my teaching are shaped by my experiences of indigenous communities living at high latitudes (the circumpolar Arctic and the Subarctic) and high altitudes (the Pamir Mountains of Central Asia), who are in the throes of sociocultural and environmental change and are therefore forced to be among the first to develop adaptation strategies for survival. The concept of the Anthropocene is founded on the recognition that the ecological footprint of humanity is now global, such that the impact of activities in industrialized areas is felt even in such seemingly remote regions as the Arctic and the mountains of Central Asia. These regions have sustained the presence of human cultures for many millennia, and their history is integral to the history of human civilization. Historical evidence of thriving settlements of indigenous peoples in the Americas and the presence of the Silk Road(s) in Central Asia remain a testimony to human adaptation and achievement.

Situated in varying ecological zones sustaining diverse cultures, these regions are in fact deeply illustrative of the fundamental questions that humanity faces regarding life on this planet. While these societies are inextricably entwined with the technological age of the twenty-first century, those who live in them generally pursue livelihoods, such as hunting, gathering, fishing, agriculture, and pastoralism, that place them in a close ecological relationship to the surrounding environment. Historically, these regions have experienced the effects of colonialism and have been at the frontiers of the Cold War. They continue to deal with imperial machinations in the form of outright war or the unsustainable exploitation of natural resources that threatens their ecosystems and thus their long-term survival. The result has been climate change and chronic poverty, to which external factors are primary contributors. These challenges are fundamentally about the well-being of households and communities, both human and non-human. It is no coincidence that the Greek *oikos*, "household," is the root of the prefix *eco-* in both ecology and economics. In a broader sense, the planet is our *oikos*: it is the dwelling place of humanity.[3] Both economics and ecology continue to have trouble, however, in dealing with complex interconnected systems. Their greatest challenge is the interface of human and non-human communities within their habitats.

Biophilia

While the notion of biophilia, namely, love of life or living systems, has been popularized by biologist Edward Wilson (1984), the idea was first articulated by Erich Fromm (1964), who was writing in the context of the excesses of narcissism and war in the twentieth century. Quoting the confrontation between the Basque philosopher Miguel de Unamuno and the fascist general José Millán-Astray at the University of Salamanca on 12 October 1936, Fromm illustrates the significance of the connection between biophilia and scholarship. The day marked the anniversary of Columbus's discovery of America, and fiery speeches were delivered, including one by Francisco Maldonado, a professor at the university. Decrying Catalan and Basque nationalism as "cancers in the body of the nation," Maldonado declared that fascism would remove them, "cutting into the live healthy flesh like a resolute surgeon free of false sentimentality." At that point, someone in the audience shouted the fascist slogan, "Long live death!" General Millán-Astray responded with "Spain!" and a fascist chant arose. Until that moment, Unamuno, the rector of the university, had been listening silently, but the fascist chant "Long live death!" stirred an immediate and emphatic response. Unamuno rose and, describing the slogan as a "necrophilus and senseless cry," denounced Millán-Astray, prompting the general to cry out, "Death to intellectuals!" Unamuno then spoke about the university as the "temple of the intellect," in which "Reason and Right" stand opposed to brute force. Unamuno said: "You will win because you have more than enough brute force. But you will not convince. For to convince you need to persuade. And in order to persuade you would need what you lack: Reason and Right in the struggle." He vehemently rejected the celebration of death, a characteristic not only of fascists then but of fanatics today, as an "outlandish paradox" that he found "repellent" (Fromm 1964, 37–38). The love of life and its pre-eminence as a value in scholarly engagement drove Unamuno to speak truth to power, even though, in fascist Spain, this power was backed by military force.

As Unamuno's reference to "Reason and Right" suggests, the ethical dimensions of science cannot be divorced from the practice of the science itself. The current and simultaneously occurring economic, energy, and environmental crises are unparalleled in human history and put all life in peril. These anthropogenic crises are a manifestation of the long-term erosion of the core value of biophilia. It is not sufficient for the university scholar to point out to students that the current predicament is leading to the reckless destruction of life on earth. Rather, it is the role of the scholar to investigate, along with those students, mechanisms that promote the conservation of life and living systems.

Intellectual Pluralism
Problems faced by societies and communities rarely present themselves neatly or in reference to a single discipline. Sociocultural and ecological predicaments such as climate change, chronic poverty, environmental degradation, intolerance, and food and energy insecurity are "wicked problems" that transcend disciplinary boundaries. These problems are "wicked" not because they are inherently evil but because they are so complex. First identified in the fields of social planning and systems science, wicked problems defy easy and singular formulations, resist resolution, and are nearly

impossible to solve because of changing circumstances that are difficult to perceive and therefore to understand (Allen and Gould 1986; Balint et al. 2011; Churchman 1967; Rittel and Webber 1973). Complex interdependencies underlie wicked problems, and attempts to solve them reveal or generate further problems. These problems have an emergent quality (Latour 1987) in that they are contingent and highly context dependent. Scientific uncertainty, combined with conflicting perceptions and values, renders an optimal solution to a wicked problem unattainable. Therefore, responses to these problems are neither right nor wrong but rather are evaluated in terms of their degree of effectiveness. Wicked problems demand engagement with cultural systems, social and institutional structures, and individual actions, all within the ecological context in which these problems manifest themselves (Kassam 2009a). Hence, responses to wicked problems have to be collaborative and participatory, involving a diversity of societal perspectives and a willingness to live with the consequences.

Participatory and collaborative approaches to problem solving engender creativity and thoughtfulness in framing solutions. Here, expertise is not sufficient; diversity is both necessary and provides hope. Cognitive diversity is the multiplicity of perspectives that are drawn from different ways of knowing, arising from a variety of livelihood activities, life experiences, and cultural backgrounds. Diversity is subtle, imbued with possibilities, and imminent; therefore, it has emergent properties, much like wicked problems. Diversity simultaneously bridges the present and the past and opens up the future. It carries with it a constant sense of becoming by enabling adaptation to change. Through the collaboration with a variety of social groups, one not only benefits from cultural and social diversity but also gains in terms of cognitive diversity. Cognitive diversity provides the ability to address wicked problems. Cognitive diversity eschews a conception of reality in which nature is reduced to a single principle. Therefore, it rejects absolutist, monolithic, or unitary explanations. Cognitive diversity among a group of problem solvers contributes to the articulation of thoughtful responses to the challenges humanity is encountering. Individual intellectual abilities are not sufficient: the diversity of our experiences and identities must combine with these abilities if we are to address the challenges we face and articulate possible solutions (Kassam 2010a; Page 2007, 2010).

One effective means of preparing future generations to address the wicked problems generated by the Anthropocene is undergraduate and graduate teaching and applied research. By building bridges across different ways of knowing, scholars draw from the diversity of their cultural backgrounds and variety of life and learning experiences. In this sense, interdisciplinary learning is not only about an ecologist working with an anthropologist but about both of them engaging with a Native hunter to tackle the question of sea ice and food security in the Arctic. Indigenous knowledge is in vital engagement with institutionalized "scientific" knowledge as *communities of inquirers* (such as students and professors) work with *communities of social practice* (such as Elders, farmers, hunters, pastoralists, and the institutions of civil society). In applied research, the border between inquiry and practice is transcended: insights resulting from inquiry are applied to human societies and thus provide the foundation for policy formulation and subsequent action. Effective policy and action are best achieved through the participation of communities of practice and inquiry.

Relevance to Sociocultural and Ecological Context

As researchers and teachers, our challenge is to make book learning at universities relevant to the needs of human societies. This requires that the teacher adopt a pedagogical framework that facilitates the transformation of students from those who know *about* the major challenges of the twenty-first century into those who know *how* to confront these challenges in particular sociocultural and ecological contexts. This demands that our research activities should inform the content of the courses we teach and our articulation of ideas in the classroom. To place an issue in context, students need to understand that the past is not merely history but is relevant to the present and to future possibilities. The idea of relevance links education to experience, or learning to community, combining critical thinking with research in the service of human societies. The very process of learning must be active and both socially and environmentally engaged in order to stimulate insight and generate practical wisdom (phronesis).

An Environment for Insight

Despite increasingly market-driven conceptualizations of universities as corporate businesses, students are not just "consumers" of information; they are also producers of insight. Advising and teaching is the raison d'être of scholarship, and the university is the context in which insights gained through research are shared. While the publication of that research brings validation by peers, teaching carries the insights generated by research into the future. Furthermore, nuanced insight and a passion for research are best conveyed in the classroom through one's own actions and experiences, which make course material come alive in the minds of students. Critical exchange through teaching produces a dynamic that allows ideas to develop and hybridize into a tapestry of possibilities. In addition, questions arising from classroom discussion often open new vistas of research or provide fresh perspectives on old problems. Thomas Kuhn noted in *The Structure of Scientific Revolutions* (1962) that paradigm shifts within a discipline generally emerge from young scholars and from those situated outside the discipline. Kuhn's observations simultaneously make a case for intellectual pluralism and emphasize the role of the young scholar. This acknowledgement of the importance of young scholars is fundamental, as it speaks to their role in advancing ideas that contribute to the development of public scholarship.

Phronesis

Phronesis, or practical wisdom, is the knowledge of how to secure the "ends of human life." It is about the well-being of the *oikos*—the place of dwelling and the web of sociocultural and ecological relationships that sustain it. Aristotle describes *phronēsis* as an intellectual virtue in his *Nicomachean Ethics* (2004). Aristotle maintained that we grasp the nature of phronesis by observing those who possess it. Although phronesis depends on our ability to reason, unlike theoretical wisdom (*sophia*), it cannot be gained solely through book learning. Phronesis requires practice. By combining critical thinking with practice, students directly experience the way that theoretical perspectives both emerge from and inform the application of their knowledge. In the course of action, the particular hints at the universal.

A conversation about learning without practice is just as vacant as a discussion of rights without responsibilities. Rights such as freedom are intimately linked to responsibilities. An applied perspective on teaching seeks to generate a cadre of young scholars who situate their thinking and ideas in the context of the universe-centered self rather than a self-centered universe. Barber (1994, 88) argued: "The language of citizenship suggests that self-interests are always embedded in communities of action and that in serving neighbors, one also serves oneself." In other words, self-interested goals do not exist in opposition to community but are realized in the course of engagement with the community.

The pedagogical approach I am describing recognizes that responsibility is embedded in knowledge. It can be characterized as participatory, in accordance with the principles described above. It facilitates constructive and thought-provoking interactions between local communities who hold indigenous knowledge and scholars from biological, physical, and social sciences as well as the humanities. Furthermore, on the basis of two decades of experience as a university scholar, I am convinced that a transdisciplinary approach provides the integrated perspective needed to conduct research related to natural resource utilization, conservation, livelihood security, climate change, and food sovereignty.

Challenging Metanarratives: Speaking Truth to Power

Challenging metanarratives—reflecting critically on otherwise unquestioned truths—requires an engagement with power. Described below are three cases in which metanarratives supported by powerful monopolies on knowledge were called into question. The first case illustrates the need for clear thinking and the faculty of empathy when a decision must be made about whether to go to war. The second establishes the importance of intellectual pluralism, or multiple ways of knowing, in addressing critical issues of human survival. The third shows that the retention of diversity even under conditions of significant stress is fundamental to survival. Together, these cases seek to speak truth to power as well as to demonstrate the pedagogical principles described above in action.

The Public Intellectual: First a Scholar, Then an Activist

The first case concerns the failure of effective analysis on the part of most (but not all) intelligence agencies to accurately predict the presence of weapons of mass destruction in Iraq.[4] Both American and British intelligence agencies conveyed to policy makers and political leaders that evidence existed of weapons of mass destruction in Iraq. In contrast, Canadian intelligence agencies, which depended primarily on data gathered by the American and British, came to the opposite conclusion. After analyzing the information, they maintained that the evidence was inadequate to support such an idea (Campbell 2010). This example is compelling because it closely links the notion of "intelligence" to the role of the "intellectual." Moreover, it clearly illustrates that information is not intelligence. Intelligence is the value added the public intellectual provides through effective analysis.

How did American intelligence analysts come to the conclusion that there was evidence of weapons of mass destruction? Their decision was strongly influenced by their own expectations of the policy needs of those who controlled institutions of power, rather than those of the public they served. In theory, the objective of intelligence is to inform policy makers and in this manner support the formulation of policies that will be of maximum benefit to society. However, "support" can also mean providing analyses that reinforce existing policies and rally others to the cause. The Iraq case illustrates the need for attention to basic social science methods in order to avoid cognitive biases. Jervis (2010, 191) argues that by focusing on the dependent variable, analysts "ignored relevant comparisons, overlooked significant negative evidence, and failed to employ the hypothetico-deductive method."[5] Unless we are careful to abide by scientific methods, we tend to interpret information so that it will accord with what we already believe (or would like to believe). Failing to recognize this, analysts overestimated the extent to which the evidence before them supported their conclusion that Iraq was harbouring weapons of mass destruction.

What did Canadian intelligence analysts do differently, given that they were using the same data as their American and British counterparts? The fact that the conclusions reached by American and British intelligence analysts were erroneous indicates that their approach was flawed. Analysts must develop hypotheses that can be empirically validated. If the proposition is correct, what predictions can be made and what evidence would one expect to be able to gather on the basis of those predictions? Similarly, a scholar would ask what information would cast doubt on, or outright disprove, their conclusions. This type of questioning alerts scholars not to neglect evidence that might falsify their assumptions and to look for areas in which potentially relevant information should be sought. Given the data before them, Canadian analysts thought to ask, What else might this equipment be used for? This approach led them to conclude that the evidence did not necessarily point to the existence of weapons of mass destruction.

Given that human lives and a nation's resources are at stake in the decision to go to war, this example is compelling illustration of what can happen when power speaks to truth, rather than the other way around. More generally, it is rigorous scholarship that informs the words and actions of the public intellectual. Activism without sound scholarship is merely a case of the tail wagging the dog. The activist believes first and then seeks evidence to support that belief, whereas the public intellectual begins with the evidence and then bases her or his belief and action on that evidence. This is well illustrated by a conversation between President Bush and Prime Minister Jean Chrétien. In his memoirs, Mr. Chrétien recalls that Mr. Bush offered to send his intelligence experts to Ottawa to convince him about Iraqi weapons of mass destruction. The prime minister responded, "'No, don't do that, George. . . . If you have proof, send it to my analysts through the normal channels. They will look at it, and I will decide" (2008, 309).

This case is, however, fundamentally about biophilia. In the long term, the bloodshed and the damage to the *oikos* of communities will generate pain, bitterness, and hatred that will continue to fester, undermining biophilia and ultimately leading to more death and destruction. The case of going to war in Iraq also illustrates a basic lack of empathy (Jarvis 2010), which is the cornerstone of biophilia. A significant literature exists on the ethical criteria for preemptive war, and, in the analysis of Franklin Eric Wester (2004), the Bush administration's justification for war did not live up to these criteria. The fact is that in the age of the Anthropocene, when human action has planetary implications, the notion of preemptive war is not only anachronistic but also ethically vacant. In the case of a conflict, the two parties may have little sympathy for each other's point of view, but the public intellectual must seek to exercise the faculties of imagination and empathy, in addition to reason. By not doing so, the public intellectual forsakes the ability to perceive the world differently and reason accordingly. In other words, his or her assumptions about the other must reflect who the other actually is.

When a nation's leaders choose to go to war using arguments of preemptive defence, this implies that they perceive their own might as greater than that of those upon whom they will wage war. Studies show that those who consider themselves powerful reveal a reduced tendency to comprehend how other people see, think, and feel (Galinsky et al. 2006). In essence, the "other" is merely a construction based on their insecurities and motivations. Their myopia, produced primarily by fear, blinds them to the diversity of perspectives and to pluralistic views of the world. In contrast, the public intellectual must have the capacity not only to think but also feel from the perspective of others. The next case illustrates how human agency is driven by empathy and the way in which multiple ways of knowing, or intellectual pluralism, contributes to survival.

Intellectual Pluralism and Survival

In the mid-1990s, following the collapse of the Soviet Union's economy, the world's most industrialized and densely populated polar region found itself facing shortages of food and fuel.[6] On the Kola Peninsula, near the Russian border with Finland, and on the Chukotka Peninsula, across the Bering Sea from Alaska, entire communities were at risk of starving or freezing to death. In Lovozero, a town on the Kola Peninsula, the price of essential food items—when these were available at all—fluctuated as the value of the ruble destabilized. Doctors could diagnose illness, but they lacked the medicines to treat those who were ill, and, even under the best of conditions, hospitals could offer only one meal a day to their patients. Russian government institutions were unable to offer much help, which arrived instead from international institutions and from other indigenous communities. Sami cultural groups from Norway, Sweden, and Finland came to the assistance of the Russian Sami, on the Kola Peninsula, while the Chukchi and Yupik living on the Chukotka Peninsula received aid from Iñupiat, Inuvialuit, and Yupik communities in Alaska (see figure 6.1).

While in some ways similar to other international emergency relief efforts, these empathetic responses were unique in that they involved the transfer of the tools and knowledge required for subsistence hunting and gathering. Far from being a matter of sport, the ability to hunt and fish was essential to feeding members of one's household and community. In such circumstances, a university degree was of virtually no use. A different kind of learning was necessary—knowledge of how to live off the land and sea. Although some individuals still had the skills needed to maintain a subsistence lifestyle, this ability had been largely neglected and devalued during decades of industrialization and collectivization. When practical and context-specific indigenous knowledge is actively suppressed by colonizing powers, it is in danger of being forgotten. This type of cognitive interruption is colonization of the mind, which seeks to eliminate intellectual pluralism and destroy cultural identity.

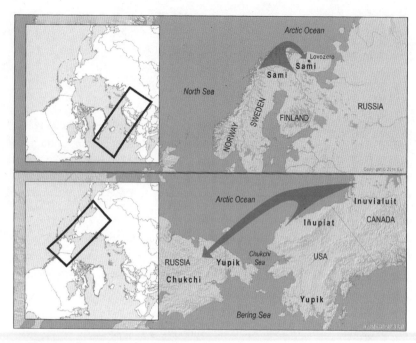

Figure 6.1. International assistance in the Arctic

To offset decades of Soviet policy that discouraged the use of local resources, Iñupiat residents of Alaska'a North Slope Borough found it necessary to send supplies and weapons to their neighbours across the Bering Sea. Before Chukotka's communities could legally hunt marine mammals, however, the Iñupiat also had to persuade the International Whaling Commission to extend quotas so as to permit subsistence hunting. In addition, for a number of years they invited community leaders, hunters, and scientists from the Chukotka Peninsula to the North Slope Borough to facilitate the transfer of knowledge and the strengthening of local institutions that would serve to safeguard hunters' rights and their capacity to use local resources effectively. Hunting demands a concomitant commitment to conservation through planning for sustainable resource use.

This case not only illustrates the empathy felt by one indigenous community for another, even across international borders, but also demonstrates how empathy is manifested in practical action. This action involved the revitalization of multiple ways of knowing by building bridges with international institutions, such as the International Whaling

Commission, and with scientists. By involving scientists as well as hunters, the Iñupiat showed practical wisdom (phronesis), which is essential to wise leadership. Intellectual pluralism was sustained by communities of social practice (indigenous leaders, hunters-gatherers, resource managers) working in tandem with communities of inquirers (scientists) in order to address a crisis.

Under conditions of stress, a public intellectual must move from critical analysis to action. To be effective, actions cannot be based solely on one individual's ability to reason but must instead draw on diverse perspectives. Learning from the example of the Iñupiat, the public intellectual must seek to encourage thoughtful action grounded in a collaborative process that incorporates the principle of intellectual pluralism. Only in this way will it be possible to address wicked problems such as food and livelihood insecurity.

Must Cain Always Kill Abel?

The Old Testament narrative in which Cain, "a tiller of the ground," kills his younger brother, Abel, "a keeper of sheep" (Gen. 4:2), out of a jealous impulse has generated social science scholarship that reinforces conflict between farmers and pastoralists.[7] While studies do confirm that conflict sometimes exists between herders and farmers (Bassett 1988; Blench 1984; Chatwin 1989; Gellner 1985; Hodgson 1974; Khaldûn 1967), there is also compelling evidence to the contrary. Despite the prevailing image of Afghanistan as a country riven by religious and ethnic differences, evidence from the Pamir Mountains suggests that ethnic, cultural, religious, and ecological diversity contributes to mutual survival and food security. This is particularly noteworthy given that the country has, for more than thirty years, been ensnared in a localized global war.

The Pamir Mountains lie in northeastern Afghanistan, in the province of Badakhshan, and extend northward into Tajikistan. Immediately to their south, a long, narrow mountain valley, known as the Wakhan Corridor, extends eastward from the central part of Afghanistan into China, and separates Tajikistan, to the north, from Pakistan, to the south (see figure 6.2). Although sparsely populated, the region is home to two distinct ethnic groups, the Kyrgyz and the Wakhi (Felmy and Kreutzmann 2004; Kassam 2010; Kreutzmann 2003; Shahrani 1978, 1979).

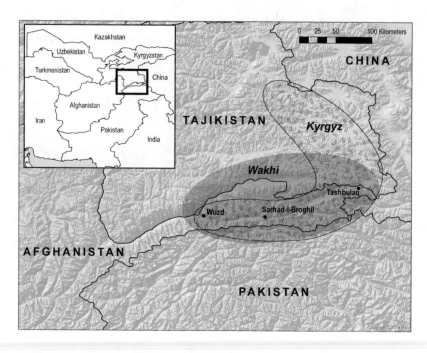

Figure 6.2. Location of Wakhi and Kyrgyz ethnic groups

Striking differences exist between the two groups. The Wakhi are primarily sedentary agriculturalists, who practice irrigated crop farming in valleys located between 2,500 and 3,500 metres above sea level. They grow wheat, barley, millet, peas, and even potatoes, although, in villages at higher elevations, the potato harvest is unreliable. Poorer households often lack a supply of grain sufficient for the entire year and must therefore decide whether to save some of their store of grain for seeding or to use it to meet their immediate needs for food. In addition to farming, the Wakhi do keep some animals, which they feed during the winter with farm-produced fodder. The Kyrgyz, in contrast, are largely nomadic pastoralists, who, in the spring and summer, migrate to high pastures to graze their herds. These consist of sheep and goats, which are generally sold in market, as well as yaks, raised for local consumption and transport, and horses, donkeys, and camels, chiefly used for the transport of supplies. Long periods of high-altitude grazing in the spring and summer, combined with shorter grazing periods in lower-lying areas during the winter months, enable the Kyrgyz to draw on natural resources in dispersed locations. In the summer, however, the Wakhi also make use of high mountain plateaus as pastures. Thus, while each of the two communities occupies a distinct ecological niche, the two niches overlap seasonally, and this overlap of land use during the spring and summer requires cooperation between the two groups.

Diversity in this region exists not only at the level of ecological habitat but also in language and religion. The Wakhi speak a language that belongs to the Iranian branch of the Indo-European family, whereas Kyrgyz is a Turkic language of the Altaic family. The Kyrgyz are Sunni Muslims, and the Wakhi are Shia Ismaili Muslims. Historically, the presence of Kyrgyz and Wakhi in the Wakhan region is the outcome of a process of competition among various groups for strategic control of resources. At times, the Wakhi, as Shia Ismaili Muslims, have faced persecution at the hands of Sunni groups who invaded and occupied the region, while the Kyrgyz suffered a similar fate at the hands of the Mongols and, more recently, the Afghan nation.

Given long-term warfare in the region, the hegemony of a fundamental-ist interpretation of Sunni Islam under the Taliban, limited arable land in mountainous regions, and religious and ethnic differences, one might expect tensions to exist between the Wakhi and the Kyrgyz. Indeed, historically, there has at times been conflict. Today, however, these two communities in fact engage in close relations that ensure their mutual survival. The Wakhi grow wheat and barley, which they trade with the Kyrgyz, and also mill the grain into flour for the Kyrgyz. The Kyrgyz, for their part, respect the pasture lands of the Wakhi and trade animals with them in return for milled grain, as well as trading rope, hide, and other items manufactured from their herds. The Wakhi obtain tea, salt, oil, and other items from the south and occasionally act as middlemen for the Kyrgyz. The Kyrgyz employ poorer members of Wakhi households to tend to their livestock, in exchange for animals. Wakhi from Sarhad-i-Broghil sometimes give their yaks (and occasionally camels) to the Kyrgyz for tending in the winter season. For the care of ten yaks, the Kyrgyz may take a one-year-old yak in payment. These interchanges generate strong relations between neighbours.

In contrast to observations from other studies (Shahrani 1979, 192), these findings do not indicate that the Wakhi and Kyrgyz hold each other in contempt on the basis of religious differences. Rather, by occupying complementary ecological niches, these two different Muslim cultures ensure economic resilience and the common good while simultaneously acknowledging differences. When they are in each other's territory, hospitality is extended, and they live at each other's homes while securing supplies and engaging in trade. Kyrgyz and Wakhi who are in regular contact can communicate in either language. Some Wakhi have Kyrgyz names because they were born in or near Kyrgyz pastures. Moreover, the two groups share religious shrines, each drawing inspiration and comfort from its own interpretation of Islam. The Kyrgyz, although among the Sunni majority, have historically faced persecution for not being sufficiently orthodox, while the Wakhi Ismailis—who, as Shia, have historically been targeted as heretics—generally resist the fundamentalist and literalist impulse (Bliss 2006). By recognizing their mutual dependence and viewing their differences as an asset, the two groups have been able to avoid the external pressure from those who seek to impose a narrow and more fanatical interpretation of Islam and maintain a largely peaceful coexistence.

What, then, is the relevance of the Cain and Abel narrative to the case of the Kyrgyz and Wakhi? The jealousy that Cain felt toward his brother is not the issue here: all human beings experience jealousy. What is significant is that, rather than attempting to reflect on his feelings and thus come to terms with them, Cain chose to use violence. More than simply a rejection of the ties of kinship, his slaying of Abel is a denial of his reciprocal connection to his brother, who represents another way of living and thinking. The very idea of mutual reliance is repudiated when Cain is asked, "Where is Abel thy brother?" and, he responds: "I know not: Am I my brother's keeper?" (Gen. 4:9). Cain's response is a refusal of the human capacity for biophilia, a concept that one would expect a "tiller of the ground" to uphold. The case of the Kyrgyz and Wakhi is not about the absence of conflict, given that, historically, conflicts have occurred. Furthermore, the two groups live in a country that has been and continues to be torn apart by a bloody civil war supported by global powers beyond its borders. What is instructive is that, despite these long-term stressors, the Kyrgyz and Wakhi choose to act in a manner that supports mutual coexistence and interdependence while safeguarding cultural difference.

How does this case speak to the role of the public intellectual? A scholar must critically engage metanarratives that seek to ignore sociocultural and ecological complexity. The conflict in Afghanistan is generally presented as an open-and-shut case of violence and the intolerance of diversity. While this interpretation is indeed possible, it also conceivable that endless repetitions of the primordial conflict between Cain and Abel are not inevitable. It is the role of the public intellectual to uncover complexities and nuances. The case of the Kyrgyz and Wakhi is informed by intricate relationships between diverse ecological habitats, variations in livelihood strategies, and socio-cultural and religious differences. This complex interaction among differences yields evidence that contradicts the narrative of perpetual conflict. Instead, it reveals agency at the level of communities—the capacity to act pragmatically and empathetically. This case is not without similarities to that of indigenous communities in the Arctic after the collapse of the Soviet Union. It again illustrates biophilia driven by food security and multiple ways of knowing, in this case arising from the differing ecological and sociocultural roles of the Kyrgyz and Wakhi. Simply put, biophilia ignites empathy, empathy appreciates difference, and difference facilitates survival in the Pamir Mountains of Afghanistan.

Discussion: Prospects for Public Intellectuals

Each of the cases described above speaks to the role of biophilia in securing the aims of human life as described by Aristotle (2004). The well-being of the *oikos*, as the dwelling place of humanity, is central to all three cases. The examples from the Arctic and from the Pamir Mountains suggest that the stewardship of the *oikos* is achieved through practical wisdom (phro-nesis). Both examples illustrate another way of knowing, and this practice enabled the continuance of life. In addition, the first case emphasizes the direct role of the public intellectual in speaking truth to power. The second case stresses the participatory nature of knowledge generation when communities of social practice work in tandem with communities of inquirers, of which the public intellectual is a citizen. The third case vividly illustrates the fundamental role of both sociocultural and ecological diversity in facilitating survival. All three cases underscore the relevance of context. To address an issue effectively, we must take into account the past and present in order to consider future possibilities, and for this it is essential that we understand the context. Intellectual pluralism also lies at the core of all three cases. Engaging and integrating multiple perspectives requires the capacity not only to reason but also to empathize and imagine. These faculties make it possible to forge connections among diverse ways of knowing, thinking, and living.

This book rests on the premise that the public space in which intellectuals operate has an impact on democratic political discourse. It is the duty of the university scholar to speak truth to power with grace and humility after substantive research and balanced reflection. It is a truism that the best hope for the preservation of biological and cultural diversity—that is, for safeguarding all the fundamental elements that together constitute life on this planet—is the next generation, our students. Their participation in research is an extension of effective teaching. Our teaching, which should provide an enabling environment for insight, is the foundation for speaking truth to power.

Acknowledgements

Funding for research on the case titled "Intellectual Pluralism and Survival" was provided by the Cooperative Institute for Arctic Research (CIFAR), supported by the National Oceanic and Atmospheric Association and the Gorbachev Foundation. Funding for research on the case titled "Must Cain Always Kill Abel?" was provided by the Christensen Fund. Morgan Ruelle helped develop figure 6.1 and Keith Jenkins helped develop figure 6.2. I am indebted to the comments of the anonymous readers and the editors of this publication.

Notes

1 "The Grey Monk" is among the poems in the Pickering MS, ca. 1807. I am quoting from *Poems and Prophecies* (Blake 1991, 332–33).
2 I use the term *objective ally* to refer to parties that share the same objective while seemingly standing on opposing sides of an issue. Arguably, in the years following 11 September 2001, the Bush administration and Al-Qaida were such objective allies. They used the so-called War on Terror to distract both political leaders and ordinary citizens from the fundamental concerns of the twenty-first century, such as structural poverty, economic and political injustice, and climate change, which take far more human lives and devastate the fabric of families (Kassam 2010b, 244).
3 The *oikos* is simultaneously a description of the sociocultural and biophysical dwelling place and an articulation of the web of relations among humans and of humans with other plant and animal life and with physical forms such as the land, rivers, and mountains upon which human

livelihoods thrive. The planet is likewise an interconnected system that sustains our livelihoods.

4 This case study emerged from personal communication with intelligence analysts and the Canadian Department of Defence staff present at the Canadian Association for Security and Intelligence Services (CASIS) Conference in 2010. I have used publicly available documents to present this case.

5 Simply put, the hypothetico-deductive method is basic to scientific method: it involves formulating an hypothesis that would serve to explain observed phenomena and that can be tested—that is, verified or falsified—through experiment. William Whewell (1837, 1840) is often credited with having laid the foundations for the method.

6 This case study, which is drawn from my research in the circumpolar Arctic, was first presented in *Biocultural Diversity and Indigenous Ways of Knowing* (Kassam 2009a).

7 This case is drawn from the author's research in the Pamir Mountains of Afghanistan (Kassam 2010a). This research provides a more detailed analysis of evidence of the practice of pluralism among the Kyrgyz pastoralists and Wakhi farmers as well as Pashtu pastoralists and the Shugni farmers. For the sake of brevity, only the Kyrgyz and Wakhi cases are presented here.

References

Allen, Gerald M., and Ernest M. Gould, Jr. 1986. "Complexity, Wickedness, and Public Forests." *Journal of Forestry* 84 (4): 20–23.

Aristotle. 2004. *The Nicomachean Ethics*. Translated by J. A. K. Thomas. Revised by High Tredennick. London: Penguin Books.

Balint, Peter J., Ronald E. Stewart, Anand Desai, and Lawrence C. Walters. 2011. *Wicked Environmental Problems: Managing Uncertainty and Conflict*. Washington, DC: Island Press.

Barber, Benjamin R. 1994. "A Proposal for Mandatory Citizen Education and Community Service." *Michigan Journal of Community Service Learning* 1 (1): 86–93.

Bassett, Thomas J. 1988. "The Political Ecology of Peasant-Herder Conflicts in the Northern Ivory Coast." *Annals of the Association of American Geographers* 78 (3): 453–72.

Blake, William. 1991. *Poems and Prophecies*. London: Everyman's Library.

Blench, Roger M. 1984. "Conflict and Cooperation: Fulbe Relations with the Mambila and Samba People of Southern Adamawa." *Cambridge Anthropology* 9 (2): 42–57.

Bliss, Frank. 2006. *Social and Economic Change in the Pamirs (Gorno-Badakhshan, Tajikistan)*. Translated by Nicola Pacult and Sonia Guss, with Tim Sharp. London and New York: Routledge.

Campbell, Tony. 2010. "The Future History of Canada's National Security: Are We Feeling the Heat Yet?" The 2010 John Tait Memorial Lecture, Canadian Association for Security and Intelligence Studies. Ottawa, 14 October. http://www.casis-acers.ca/wp-content/uploads/2014/06/Tony-Campbell-2010.pdf.

Chatwin, Bruce. 1989. "Nomad Invasions." In *What Am I Doing Here?* 216–29. New York: Viking.

Chrétien, Jean. 2008. *My Years as Prime Minister*. Toronto: Vintage Canada.

Churchman, C. West. 1967. "Wicked Problems." *Management Science* 14 (4): B141–42.

Cronon, William. 1983. *Changes in the Land: Indians, Colonists, and the Ecology of New England*. New York: Hill and Wang.

Crutzen, Paul J., and Eugene F. Stoermer. 2000. "The 'Anthropocene.'" *Global Change Newsletter* 41: 17–18.

Crutzen, Paul J., and Will Steffen. 2003. "How Long Have We Been in the Anthropocene Era?" *Climatic Change* 61 (3): 251–57.

Felmy, Sabine, and Hermann Kreutzmann. 2004. "Wakhan Woluswali in Badakhshan: Observations and Reflections from Afghanistan's Periphery." *Erdkunde* 58 (2): 97–117.

Fromm, Erich. 1964. *The Heart of Man: Its Genius for Good and Evil*. New York: Harper and Row.

Galinsky, Adam D., Joe C. Magee, M. Ena Inesi, and Deborah H Gruenfeld. 2006. "Power and Perspectives Not Taken." *Psychological Science* 17 (12): 1068–74.

Gellner, Ernest. 1985. *Muslim Society*. Cambridge: Cambridge University Press.

Hodgson, Marshall G. S. 1974. *The Venture of Islam*. 3 vols. Chicago: University of Chicago Press.

Innis, Harold A. 1995. *Staples, Markets, and Cultural Change: Selected Essays*. Edited by Daniel Drache. Montréal and Kingston: McGill-Queens University Press.

Jervis, Robert. 2010. *Why Intelligence Fails: Lessons from the Iranian Revolution and the Iraq War*. Ithaca: Cornell University Press.

Kassam, Karim-Aly. 2009a. *Biocultural Diversity and Indigenous Ways of Knowing: Human Ecology in the Arctic.* Calgary: University of Calgary Press and the Arctic Institute of North America.

———. 2009b. "Viewing Change Through the Prism of Indigenous Human Ecology: Findings from the Afghan and Tajik Pamirs." *Human Ecology* 37 (6): 677–90.

———. 2010a. "Pluralism, Resilience, and the Ecology of Survival: Case Studies from the Pamir Mountains of Afghanistan." *Ecology and Society* 15 (2): article 8. http://www.ecologyandsociety.org/vol15/iss2/art8/.

Kassam, Karim-Aly, ed. 2010b. *Understanding Terror: Perspectives for Canadians.* Calgary: University of Calgary Press.

Kassam, Karim-Aly, and Leanne M. Avery. 2013. "The *Oikos* of Rural Children: A Lesson for the Adults in Experiential Education." *Journal of Sustainability Education* 5: 1–17.

Kassam, Karim-Aly, George Melnyk, and Lynne Perras, eds. 2002. *Canada and September 11: Impact and Response.* Calgary: Detselig.

Khaldûn, Ibn. 1967 [1377]. *The Muqaddimah: An Introduction to History.* Translated by Franz Rosenthal. Edited and abridged by N. J. Dawood. Princeton: Princeton University Press.

Kreutzmann, Hermann. 2003. "Ethnic Minorities and Marginality in the Pamirian Knot: Survival of Wakhi and Kirghiz in a Harsh Environment and Global Contexts." *Geographical Journal* 169 (3): 215–35.

Kuhn, Thomas. 1962. *The Structure of Scientific Revolutions.* Chicago: University of Chicago Press.

Latour, Bruno. 2002 [1987]. *Science in Action: How to Follow Scientists and Engineers Through Society.* Cambridge, MA: Harvard University Press.

Mann, Charles C. 2005. *1491: New Revelations of the Americas Before Columbus.* New York: Alfred A. Knopf / Random House.

Page, Scott E. 2007. *The Difference: How the Power of Diversity Creates Better Groups, Firms, Schools, and Societies.* Princeton: Princeton University Press.

———. 2010. *Diversity and Complexity.* Princeton: Princeton University Press.

Rittel, Horst W. J., and Melvin M. Webber. 1973. "Dilemmas in a General Theory of Planning." *Policy Sciences* 4 (2): 155–69.

Sayre, Nathan F. 2012. "The Politics of the Anthropogenic." *Annual Review of Anthropology* 41: 57–70.

Shahrani, M. Nazif Mohid. 1978. "Ethnic Relations and Access to Resources in Northeast Badakhshan." In *Ethnic Processes and Intergroup Relations in Contemporary Afghanistan: Papers Presented at the Eleventh Annual*

Meeting of the Middle East Studies Association in New York City, November 10, 1977, edited by Richard F. Strand and Jon W. Anderson, 15–25. New York: Afghanistan Council of the Asia Society.

———. 1979. *The Kyrgyz and Wakhi of Afghanistan: Adaptation to Closed Frontiers*. Seattle: University of Washington Press.

Smith, Nigel J. H. 1980. "Anthrosols and Human Carrying Capacity in Amazonia." *Annals of the Association of American Geographers* 70 (4): 553–66.

Steffen, Will, Paul J. Crutzen, and John R. McNeill. 2007. "The Anthropocene: Are Humans Now Overwhelming the Great Forces of Nature?" *Ambio* 36 (8): 614–21.

Wester, Franklin Eric. 2004. "Preemption and Just War: Considering the Case of Iraq." *Parameters* 34 (4): 20–39.

Whewell, William. 1837. *History of the Inductive Sciences: From the Earliest to the Present Times*. London: John W. Parker, West Strand; Cambridge: J. and J. J. Deighton.

———. 1840. *The Philosophy of the Inductive Sciences, Founded upon Their History*. London: John W. Parker, West Strand; Cambridge: J. and J. J. Deighton.

Williams, Raymond. 1976. *Keywords: A Vocabulary of Culture and Society*. London: Fontana Press.

Wilson, Edward O. 1984. *Biophilia*. Cambridge, MA: Harvard University Press.

7   Reflections on My Dubious Experience as a Public Intellectual

BARRY COOPER

As is often the case when a political scientist is tasked with discussing a modern question such as the transformation of public intellectuals in Canadian democracy, he or she begins with some remarks on the early political scientists, the Greeks. This is not merely a bow to tradition but an attempt to begin with some clear distinctions, distinctions that tend to be blurred or obliterated by modern and contemporary usage. And so I begin with Aristotle.

Aristotle distinguished three ways of life that human beings might choose freely, which is to say, in a manner independent of the necessities of life. Human beings can, moreover, choose to submit, temporarily or forever, to necessity, as do slaves, craftsmen, and money makers (*Politics* 1337b5). Beyond what he called the banausic ways of life are those that are concerned with the beautiful, which is neither useful nor necessary. More specifically, they are: (1) the life of enjoyment, in which the beautiful is consumed; (2) the life devoted to the polis, in which the practice of *arete* leads to beautiful and memorable deeds; (3) the life of the philosopher, which is devoted to the contemplation of everlastingly beautiful things (*Politics* 1333a 30 et seq., 1332b 32). For present purposes, we can ignore the first non-banausic option and look only at what Aristotle called the *bios politikos* and the *bios theoretikos*. With the end of the polis, a life of practice lost its specifically political orientation, and the theoretical life thus remained as the only genuinely free way of life throughout the Middle Ages and into modern times. There are many qualifications that could be made to this distinction between practice and theory or between politics and philosophy, but, like the distinction between war and peace, it is evident enough to serve as a starting place.

This distinction, however qualified, and like all distinctions, is a theoretical one. For the man of action, the contemplative is understood, as Pericles said in his famous funeral oration, to be an *idiot*—a private person who minds his own business and is, in consequence, politically useless (Thucydides, *History* 2:40). Why? Because he refuses to undertake noble and beautiful deeds that bring glory to the city. But even here, in this best-known praise of democracy at its best, directed toward a democratic assembly that liked to think well of itself—which is to say, in the flattering words of a democratic politician—action is subordinated to speech, *logos*. This is so in two ways: first of all, because the glorious deeds of the dead Athenian soldiers were praised by Pericles in words and, second, because Pericles's glorious words were recorded in a book written by Thucydides, who, I would argue, is a political philosopher *avant la lettre*.

Consider another example, also from Greek antiquity. In 389 BCE, at about forty years of age, Plato left Athens for extended travels that eventually took him to Sicily. In Syracuse, he formed a friendship with Dion, who was about twenty and was the brother-in-law of the tyrant Dionysius I. When Dionysius I died in 367, Dion sought to influence his nephew, Dionysius II, and help him to reform the government. To that end he asked Plato, who was then about sixty, to return to Syracuse and instruct the new ruler. Plato says he did so reluctantly and with misgivings (*Epistles* VII, 328b). He had good reason to mistrust the new tyrant. Dionysius II lacked the discipline and commitment necessary to a philosophic life, although he was keen to acquire the appearance of learning and apparently published what he understood of Plato's philosophy, which was not much. In Plato's language, Dionysius II was a lover of opinion, a philodoxer, not a philosopher (*Republic* 480). Or, as Eric Voegelin (2004, 100) once remarked, "what Plato called a *philodox[os]* we generally term *intellectual*." In any event, Dionysius II banished Dion, and Plato left Syracuse for Athens. Dion, still in exile, again appealed to Plato, and he returned, now about sixty-six. Three years later, Dion deposed Dionysius II, and three years after that was killed. Plato's influence on the unhappy course of Sicilian politics was negligible. There was a brief interlude of order under Timoleon, starting around 344 BCE, which had some faint echoes of the Platonists' aspirations, but civil war broke out soon after. Eventually, around 323, this most promising island of Hellenic colonization was conquered by the Carthaginians and later fell to their successors, the Romans.

At the end of his book on intellectuals in politics, Mark Lilla appended an afterword, "The Lure of Syracuse." This "lure" was perfectly captured by a query of one of Heidegger's colleagues when, in 1934, he returned to teaching following his tenure as (Nazi) Rektor of the University of Freiburg: "Back from Syracuse?" his colleague asked. Dionysius, Lilla said, "is our contemporary" (Lilla 2001, 194, 196). As the list of intellectuals and the tyrants' intellectuals admired so eloquently analyzed by Lilla attests, Dionysius has assumed many names today. This is another way of saying, along with Leo Strauss, that Xenophon's *Hiero* remains a useful discussion of the relationship of the tyrant and the poet-philosopher. What was new in the twentieth century, Lilla argued, was the advent of what he called the philotyrannical intellectual. Such a creature cannot be found in antiquity, despite the arguments of Strauss's great interlocutor, Alexandre Kojève. A few major thinkers—besides Heidegger, there was Carl Schmitt, who also admired Hitler, and Georg Lukács, who faithfully followed Stalin—and scores of second- and lower-rank ones, along with poets, professors, and celebrities, made pilgrimages to new Syracuses in Moscow and Berlin, and, more recently, in Hanoi and Havana, or even Tehran.

How philosophically grounded criticism of and opposition to tyranny became the philotyranny of the intellectuals is a large, complex, and puzzling question. A thorough account of the growth of these *fleurs du mal* even within the smaller Epicurean garden of French intellectual life, with which I am at least somewhat familiar, is beyond the scope of these reflections. Even so, a summary account of changes from the Dreyfus affair, which effectively introduced the term *l'intellectuel* to modern discourse, would disclose not only an absence of philosophy but a love, precisely, of opinion, *doxa* (Datta 1999). A great divide, for example, is disclosed between Aron's *L'opium des intellectuels* (1955) and Sartre's *Plaidoyer pour les intellectuels* (1965). The division was not so much between Plato's philosopher and philodoxer as between Aron's *bon sens* and Sartre's philotyranny. That is, substantially, Aron was unquestionably correct to consider the opposition, in Aron's words, of "humanity" and "power," so central to the critiques of the left following the affair, to be simple-minded—evidence, for example, of Sartre's refusal, at once naïve and romantic, to confront the realities of twentieth-century politics.

Across the Rhine, as Aron also remarked, the problem was not so much *engagement* as *Innerlichkeit*, a kind of internal retreat from political reality in the name of *Bildung* and *Kultur* and *Wissenschaft*. Thomas Mann's *Reflections of an Unpolitical Man*, published a month before the 1918 armistice, was probably the *locus classicus* of this aesthetic attitude toward politics. For Aron, but also for Jürgen Habermas and Eric Voegelin, who otherwise had very little in common, the refusal to confront reality by embracing the escapism of *Innerlichkeit* was as imprudent as the escapism of French commitment. Moreover, both Aron and Voegelin, who had a great deal in common, stressed the importance of common sense in politics, as did Hannah Arendt.

In other words, from the old distinction of theory and practice we are directed to a kind of hierarchy based, in Platonic terminology, on desire, *eros*. The desire of the philosopher, we know, is for wisdom and of the *politikos* for glory. But what do the philotyrannical intellectuals desire? And what do those who desire only the tranquility of *Innerlichkeit* expect their lives to be like? However those last questions are answered, we must begin with an analysis of common sense.

Philosophically speaking, common sense—as used by Thomas Reid, for instance—refers to the human capability of "managing our own affairs, and [being] answerable for our conduct towards others: this is called common sense because it is common to all men with whom we can transact business, or call to account for their conduct" (Reid 1850, chap. 2, "Of Common Sense," 332–33). It is, in other words, a habit or attitude rather than philosophically articulate knowledge. As Voegelin (2002, 411) remarked, "the civilized *homo politicus* need not be a philosopher, but he must have common sense." Arendt makes the same point, but, as it were, commonsensically: "Common sense occupies such a high rank in the hierarchy of political qualities because it is the one sense that fits into reality as a whole our five strictly individual senses and the strictly particular data they perceive." The existence of common sense allows us to know that our sense perceptions disclose rather than obscure reality. As Arendt (1958, 208–9) further observes, "A noticeable decrease in common sense in any given community and a noticeable increase in superstition and gullibility are therefore almost infallible signs of alienation from the world."

Let us make a preliminary conclusion, then, that at best the thinking of an intellectual, as distinct from that of a scholar or a scientist, to say nothing of a philosopher, aims to be commonsensical. In contrast, scientific, scholarly, and philosophical thinking aims as well to justify the grounds of common sense, namely, those habits of mind that are presupposed or taken for granted by common sense (Schutz 1962, 3).

By this argument, intellectuals were present long before the word was invented. Even more so, *public intellectual* is a term that, by virtue of certain aspects of their writings, could equally have been applied to scholars, scientists, and philosophers long before the term was coined, apparently in 1987 (Jacoby 1987, 5). Richard Posner (2001) distinguished public intellectuals from scholars, scientists, and philosophers not in terms of the substantive content of their work or whether it was commonsensical but in terms of their rhetoric and their audience.

The question of the public intellectual, Posner (2001, 1) said, refers to "the phenomenon of academics' writing outside their field or, what often turns out to be the same thing, writing for a general audience." A few pages later, he wrote:

To an approximation only, the intellectual writes for the general public, or at least for a broader than merely academic or specialist, audience on "public affairs"—on political matters in the broadest sense of that word, a sense that includes cultural matters when they are viewed under the aspect of ideology, ethics, or politics (which may all be the same thing). (23)

And, as a final formulation, he said:

To summarize, a public intellectual expresses himself in a way that is accessible to the public, and the focus of his expression is on matters of general public concern of (or inflected by) a political or ideological cast. Public intellectuals may or may not be affiliated with universities. They may be full-time or part-time academics; they may be journalists or publishers; they may be writers or artists; they may be politicians or officials; they may work for think tanks; they may hold down "ordinary" jobs. Most often they either comment on current controversies or offer general reflections on the direction or health of society. In their reflective mode they may be utopian in the broad sense of seeking to steer the society in a new direction or denunciatory because their dissatisfaction with the existing state of the society overwhelms any effort to propose reforms. When public intellectuals comment on current affairs, their comments tend to be opinionated, judgmental, sometimes condescending, and often waspish. They are controversialists, with a tendency to take extreme positions. Academic public intellectuals often write in a tone of conscious, sometimes exasperated, intellectual superiority. Public intellectuals are often careless with facts and rash in predictions. (35)

Posner (2001, 26) also accepted the view that public intellectuals filled a market niche that opened up when academics fell under the influence of "continental, mainly French, social theorists" and then adopted "an esoteric, jargon-laden, obscurantist style." That is, the intellectuals involved may have written about public affairs, but no ordinary member of the public could understand them. By this account, one of the tasks of a public intellectual is to translate, for instance, esoteric postmodern "discourse" into a more persuasive, though not often a commonsensical, idiom.

These aspects of what public intellectuals might aspire to be and how they might be effective was the subject matter of a rather comic exchange in the pages of the *Literary Review of Canada*. In the December 2010 issue, Sylvia Bashevkin, a self-described "progressive" political scientist at the University of Toronto, lamented the absence of "centre-left voices" from the public discourse of Canadian politics. According to her, there remained within political science but "a relatively narrow, shrunken conduit linking left-of-centre elements of the discipline with the wider general community" (20). She was particularly "troubled" by the fact that "conservative advocates have been better communicators, finding new ways to dress up old ideas such as laissez-faire capitalism and patriarchal family organization in spiffy new outfits for each debating season" (20). In contrast, she lamented of progressives such as herself that "our work is often so theoretically inclined and academically focussed as to be publicly inaccessible" (20).

Her complaint was that the rhetoric of the "progressive" left was defective. Leaving aside the questionable assertions made in passing, Bashevkin's major observation is undoubtedly correct. In fact, this short piece in a popular magazine exemplified that regrettable combination of opacity and cliché that both Posner and Jacoby noted as well. What Bashevkin called "theoretically inclined and academically focussed" writing is often pretentious po-mo gibberish. Not for her the advice of George Orwell, to write prose as clear as a windowpane, or even of Kant, who hoped his philosophy could be made intelligible to a plow-boy.

In the next issue, my friend and colleague Tom Flanagan (2011, 30) offered some "helpful hints" on how the "progressive" political scientists might do better. His first and most serious hint was simple: "Learn to write clearly." This meant, among other things, avoid the locutions of postmodernism and, in particular, the "misguided insistence on using nouns .as verbs." Instead, he said, "Read Hemingway and learn to write short, declarative sentences. Do it. Now." Other helpful hints followed: discuss topics that citizens actually care about; get involved in political life. He also illustrated in his advice the kind of playfulness that typically serious "progressive" activists deliberately avoid when he noted the need of a plan for world domination: "The Calgary School is now grooming Sarah Palin to be the next president of the United States." We saw how that worked out. On cue, two readers replied in the next issue with separate letters to berate Flanagan for advocating the building, as he had playfully said, of "a Hayekian Jerusalem in Canada's green and pleasant land."[1] One of the two, Erna Paris, a very serious Toronto writer, recalled another bit of levity in which Flanagan indulged on CBC television, namely, his "manly" advice to President Obama that a Predator strike on the founder of WikiLeaks, Julian Assange, whose actions had imperilled the lives of countless Afghans and NATO troops, might be worth considering. Making such a suggestion was, she said, an indictable offence under section 464 of the Criminal Code (Paris 2011, 30). Now, Leo Strauss once observed, in his discussion of Xenophon's rather subtle way of writing, that there is little more tedious than explaining a joke to someone with no sense of humour. Likewise, no one could reasonably expect serious "progressive" academics to see the comedy in their own actions and words.

To summarize these preliminary observations, the philosophical insights of intellectuals are limited. By and large, they can aspire no higher than to common sense—and often aim lower. In "Evil by Any Other Name," Christopher Hitchens (2011) made much the same point: "The proper task of the 'public intellectual' might be conceived as the responsibility to introduce complexity into the argument: the reminder that things are very infrequently as simple as they can be made to seem." A good example of complexity, to which I will return, is climate change. "But," Hitchens added, "never, ever ignore the obvious either." Hitchens was referring to the attacks of 11 September 2001: the complexity provided by conspiracy theories served scant purpose there. The offering of commonsensical advice such as this is supplemented by the need, as Flanagan said, to write or speak in a way that audiences understand. Hitchens's prose is in this respect exemplary.

The philosophical version of this approach is Socratic rhetoric. Likewise, there's no rule against making fun of your opponents or making the occasional joke. Again, the philosophical version of this approach is Socratic irony. It seems to me that no one who is aware that one of the constituent elements of philosophy is comedy could ever be lured by philotyrannical temptations. Such temptations hold appeal only to those who are serious— and they, as Johan Huizinga (1955) recalled, are devoid of both culture and civility. In short, I am suggesting that it is possible to act as a public intellectual in Posner's sense only so long as you retain your common sense and your sense of irony. This remains even more necessary when one writes as a scholar or a philosopher, even a political philosopher. Of course, there are non-commonsensical public intellectuals as well, so there are often conflicts in the media among members of different "schools"—such as Bashevkin's Progressive School and the presumably non-progressive Calgary School.

—⁓—

The next part of this chapter is a kind of confessional. It is intended to justify the phrase in the title referring to my dubious experiences.

In high school and then as an undergraduate at the University of British Columbia I would write occasional pieces for the student newspaper. At UBC I even dated a reporter for *The Ubyssey*, who later became a ferocious lawyer in Vancouver. One of my good friends at the time was Mike Valpy, who went on to become a major writer at the *Globe and Mail*. When I lived in Toronto, I wrote occasional op-ed articles for the *Globe*. The last one I penned as a resident of that city explained why I was leaving for Calgary.

My editor called it "New Barbarism: The Young Man Goes West" (Cooper 1981). It was published in the "Trends" section. After about a decade of writing intermittently for the *Globe* and for the *Financial Post*, I wrote a longer article titled "Thinking the Unthinkable," which appeared in a *Globe* supplementary magazine called *West* (Cooper 1990). It was not about the effects of nuclear war, as was Herman Kahn's book of that name, but about how to help Québec gain independence because of the incessant monetary demands of the province, Quebeckers' and their government's sense of entitlement, and their obnoxious lack of gratitude for the largesse Albertans and other productive Canadians had sent their way.

David Bercuson, whom I had met once in Toronto, called me up and suggested we write a book on this problem. I had never written a book for a general audience before and had never engaged an agent to negotiate with publishers and secure an advance, which I had never previously received. It was all very exciting.

The aftermath of the book we produced, *Deconfederation: Canada Without Quebec* (1991), was also exciting. On 5 October 1991, *Deconfederation*, according to the *Globe and Mail*, was the best-selling book in the country. David and I went on book tours. I had the enjoyable experience of speaking *en français* to my erstwhile fellow citizens in Québec to explain why we wanted them gone. The editor of the *Montreal Gazette*, Norman Webster, wrote a threatening editorial denouncing us. We made fun of him as the Ayatollah Webster. We wrote a sequel, *Derailed: The Betrayal of the National Dream* (1994), but it was not nearly as successful. Writing these books with Bercuson led to a collaboration over several years in which we produced regular newspaper columns for the *Calgary Sun*, the *Globe and Mail*, and the *Calgary Herald*. In addition, and starting with that initial book tour promoting *Deconfederation*, I have regularly been interviewed for radio and television.

By Posner's understanding, this production of more-or-less popular books and newspaper writing, along with electronic media appearances, counts as an activity certifying one as a public intellectual. Fair enough. But such a category does not address the actual experience of writing such material. Here I would have to add that, invariably, there exists an element of entertainment and provocation in writing for a general audience. That is, for one who has at least a remote understanding of philosophy, writing for non-philosophers and for human beings who do not aspire even to become aware that they are non-philosophers, let alone do something about it, necessarily emphasizes the comic side of the philosophical way of life. One cannot avoid irony under those circumstances.

There are also occasions when irony is thrust upon you whether you seek it or not. Apart from my experience at a think tank, which should more accurately be called a dogma tank, and of which I have written elsewhere (Cooper 2009, 247–57), twice I have been the object of attention in the media in a way that I did not seek. These occasions, too, constitute important elements of my dubious experience as a public intellectual.[2]

During the 1980s, the Government of Alberta made money available to hire research assistants. They were called, for reasons I can no longer recall, PEP grants and STEP grants. Professors were urged to apply in order to support our students. Having secured three months support for four students, I asked one of my MA students, Lydia Miljan, to design a research program to put them to work. She had them do a content analysis of CBC national network radio programs, including such flagship productions as *As It Happens* and *Morningside*, starring Barbara Frum and Peter Gzowski, respectively. Lydia was working on politics and the media, so it was also on-the-job training for her. The team developed a code book, protocols for resolving disagreements over coding and for monitoring inter-coder reliability, and so on. I had very little input into the whole process. Lydia and I then wrote a paper for the next Canadian Political Science Association meeting presenting the data. The data revealed, and we attempted to account for, a persistent left-wing bias and a kind of enduring animus against the western parts of the country.

We left a few copies of the paper in the press room, and, much to our surprise, it made the front page of the *Globe* next morning, below the fold. Lydia, who now teaches at the University of Windsor, thought this was amusing. Neither of us expected the flurry of letters to the editor denouncing our findings. Perhaps the letter-writers had read the paper, perhaps not. We replied, restating our findings, and the disturbance subsided.

Back in Calgary, toward the end of the summer of 1987, so far as I can recall, I received a letter from Norm Wagner, the president of the university at the time. Wagner was a scholar of the ancient Near East as well as a dynamic administrator, and he had a wonderful sense of humour. He had received a letter from the president of the CBC, Pierre Juneau, demanding that I be fired. "Would you care to draft a reply?" Wagner asked. I did.

Moreover, I was curious about the, to me, strange sensitivity of the journalists and bureaucrats at the CBC. We had not set out to *attack* them but to discover whether a vague sense of imbalance in their news and magazine shows could be measured using a well-known and long-accepted method of content analysis. Personally, I was not astonished by what we found, and the interesting problem was how to account for both the left-wing bias and the central Canadian bias of CBC news coverage. Some of this problem I worked out later in discussing the several competing regional myths at play in Canada, but my immediate response was to write a book that further documented the shoddy job done by the CBC, *Sins of Omission: Shaping the News at CBC TV* (1994). A few years later, Lydia and I rewrote her PhD thesis, which examined the political attitudes of journalists, both print and electronic, in Canada (Cooper and Miljan 2003). This book was runner-up for the Donner Prize for the best book in public policy. In all modesty, we ought to have won.[3]

I would emphasize, however, that I did not set out to study the media and their influence on politics as part of my political science research agenda. This work was simply occasioned by the availability of funding, which provided a means to support students over the summer, which led to the paper, which chanced to encounter an interested journalist, who brought it to the attention of a *Globe* editor, who publicized our findings. Who could have anticipated the response of Pierre Juneau or the people at the CBC responsible for showing how balanced the organization was? Having been attacked by CBC, however, and then having that organization's CEO write the president of my university asking that I be fired, I felt that a thymotic response on my part was appropriate, as well as satisfying. In fact, I was never concerned about getting fired, but I was curious and suspicious about the CBC. Why did they object *so strenuously* to an outsider examining their work? Could the bias that the students' content analysis brought to light be systemic? In my more suspicious moments I wondered, What are they hiding? And why? Curiosity led me to write *Sins of Omission* and some further papers, as well as to help Lydia turn a very interesting thesis into a more accessible examination of the attitudes of Canadian journalists and document the influence of those attitudes on the production of news.

There is an accidental aspect to the second event as well. When the Chrétien government signed the Kyoto Protocol in December 1997, it reversed initial commitments made to the provinces, especially to Alberta, that they would be consulted regarding the provisions of this agreement. At the time, I thought this was just run-of-the-mill treachery from Ottawa, but it soon became apparent that the increase in the reach of the federal bureaucrats was advanced in the name of climate science, global warming, anthropogenic climate change, the production of greenhouse gases, and so on. To my way of looking at federal politics, it was an updated version of the National Energy Program initiated by Pierre Trudeau during the early 1980s.

Even in the late 1990s, it was clear that the issues surrounding the actual causes of climate change were not settled but hotly disputed by the climatologists; it seemed to me that the bureaucrats in Environment Canada were being highly selective in what they considered to be scientifically acceptable. Of course, this is not surprising. Bureaucrats are not likely to look for reasons to diminish their own power. In any event, the more I looked into Kyoto and the justification for it, the more it looked as if federal bureaucratic politics, not science and the debates among climate scientists, was driving the Ottawa agenda.

In the summer of 2004, one of my friends in business introduced me to several individuals, mostly retired geologists and geophysicists, who had formed a group called "Friends of Science" (FOS). They were concerned to promote discussion of the data, models, conclusions, measurement problems, and so on relating to climate science, meteorology, and climatology. We held a number of meetings, and I explained my interest in the politics of the debate about anthropogenic global warming, as it was then called. In the fall of 2004, I set up a project, "Research on the Climate-Change Debate," and, in collaboration with FOS, an associated trust account to receive funds that would pay for the production of a DVD documenting the many complexities of the climate-science debate and would also be used to publicize the existence of the DVD. My thinking was, and is, that the media's presentation of the problem of climate change, particularly in the early 2000s, was one-sided and that the political consequences for Alberta and for Canada were significant. To my way of thinking, producing a DVD was akin to writing a book; publicizing its existence was akin to publishing a book. After all, there is not much point in writing a manuscript or making a DVD if no one knows it exists.[4]

The production, distribution, and publicizing of a DVD is an expensive operation. In this instance, the whole thing cost slightly more than half a million dollars. Contributions to the trust account, which was administered by the university, came from individuals, foundations, and companies; donors were given tax receipts because, in the eyes of the Canada Revenue Agency, the University of Calgary is a registered charity. This was the same administrative structure I had used for many other research projects.

In the early spring of 2005, the DVD was released and remains available on the FOS web site. Initially, it had the University of Calgary logo on it, in order, I presumed, to acknowledge the collaboration with the university. A couple of days later, on 5 May 2005, FOS received a letter from the university lawyer instructing FOS to remove the name and logo of the university from the DVD or face legal action. The reasons given by the university were "that it did not support the position set out in the video, that it had not entered into any affiliation agreement with FOS," and that the Board of Governors had not approved the use of the U of C's coat of arms or crest. It was certainly true that the Board of Governors had not approved anything, and the identifying symbols were removed. It was not clear to me what an "affiliation agreement" was other than the standard agreement supplied by Research Services to administer research funds accumulated in the usual way in a trust account. So far as "the position set out in the video" is concerned, what it set out was a respectable and scientifically well-qualified argument to the effect that the view reported widely in the media, namely, that something approaching a consensus existed on the question of global warming, was wrong. At the time, the significance of the response of the university escaped me.

Meanwhile, a blogger and public relations consultant based in Vancouver and affiliated with the David Suzuki Foundation began posting the most alarming reports, most of which concerned my being a "conduit" for money from "big oil" to produce propaganda for my good friend and "fishing buddy" Stephen Harper. For the record, none of this is true: (1) I was not a conduit for anything; I was an account holder of research money; (2) we received money from one medium-sized oil and gas company, Talisman Energy, about which I will have more to say (unfortunately, "big oil" contributed nary a cent); (3) it is a great exaggeration to say that the prime minister and I are good friends, notwithstanding my qualified admiration for his achievements as compared to his predecessors, and so far as I know he does not fish. None of this mattered because the focus was on the FOS video and the doubt it cast on the fantasy that the science surrounding anthropogenic climate change was conclusive and "settled."

Someone, identified only as "a citizen," complained to the university about the project and the video, alleging that it was an illegal and illegitimate operation. The allegation of illegality concerned radio advertisements drawing attention to the contested state of climate science that were aired in Ontario during the 39th federal general election in the fall of 2005. The illegitimacy, apparently, concerned the content of the FOS video. Regarding the legal question, the issue concerned "third-party spending," which is prohibited by section 353 of the Canada Elections Act. I had, in fact, served as an expert witness, *for the Crown*, in the third-party spending cases brought against the National Citizens Coalition led at the time by my alleged fishing buddy, Stephen Harper. Before FOS negotiated with radio stations in Ontario about running the ads, I told them that, in the event of an election (it had not yet been called, but there was considerable speculation during the summer and early fall), the content of the ads would not violate the Canada Elections Act because it did not endorse any political party. I was right. Three years later, in response to this citizen's complaint, Elections Canada issued a ruling to that effect.

This leaves the question of the significance of the content of the FOS video. At the time, I was simply puzzled about why the university—which had several times provided a forum for David Suzuki, and awarded him an honorary degree, and later co-sponsored an appearance in Calgary by Al Gore—would not dismiss the complaint with some high-sounding talk about academic freedom. What are universities for, after all, if not to discuss all sides of controversial questions? Indeed, Allison MacKenzie, the university's director of community relations, agreed that bringing Gore to town was controversial, "but the university is a place to discuss different ideas, and climate change is a hugely important issue." So important was this issue that the university set aside twenty tickets to reward students who developed ideas on how to make the campus "more sustainable" and greener (Anderson 2007).

One of the oddities about the discussion of anthropogenic climate change is that the "skeptics," as they are called, tend to be dismissed by what we might call the orthodox. For anyone even slightly familiar with the history of science, skepticism seems to be one of the few constants. Why is climate change so different? One answer seems plausible. The response to criticism of the reports of the Intergovernmental Panel on Climate Change (IPCC) to the United Nations or to such comic episodes as the hacking of computers in the United Kingdom and the publicizing of some embarrassingly unscientific emails suggests that, within the orthodox community of climate scientists, great value is accorded political solidarity. That is, the debate regarding climate change is first of all political rather than scientific, rather like the exclusion of Alberta's interests and Alberta's voice from the Kyoto "process."

The immediate effect, however, was rather different. I was summoned to a meeting with the provost, the university lawyer, the vice-president for research, and the chief fundraiser for the university. I was asked to explain myself, which is what I did along the lines just indicated. I was told that the university was shutting down the research accounts because I had violated several rules, which was news to me.[5] The upshot was that a cheque from the Calgary Foundation, which was going to produce an updated version of the original DVD, was to be returned to them. It was also clear from the conversation that these senior managers were most unhappy with me. One of them went so far as to suggest that I would be liable for some $30,000 that the university had spent on legal and accounting advice. They were not amused when I said that perhaps FOS could pick up the tab. That evening I spoke to one of my genuine fishing buddies, a much-admired (and feared) litigator. He wrote the university lawyer and received the reply that it was all a great misunderstanding.

This was as curious an episode as the response of the CBC, only this time it was the university, not the public broadcaster, that was the source of the threats. So what, in turn, was the threat posed by the FOS DVD? As Hitchens advised: Do not ignore the obvious. A plausible principle might therefore be found by bearing in mind the following: by analogy with "big oil," where "big science" is concerned, the old adage of detectives, "Follow the money," may be correct.

Because the correspondence between the university and several funding agencies involved is not public, all one can do is note that the university has received a great deal of money to support infrastructure and personnel working in two organizations the premise of which is that anthropogenic climate change is a genuine threat and that the FOS video cast that premise into doubt. These organizations are the Institute for Sustainable Energy, Environment, and Economy (ISEEE) and the Canada School of Energy and Environment (CSEE). They conduct research on such questions as carbon capture and sequestration (CCS), for example, which assumes not only that

CO_2 is a significant "greenhouse gas" which is questionable, that it is produced by humans, which is true, but that it is the chief cause of potentially catastrophic climate change, just as Al Gore and the IPCC have said, which is even more questionable. The numbers are impressive: press reports indicate the ISEEE is in the process of receiving hundreds of millions of dollars (Alberta Energy 2011; Cryderman 2011; Lowery 2004).

The CSEE story is even more interesting not so much because of the money at stake (though that is considerable) but because of the colourful individuals involved. The initial memorandum of understanding, which established the CSEE as a joint venture among the three largest Alberta universities and the Government of Canada, was signed in 2004. This MOU was followed by others in 2007 and 2008. In 2008, Bruce Carson was appointed executive director and in 2009 the funding agreement was extended to 2013–14.

According to Andrew Nikiforuk, writing in *The Tyee* (Nikiforuk 2011), which is to say, a strong environmentalist writing in a strongly environmentalist paper, Bruce Carson, despite his questionable past and the somewhat lurid scandals that later surrounded him, managed to secure over $30 million in funding for CSEE. Carson was, at the time, Harper's senior policy advisor. When asked by the *Calgary Herald* about Carson's criminal record, a university spokesperson refused to discuss "second or third hand information" (quoted in Nikiforuk 2011). Much of the information regarding Carson was in fact not gossip, however, but part of the public record.

In any case, it is not Carson's character that deserves attention in the present context. Rather, as Nikiforuk reported, it is that the university actually *was* lobbying the Government of Canada, whereas FOS was merely accused of having done so but in fact had not.

The latest chapter in the FOS-university story appeared in mid-September 2011, when Mike De Souza, who had written several earlier stories in the *Calgary Herald* about the video and my part in securing its production, wrote a couple more stories after having learned from a freedom of information request that one of the sponsors of the original project was Talisman Energy (De Souza 2011a, 2011b). He was particularly interested to report that Talisman now disavowed their previous support for FOS (De Souza 2011c). The interesting aspect of this story is not the allegation that research money was used for lobbying, which was not true; it is the curious fact that, of all the CEOs in the major and junior oil and gas companies in

Calgary, only one, Talisman, ever gave serious money to this project. One reason for this oddity, it seems to me, is that most oil and gas companies are run by engineers or MBAs or engineers with MBAs. Talisman, at the time, was run by Jim Buckee, who had a PhD in astrophysics from Oxford. In other words, Buckee was a scientist as well as a manager. When he spoke about climate change and associated topics, he spoke the way genuine scientists do, with a fiduciary concern for truth.

To conclude, let me cite one final comic episode. On 15 September 2011, in an editorial titled "Ethics 101" written in the wake of the latest revelations concerning the connection of FOS and the University of Calgary, the *Ottawa Citizen* opined that "it is not the role of the university to lend its legitimacy, good name—and possibly, donation tax receipts—to a lobbying campaign, funded in part by a company with a direct interest in the issue, and aimed at presenting the results of scientific research in a particular light." Of course, the university administration and celebrated researchers, not FOS, had been doing just that for several years . The lobbying was a success and the university was handsomely rewarded for it.

—⁂—

There are a few conclusions that can be drawn from these reflections. The first is that whether one becomes a public intellectual is in no small measure a matter of contingency. Second, those who are sometimes called celebrity journalists (who are, perhaps, just individuals with PhDs who are unable to find academic employment) might seek such a status for the monetary rewards it brings. Here, my own experience cannot really serve as an example since the rewards have been relatively meager compared to my regular employment as a university teacher. (Notwithstanding the fact that environmentalist bloggers think I am a lackey and shill for big oil, I still have a substantial mortgage to pay.) That said, I do not think I would write a newspaper column for free. George Grant once remarked that it was a matter of vanity to hope that one's views will have an effect. There is something to his observation, but that is not the whole story. One hopes that one's views will be effective in teaching, say, Plato's *Republic* not just because they are one's own interpretations but also because what Plato says is true.

It seems to me that, one way or another, we cannot avoid the question of truth. I mentioned that this was probably why Jim Buckee, a scientist, responded to the climate change alarmism by principled action whereas the ordinary CEO today is more likely to manage a disturbance by buying some tranquility rather than, as the Bible says, "kick against the pricks" (Acts 9:5). Finally, I would say that a combination of common sense, a reasonable rhetorical style, and a sense of the absurd or of irony is necessary for life as a public intellectual in Canada today. Such at least is my experience.

Notes

1 For anyone who has read Hayek and grasped his notion of spontaneous order, the echo from Blake's poem was a line of wit. Progressives seem not to have got the joke, but whether it was from ignorance of Hayek or of Blake is not clear.

2 There is a third and minor occasion as well, to which Flanagan adverted: the Calgary School. This, too, is an ironic label foist upon Bercuson, Flanagan, and me, along with Ted Morton and Rainer Knopff, by journalists who think that ideas are more important than interests or ambitions in politics. Even more specifically, it was a convenient portmanteau term that allowed Toronto and other eastern and left-wing journalists and bloggers to make sense of the success, otherwise unintelligible to them, of Stephen Harper. For such intellectuals, Harper was a creature of the Calgary School, which makes as much sense as saying Dionysius was a creature of Platonic philosophy. An especially comic rendition of this tale is Marci McDonald, "The Man Behind Stephen Harper" (2004).

3 Granted, both these books were published by university presses and so might be disqualified from contributing to any public intellectual profile. However, the narcissism of media ensured that they received extensive media attention, so I include them.

4 In fact, I set up two trust accounts. The second was to comply with the conditions of a donor who wished to ensure that his funds were used only for the production of the DVD and not for ancillary matters, such as publicity.

5 A report by the university auditor found that there was insufficient oversight, which is probably true. But then such people have a vocational commitment to the proposition that you can never have too much oversight. There was no serious wrongdoing, however, although I did violate some minor provisions of reporting.

References

Alberta Energy. 2011. "Carbon Capture and Storage." News release, 11
 March.

Anderson, Katy. 2007. "Al Gore Coming to Calgary." *The Gauntlet*, 12 April.

Arendt, Hannah. 1958. *The Human Condition*. Chicago: University of
 Chicago Press.

Bashevkin, Sylvia. 2010. "Canadian Political Science: Missing in Action? A
 Practitioner Wonders Why the Progressive Side of the Discipline Has Gone
 Mute." *Literary Review of Canada*, December, 20–21.

Bercuson, David, and Barry Cooper. 1991. *Deconfederation: Canada Without
 Quebec*. Toronto: Key Porter.

Bercuson, David, and Barry Cooper. 1994. *Derailed: The Betrayal of the
 National Dream*. Toronto: Key Porter.

Cooper, Barry. 1981. "The New Barbarism: The Young Man Goes West."
 Globe and Mail, 14 August 1981.

———. 1990. "Thinking the Unthinkable," *West*, May, 22–28.

———. 1994. *Sins of Omission: Shaping the News at CBC TV*. Toronto:
 University of Toronto Press.

———. 2009. *It's the Regime, Stupid! A Report from the Cowboy West on
 Why Stephen Harper Matters*. Toronto: Key Porter.

Cooper, Barry, and Lydia Miljan. 2003. *Hidden Agendas: How Journalists
 Influence the News*. Vancouver: University of British Columbia Press.

Cryderman, Kelly. 2011. "University of Calgary Plans Carbon Capture
 Research Facility," *National Post*, 17 January.

Datta, Venita. 1999. *Birth of a National Icon: The Literary Avant-Garde and
 the Origins of the Intellectual in France*. Albany: State University of New
 York Press.

De Souza, Mike. 2011a. "Talisman Backed Anti-Global Warming Campaign."
 Calgary Herald, 14 September.

———. 2011b. "U of C 'Research' Dollars Used for Lobbying." *Calgary
 Herald*, 15 September.

———. 2011c. "U of C, Talisman Distance Themselves from Friends of Science
 Group." *Calgary Herald*, 17 September.

Flanagan, Tom. 2011. "Letter." *Literary Review of Canada*, January–February,
 30.

Hitchens, Christopher. 2011. "Evil by Any Other Name." *National Post*, 6
 September.

Horn, Michiel. 2011. "Letter." *Literary Review of Canada*, March, 30.

Huizinga, Johan. 1955. *Homo Ludens: A Study of the Play-Element in Culture*. Boston: Beacon Press.

Jacoby, Russell. 1987. *The Last Intellectuals: American Culture in the Age of Academe*. New York: Noonday Press.

Kintisch, Eli. 2010. *Hack the Planet: Science's Best Hope—or Worst Nightmare—for Averting Climate Catastrophe*. Hoboken, NJ: John Wiley.

Lilla, Mark. 2001. *The Reckless Mind: Intellectuals in Politics*. New York: New York Review of Books.

Lowery, Mark. 2004. "Unlocking Buried Oil Reserves." *On Campus Weekly*, 15 October.

McDonald, Marci. 2004. "The Man Behind Stephen Harper." *The Walrus*, October.

Nikiforuk, Andrew. 2011. "Bruce Carson Scandal Greased by Harper's Oil Sands Agenda." *The Tyee*, 27 April.

Paris, Erna, 2011. "Letter," *Literary Review of Canada*, March, 30.

Posner, Richard A. 2001. *Public Intellectuals: A Study in Decline*. Cambridge, MA: Harvard University Press, 2001.

Reid, Thomas. (1785) 1851. "On Judgment." Essay 6 in *Essays on the Intellectual Powers of Man*. Cambridge, MA: John Bartlett.

Schutz, Alfred. 1962. "Common-Sense and Scientific Interpretation of Human Action." In *Collected Papers*, vol. 1, *The Problem of Social Reality*, 3–47. Edited by Maurice Natanson. The Hague: Martinus Nijhoff.

Voegelin, Eric. 2002. *Anamnesis: On the Theory of History and Politics*. Edited by David Walsh. Translated by M. J. Hanak. Vol. 6 of *The Collected Works of Eric Voegelin*. Columbia: University of Missouri Press.

———. 2004. *The Drama of Humanity and Other Miscellaneous Papers, 1939–1985*. Edited by William Petropulos and Gilbert Weiss. Vol. 33 of *The Collected Works of Eric Voegelin*. Columbia: University of Missouri Press.

Intellectual Discourse Online

MICHAEL KEREN

With much of public discourse today moving online, democracies that aim at a degree of civility in their internal and international politics face a major challenge: how to maintain the standards and norms of public discourse that have developed over the course of many centuries. Although the discourse of the marketplace, or of government, or of the mass media generally bears little resemblance to conversations in university seminars or at scholarly meetings, book readings, or exhibition openings, intellectuals—defined by Russell Jacoby (1987, 5) as "writers and thinkers who address a general and educated audience"—have played an important role in setting the standards for public discourse. Foremost among these are the need to rely on statements supported by factual evidence and the willingness to listen to others. Intellectuals introduced a degree of structure, style, and self-reflection into public discourse—three qualities seen since the time of Socrates as functional to the quest of truth in intellectual life and justice in public life (Shils 1973).

Democratic political regimes place restraints on excessive power and abusive language. Intellectuals have contributed to restraining both by setting the boundaries of truth and justice and by occasional interventions in the public sphere when these boundaries are breached. While intellectuals rarely have more than a limited impact on politics—which, even in a democracy, is more inspired by practical considerations than by intellectual discourse—interventions by intellectuals, such as Émile Zola's cry "J'accuse!" during the Dreyfus affair, have served as important reminders of the distinction between good and evil, even when evil abounded.

This is not to say that intellectuals necessarily have a better sense of good and evil than do political representatives. However, ongoing intellectual discourse within a society and practices of public discourse that are inspired by the rules of restraint and inhibition developed in scholarly and other intellectual enterprises help to prevent the association of political might with right. In societies in which intellectual discourse has been muted and the practice of speaking truth to power banned, political leaders can more easily exceed the boundaries of truth and justice. It is therefore worthwhile to explore the effects of online public discourse—in which some of the restraints and inhibitions associated with traditional intellectual discourse are dismissed—on democracy.

Public Thinkers and "Putative Revolutionaries"

Let me begin by adding to Russell Jacoby's definition of public intellectuals as writers and thinkers who address a general and educated audience an idea proposed by Václav Havel. Havel argued that intellectuals do not merely devote themselves to thinking in general terms about the affairs of the world and the broader context of things but "do it professionally" (quoted in Jennings and Kemp-Welch 1997, 13). I thus abandon the tradition associated with Karl Mannheim's *Ideology and Utopia* ([1936] 1968), in which intellectuals were treated as a free-floating stratum, and focus instead on the professional base that grants them the authority to comment on public affairs. As Jennings and Kemp-Welch (1997, 14) point out, intellectuals have never lived what literary scholar Bruce Robbins called a "gloriously independent life" but have had to devise a variety of strategies in order to speak and engage with a wider public.

Pointing at one's vocational credentials is a major component of these strategies. These credentials may include academic research, published novels, or acclaimed artwork, accomplishments that may or may not be relevant to the public discourse at hand but help to establish public authority and recognition. As Elshtain (2001) notes, political theorists have often expressed widespread discontent over such issues as the disaffection of American citizens from the work of civil society, but it was not until the publication of *Bowling Alone*, Robert Putnam's empirical work on the subject, that these concerns won a broad public hearing.

Once public intellectuals are no longer treated as a free-floating stratum, we may consider them as actors in a public arena who compete for scarce resources, including access to the mass media, public recognition and the symbolic rewards associated with it, money, social and political ties, and sometimes power. Magali Sarfatti Larson, a sociologist who writes on professionalism, narrows down the public arena to what she calls "discursive fields" (1990, 35), defined as battlefields in which professionals fight with non-professionals for pre-eminence. And although the "public intellectual" category differs from that of the "professional" in its emphasis on the concern with ideas that extend beyond one's vocation, public intellectuals can also be conceptualized as participants in the battles over pre-eminence in the discursive fields in which issues of public interest are debated. This is especially evident at times in which a new breed of public intellectuals, with new claims to authority, comes on stage.

This theoretical base is consistent with the market model advanced by Richard Posner in *Public Intellectuals: A Study of Decline* (2001). Posner calls for an investigation of the factors that create a demand on the part of the general public for access to the ideas and opinions of public intellectuals on issues of general interest, as well as of the factors that determine the supply in response to this demand. The market for public intellectuals, he writes, is highly competitive because many consumers and suppliers exist, both actual and potential, and because entry into the public sphere is not restricted by such requirements as obtaining a licence. Posner's market model is useful because it directs us to look at the public intellectual not only as a person who speaks truth to power but also as a player in a competitive arena and this model can be applied to the study of online discursive fields because, in spite of claims that the Internet provides "a democratic distribution of access" (Hurwitz 2003, 101), the Internet is indeed a competitive arena. As David Park (2006, 12) writes, "The Internet may support different public intellectuals, and may also support a different kind of interaction between public intellectuals and their audiences."

The Internet is particularly challenging to "traditional" public intellectuals, that is, those who established their public authority prior to the late 1990s. The Internet has given rise to bloggers who claim authority on an alternative basis, one that does not always put professionalism on center stage. As Park (2009, 267) points out, "They play their cards as putative revolutionaries who represent the true voice of the people." Indeed, bloggers often argue that they are now fulfilling the role of public intellectuals, a claim not without merit if we consider Etzioni's portrayal of public intellectuals as persons who "opine on a wide array of issues, are generalists rather than specialists, concern themselves with matters of interest to the public at large, and do not keep their views to themselves" (2006, 1).

The claim of bloggers to the public intellectual's role is based on the expansion of "public" to incorporate private concerns that were formerly excluded from the public sphere but are acceptable topics of discussion in blogs, while it also reflects the opportunity now given to many more people than before to comment on public affairs. Daniel Drezner argues that the growth of online venues has in fact stimulated the quality and diversity of public intellectuals. "The Internet," he writes (2009, 49), "is viewed as a vital aid for the renaissance of public intellectuals. The explosion of online publications, podcasts, dialogs, and especially weblogs has enabled public intellectuals to express their ideas beyond the narrow confines of elite op-ed pages and network television." Annabelle Sreberny and Gholam Khiabany, studying the blogosphere's contribution to a realignment of public debate in Iran, make a similar claim. Noting that the social production of intellectuals and, more importantly, of intellectual debate requires public space sufficient to permit debate to emerge, they argue (2007, 272) that the Internet provides such a space, allowing for a "far greater range of voices speaking 'intellectually' than ever before."

In the competitive market of intellectual life, the emergence of new suppliers who have a broader class, gender, and ethnic composition warrants careful attention. In what follows, I offer a case study drawn from my own experience. Although quite limited in scope, it allows for some preliminary observations on this process.

"To the Crowd in its Nakedness Everything Seems a Bastille"

At the end of January 2007, comments I made at the University of Calgary in connection with my recently released book, *Blogosphere: The New Political Arena* (Keren 2006), were picked up by the Canadian media, which resulted in hundreds of responses in the blogosphere. It appears that my comments on blogs as reflecting an existential state of loneliness in contemporary life had hit a nerve. While of course I stopped short of providing a full account of the book's theory about the relation between the emancipatory and the melancholic dimensions of cyberspace, my comments challenged bloggers to think about ways to overcome the constraints on their newly acquired emancipation posed by political parties and marketing agencies, as well as about the difficulty of translating their self-expression in virtual reality into actual political power. The comment that provoked the greatest response was: "Bloggers think of themselves as rebels against mainstream society, but that rebellion is mostly confined to cyberspace, which makes blogging as melancholic and illusionary as Don Quixote tilting at windmills" (quoted in Graveland 2007).

Here are two examples of bloggers' responses. "Bea," who describes herself as a young mother and university instructor in Ontario interested in theology, Victorian literature, children's books, autism, the Turin shroud, and Buffy the Vampire Slayer, used the above comment to reflect on the contributions that blogging made to her life and the support she received online. Her reflections inspired other introspective posts and sparked a civil and thoughtful deliberation ("Bea" 2007). On the other hand, "CK"—an American blogger who, according to her profile, is passionate about ideas, programs, and people, focuses on creating value for the companies she works for, and excels at developing clever ideas and programs that engage people around businesses, brands, or causes—took a different line. Readers who approached her blog on 5 February were met with an illustration of a finger pointed at them with the word "LOSER" printed in large type on top of the page. This illustration was accompanied by an open letter, "Dear Dr. Michael Keren," in which the blogger made harsh comments about *Blogosphere: The New Political Arena*, a book she admittedly had not read and had no clue about its content or methodology, which did not prevent her from "quoting" from it or implying that the nine case studies analyzed in it were intended as a representative sample of the blogosphere. In no time, the mob was enthused:

Bloggers Swarm Against This Jerk!
    Posted by: vaspers the grate | Monday, February 05, 2007 at 09:18 AM

Let 'em have it, CK! That will teach him to generalize too hastily. :)
    Posted by: Cam Beck | Monday, February 05, 2007 at 09:37 AM

Yeah Cam, go buddy!
    Posted by: vaspers the grate | Monday, February 05, 2007 at 10:51 AM

There are good reasons for these schmucks to fear us bloggers. Let's "geet er dunn."

Posted by: *vaspers the grate* | *Monday, February 05, 2007 at 10:52 AM* ("CK" 2007).

Such online talk can be dismissed as esoteric, but not so its exploitation by "CK," the marketing blogger, who works the mob up, addressing many of them directly:

Hey all you lonely-loser-terrorists: Thank you for voicing-in . . . my jaw just dropped when I read his quotes. So many great points above.

Vespers: Indeed we are more informed than most, great point. I like your note to the "Doctor of Deception" . . . I'd love to see him go a few rounds with you.

Gay: Yep, we have made change and with more consumers coming online co's are having to let go of more control—that's change. . . .

Cam: People just need to generalize I guess; such a shame as this guy is clearly missing out and out-of touch as a result ("CK" 2007).

In *Crowds and Power*, Elias Canetti ([1962] 1991, 20) wrote that "to the crowd in its nakedness everything seems a Bastille." Although the crowd forming on CK's blog does not necessarily resemble the historical crowds Canetti had in mind (and no analogy is attempted here), one cannot avoid thinking that online discourse is also not immune from opinion leaders who stir mass behaviour in order to fulfill political, promotional, or personal goals. The tendency of human groups to turn into mobs under certain conditions has not diminished with the advent of the Internet; if anything, it may even be encouraged by clever political and marketing forces that have learned how to manipulate the free expression it allows.

Bloggers and other Internet users have often emphasized the democratic nature of the new medium, claiming that it provides an open arena for public deliberation similar to the ancient Greek agora, gives public voice to private issues excluded from the formal public sphere, and encourages a politically engaged citizenry. As one blogger writes, "The Internet is the best thing to happen to free choice since Erasmus, the best thing to happen to democracy since John Locke, and the best thing to happen to commerce since Adam Smith. The Internet is the new Agora, a new market for ideas" (Donovan 2012).

Such references to the agora analogy have been supported by communication researchers such as Vincent Price, in his study of citizens deliberating online. Price (2011, 233) admits that public discussion online differs in fundamental ways from that carried out face to face but argues that its distinctive features "may well prove to help rather than hinder the core attributes of deliberation." He goes on to emphasize three such features of online discussions: the reduction in social cues, which limits the scope for the projection of social status and may thus encourage less deferential behaviour, thereby undermining status hierarchies; the fact that multiple statements can be input simultaneously, which may promote the sharing of ideas; and the anonymity, which can work to reduce inhibitions and anxieties about expressing one's honest views, including potentially unpopular ones.

Price's three features of Internet deliberation stand in contrast to some of the familiar characteristics of intellectual discourse, such as the emphasis on status hierarchies stemming from the need to establish one's credibility before speaking, the expectation that statements will be made in a linear order rather than simultaneously, and, most notably, the adherence to certain procedures guiding scholarly inquiry, literary work, and other intellectual endeavours, which force a degree of inhibition in the form of structural, stylistic, and other constraints expected to be maintained even in conversations on issues, such as politics, that involve high emotions. Traditional intellectual discourse is thus replaced in online environments by a different mode of deliberation, and the question then arises: what are the political consequences of this transformation?

Online Commentators

In pursuit of an answer to this question, I studied the responses to the *Globe and Mail*'s online article of 31 January 2007 in which my "Don Quixote" comment appeared (Graveland 2007). The article was open to comments from 31 January to 5 February. I tried to place these comments in a typology I developed (Keren 2010) which classifies online statements by their structure, their style, and the degree of self-reflection found in their content. Before showing how the above comments fall into the different cells of the typology, let me go over its main features.

In terms of structure, the typology guides one to ask whether online comments involve a discursive structure, that is, whether the online commentator proceeds by some form of deductive reasoning, mainly by the use of syllogisms or enthymemes (syllogisms lacking one or more components, which can however be inferred), or rather by an intuitive structure in which truisms replace reasoning. In terms of style, it asks whether the writing is generally restrained, temperate, and prudent or instead tends to be aggressive, uncompromising, and bigoted, labelling the former "moderate" and the latter "rabid." In terms of content, the typology distinguishes between introspective comments, which involve an element of self-reflection and vacuous ones, which lack such an element.

The three variables—structure, style and content—each with two variants yield a total of eight ideal types of online commentators, which can now be applied to the present case.

Civilized

The civilized commentator is characterized by a discursive, moderate, and introspective style. He or she uses some form of deductive reasoning, avoids highly charged, tendentious language, and exhibits the capacity for self-reflection, corresponding to Aristotle's observation in Book III of the *Rhetoric* that "it is not enough to know what to say; we must also say it in the right way." Here is a representative statement by one commentator:

> Perhaps that is a downside to the growth of the Internet. A technology that is doing so much to bring people together—breaking down barriers across national and cultural boundaries—is also able to separate us physically from . . . fellow human beings. This conversation is a good example of my point. I can share my thoughts about common issues with other readers from across Canada, and even around the world. Yet I could bump into anybody commenting here on a street corner, and never know who they are. I don't know what they look like. I don't know what they sound like. I don't know how the[y] dress or style their hair. All I see is their ideas.[1]

Egghead

The egghead maintains the deductive structure of argument and the moderate style associated with the civilized commentator; however, the element of introspection is missing. I have characterized this style as "vacuous" because it relies on abstract observations that, in the absence of the evaluative dimension associated with the process of self-reflection, easily become airy assertions offered without benefit of critical scrutiny. For example:

> Blogs aren't literature but they provide a good forum for free speech. With objectivity in journalism an oxymoron, blogs provide people the opportunity to present balanced views of the world. If [we] rely on authors and journalists to direct societies, we can end up with the biased and misinformed views that are a detriment to society. Blogs also provide important information such as the "whistle blowing" we were able to see in the corporate scandals in the US.

Contentious

Some online commentators, while adopting a discursive mode of argument and demonstrating a degree of introspection, choose to abandon the temperate, detached style that characterizes civilized discourse. Their statements tend to be opinionated and not necessarily very polite, as in the following case:

> Pure rubbish, and I second Mr. Cyr's statement that the Lonely Blogger is a meaningless characterization. It certainly depends on the blog community. I wouldn't know about myspace, but blogger and vancouverbloggers organize and encourage social events and meetups. I think most bloggers are just venting about aspects of their lives, or societies and gain a sense of empowerment through their writing. Speaking for myself, it's cathartic. I don't really care about my visitor count. I just like the fact that I can speak my mind without any politically correct restrictions. Talk hard.

Pretentious

Sometimes the rabid style illustrated just above accompanies not introspection but vacuous assertions, such as these: "What's a book if it's not the original form of blogging? Michael Keren should get a life, maybe." The above statement could be seen, with some effort, as containing an enthymeme, but the other two characteristics of civilized discourse—moderation and self-reflection—are clearly missing.

Pristine

The four ideal-types discussed thus far follow the classical Aristotelian emphasis on reasoned argument—on what I have described as a "discursive" structure. A discourse can, however, adopt a more intuitive approach, abandoning deductive structures of argumentation in favour of appeals to personal experience and statements grounded in standard assumptions and truisms—that is, in "gut sense." The category in the typology labelled "pristine" refers to those whose writing lacks the discursive structure traditionally associated with intellectual activity and yet remains temperate and introspective. For example:

> I tend to agree with Michael Keren on a few points. I tried blogging
> once, and found it to be fruitless. Nobody pays attention to it unless
> you have some sort of celebrity or purpose. Incidentally, those who did
> pay attention were friends of mine that I communicated with regularly
> outside the internet.

Noble Savage

Intuition can be an important source for introspection, but this is not always so. The intuitive thinker, no less than the egghead, may make assertions that involve no element of self-reflection. While the egghead is often ridiculed because we expect that someone who is otherwise immersed in the structure of civilized discourse would be adept at self-reflection, this expectation does not apply to the intuitive thinker. A commentator who maintains a moderate style but lacks the two other qualities of civilized intellectual discourse—namely, reasoned argument and the ability to engage in introspection—is called in the typology a "noble savage." The following example comes close to this type:

> The good and bad thing about blogs is that, being as diverse and popu-
> lous as the people who surf the web, you can find ample evidence for
> any pre-conceived notion you may have about them. I think Michael
> Keren is looking at the phenomena with too narrow and prejudiced
> an agenda (though admittedly it will sell books to those who are too
> lazy to question this belief). It's obvious this is an academic exercise for
> someone not very acquainted with blogging; it's not difficult to refute
> his points by even a cursory glance at what's out there.

Adolescent

The intuitive form of introspection characteristic of the pristine type may be expressed in a rabid style, rather than in civil, temperate language. This combination yields a method of argument we often witness among self-reflective adolescents, as demonstrated in our case by the following comment:

Excuse me? An academic is pointing fingers and saying that others are lonely and pathetic? How much social time and development did the Professor sacrifice so he could get his PhD? Most Profs I know are pretty anti-social. I understand if he can't survive by just selling his books to his students as part of the course curriculae he felt he should pick a different topic to publish on. But "bloggers are losers"? Why didn't he just write a book on how to get rich quick like every other wannabe who wants to boost their sales? It'd be less embarassing for him. As for examples to the contrary, I know professional business people who link their blogs to assist their clientelle, support groups for parenting, soldiers in Iraq, Doctors serving up north, space tourists, you name it, they've blogged it. And we're supposed to see these people as social misfits? This guy's on crack! If this is what counts for research from a Prof at U of C I really feel for the students.

"Mass Man"

This brings us to the ideal type I called "mass man" (Keren 2010, 117), a term coined by José Ortega y Gasset in *The Revolt of the Masses* (*La rebelión de las masas*, 1930). Ortega's "hombre-masa" was someone who expresses ideas without accepting the standards one needs to appeal to in a civilized discussion. Indeed, the mass man represents the very antithesis of the civilized commentator. Statements made by this type lack discursive structure, moderate style, and evidence of introspection, as in this example:

Stereotypes are fun, let me give it a try. I see a photo of Phd with what appears to be a bowl cut, and a laptop in the foreground not exactly the archetypal extrovert, is he? This is just such a joke. He's basing his observations on a whole nine instances, and doubtless, handpicked. If he were doing his Masters he wouldn't get this past the proposal stage, let alone have the media cover his "research." It makes me wonder if he isn't trying to compensate for his own life, or lack their of.

Disinhibition and the Totalitarian Spirit

In an article published in *CyberPsychology and Behavior*, John Suler (2004) analyzed the psychological effects of online discourse, focusing on the loss of inhibitions behind a veil of anonymity. Because anonymity allows online actors to sever the link between their actions and their real-world identity, they tend to be more comfortable about opening up, but they are also more likely to act out. A process of dissociation occurs, whereby "the online self becomes a compartmentalized self" (2004, 322), disconnected from the offline self. This "toxic" form of disinhibition encourages an attitude of irresponsibility toward others, inasmuch as the real person cannot be held accountable for his or her actions online. The ability to avoid the immediate consequences of one's words and actions may prompt the online actor to express hostilities more freely and to engage in behaviour that is rude, cruel, or otherwise socially unacceptable. As Suler points out, it is "almost as if superego restrictions and moral cognitive processes have been temporarily suspended from the online psyche" (2004, 322).

The responses to the *Globe and Mail* article were varied. Although all eight ideal types could more or less be identified, special attention must be paid to the "mass man" category, which was represented in a high number of responses. What makes the mass man's disinhibited behaviour important is its rejection of anything associated with intellectualism in the past: the inhibitions stemming from the traditional need to adhere to rules of structure, style, and self-reflection are abandoned. Public discourse requires rules and procedures—a condition that has not been sufficiently stressed by Internet theorists. Such theorists often compare online discourse to the deliberative public sphere described by Jürgen Habermas in relation to Europe of the modern era. However, Habermas did not ignore the importance of the laws and procedures that guide public deliberations. According to Habermas, "Discourse theory has the success of deliberative politics depend not on a collectively acting citizenry but on the institutionalization of the corresponding procedures and conditions of communication" (1994, 7).

Public discourse that lacks rules and procedures and is conducted within a setting that allows human inhibitions to be abandoned may in fact be more consistent with totalitarianism than with deliberative democracy. The warnings issued by Jacob Talmon to this effect are worth recalling. In *The Origins of Totalitarian Democracy* (1952), Talmon was concerned with the emergence, in the eighteenth century, of a totalitarian form of democracy concurrently with the liberal variety. These two currents have continued to exist side by side, and Talmon regards the tension between them as the most vital issue in modern history. Although his analysis deals with eighteenth-century political philosophy, some of the origins of totalitarian democracy resemble the features attributed, often in tones of praise, to online discourse. Talmon ([1952] 1970, 5) points to the "decline of the idea of status consequent on the rise of individualism," which "spelt the doom of privilege"; the view of human beings as an "abstraction," independent of the historical groups to which they belong; the blurring of the distinction "between the sphere of personal self-expression and that of social action"; and the rise of a "vanguard of the enlightened." These trends are associated with democratic ideals but are also powerful vehicles of totalitarianism, the use of extreme compulsory measures by, or in the name of, an enthused mob.

Talmon saw the origins of totalitarian democracy in Rousseau's appeal, in *The Social Contract* (1762), that the people as a whole, not just a small representative body, should take part in the political process. For Talmon, Rousseau demonstrated the close relation between popular sovereignty, taken to an extreme, and totalitarianism. "It is commonly held that dictatorship comes into existence and is maintained by the indifference of the people and the lack of democratic vigilance," writes Talmon, and "there is nothing that Rousseau insists on more than the active and ceaseless participation of the people and of every citizen in the affairs of the State" ([1952] 1970, 47). But this is where Rousseau abandons the democratic practices developed by the ancient Greeks and unwittingly provides the ideational base of modern totalitarian dictatorships:

Saturated with antiquity, Rousseau intuitively experiences the thrill of the people assembled to legislate and shape the common weal. The Republic is in a continuous state of being born. In the pre-democratic age Rousseau could not realize that the originally deliberate creation of men could become transformed into a Leviathan, which might crush its own makers. He was unaware that total and highly emotional absorption in the collective political endeavor is calculated to kill all privacy, that the excitement of the assembled crowd may exercise a most tyrannical pressure, and that the extension of the scope of politics to all spheres of human interest and endeavor, without leaving any room for the process of casual and empirical activity, was the shortest way to totalitarianism. (Talmon [1952] 1970, 47)

The participants in online discourses of the twenty-first century differ in many ways from the excited crowds associated with totalitarian democracy. The breakdown of status hierarchies in cyberspace generally does not involve the guillotine, and political activism often consists of no more than pressing a "Like" button on Facebook. But the seeds of totalitarian democracy that Talmon detected in the context of the Enlightenment may be found in any political process marked by disinhibition.

Let me stress again that no analogy between the participants in online discourse and the frenzied mobs of the French revolution or the interwar era is intended here, nor am I trying to apply a unified behavioural model to the varied individuals in cyberspace. My argument is rather that the new media cannot simply be equated with the agora without considering warnings, such as those issued by Ortega, on the political consequences of public discourse that lacks inner inhibitions or constitutional constraints. Political discourse that does not respect norms and standards, Ortega argued, does not allow a civil society to emerge: "Niceties, norms, courtesy, mediation, justice, reason ... What was the original point of such inventions, of creating all these subtle complications? They are all summed up in the word 'civilization,' which in its root, *civis*, 'citizen,' discloses its authentic origin. It is this concept which strives to make possible the city, the community, life in common (1985, 64)." Indeed, civil life is hard to imagine when intellectual discourse turns into mob rule.

Righteous Mobs and Civil Society

Internet researchers have often adopted an optimistic view of the potential contribution of online discourse to the renewal of a sense of citizenship and the revitalization of civil society. As a medium that encourages both chaos and consensus—in that it lacks order and authority but allows thousands of individuals to form affective bonds—the Internet has seemed to many to hold political promise. In his *Spirit of the Web*, published in 1999, Wade Rowland expressed his hope that the age of information, blossoming at the end of the bloodiest century in history, would help to usher in an era of greater humanity:

The world suggested by digital networks . . . finds beauty, meaning,
order and life in chaos. It suggests a civilization that promotes and
values diversity, even anarchy. It suggests a politics that organizes
from the bottom up, valuing nimbleness above persistence, honor
above duty, freedom above security, cooperation above competition,
consensus above authority, and [an] approach to communication that is
bilateral rather than unilateral, valuing the informal conversation over
the formal address. (1999, 377)

Internet theorists have been particularly enthusiastic about the advent
of blogs, with their blurring of the divide between the private and public
spheres. In *A Private Sphere: Democracy in a Digital Age*, Zizi Papacharissi
argues that, by providing citizens with a space within which to express private concerns and give voice to marginalized interests, blogs offer a means
to revive a civic arena. "Blogs," writes Papacharissi (2010, 148), "present
the contemporary terrain where ascetic practices of narcissism untangle
the complex relation of the self to its own self, and, by extension, to the
democratic environments that it inhabits" (148). Acknowledging that participation in civil society requires a consideration of the public good, she
correctly raises the question of how it is that "the private sphere can sustain
a new civic vernacular through which individual citizens may connect back
to publics, counter-publics, and hybrid spheres as they choose" (132). Her
response:

The unique contribution of blogs lies not in enabling the public good,
but rather in challenging the premises upon which it rests. Their function is expressive first and deliberative only by accident. . . . Thus blogs
and similar media are best understood in terms of their potential for
debasing the stability of political environments, including democracies
and non-democracies, rather than revitalizing the structures within
which they come to be. (149)

This response points at a new conception of civil society, one that shifts
away from the citizen as a participant in public deliberations that produce
compromise and duty-based action toward the construction of a pluralistic
community engaged in the collective expression of affect-laden opinion,
reminiscent of Rousseau's "general will," a process in which thousands of

individuals form consensus on their digital devices about the social structures to be destroyed and the sinners to be shamed.

This may be an extreme interpretation of Papacharissi's dismissal of the public good, but the view of the blogosphere as a new political arena based on affective bonds rather than on deliberation is not hard to find in works by early promoters of digital media. Consider Hugh Hewitt's *Blog: Understanding the Information Reformation That's Changing Your World*, in which he compares the swarming of bloggers against well-known American political and media figures to the "great mounted armies" of seventh-century Muslims and thirteenth-century Mongols (2005, 4). "Swarming," writes Hewitt, "is a seemingly amorphous but carefully structured, coordinated way to strike from all directions at a particular point or points, by means of a sustainable 'pulsing' of force and/or fire" (4). To him, success in achieving ascendancy, whether "of a brand, a candidate, or a cult," depends in part on the destruction of the opposition (6). Although Hewitt expects blogging to demonstrate its constructive potential in the future, he emphasizes its power in mocking and shaming people who say or do the wrong things—in beating them, to borrow one of his metaphors, "like a bongo drum" (26).

A more balanced approach to the burgeoning of new media can be found in Howard Rheingold's *Smart Mobs: The Next Social Revolution*, in which he analyzes the convergence of wireless technology and social communication in mobile devices, which allow people who do not know each other to act in concert and cooperate in ways never before possible. The author is aware that, while some of the ensuing changes will benefit the public good, others will erode it. "As indicated by their name," writes Rheingold (2002, xviii), "smart mobs are not always beneficial. Lynch mobs and mobocracies continue to engender atrocities. The same convergence of technologies that open new vistas of cooperation also makes possible a universal surveillance economy and empowers the bloodthirsty as well as the altruistic." In particular, he expresses concern over the misuse of the new media by malicious governments and groups: "Cooperative effort sounds nice, and at its best, it is the foundation of the finest creations of human civilizations, but it can also be nasty if the people who cooperate share pernicious goals. Terrorists and organized criminals have been malevolently successful in their use of smart mob tactics" (xxi). This insightful prediction ignores, however, the potential of smart mobs to disrupt civil society even when their intentions are not malicious but righteous.

Some scholars have pointed at that potential. In *Speaking into the Air*, John Durham Peters (1999, 1) warned of the human tendency to replace imperfect down-to-earth deliberations by the "dream of communication as the mutual communion of souls." In *Critique of Information*, Scott Lash (2002, 37) criticized political movements based on affective bonding, which "have more in common with the sect than the church, with *Gemeinschaft* than *Gesellschaft*." And among the insights that emerged from a brainstorming session on governance and social media held in 2012 was the idea that the present crisis of governance in democracies results from a lack of deliberation—that "deliberation is necessary so that democracy produces collectively-intelligent decisions instead of dumb politics":

> Without deliberative mechanisms for making decisions that weigh
> consequences and balance trade offs, social networks that only enhance
> unmediated participation and information also just enhance the "dumb
> mob." Turning the "dumb mob" into the "smart mob" is one of the
> key challenges for the immense participatory power of social media.
> As it is now, social media like Twitter or Facebook are good for simple
> minded mobilization of those prepared to act, but not for the processes
> of negotiation and consensus building required for intelligent decision
> making. (Gardels 2012, 14)

The dangers posed to civil society by "righteous mobs" have become more apparent with the growing phenomenon of online swarming against individuals who make what others consider racist, sexist, or otherwise misguided statements, prompting Tarun Wadhwa (2013) to comment that "the severity of collective punishment is taking a disturbing direction." One such incident occurred in 2013 when a racist comment tweeted by the director of communications for InterActiveCorp, Justine Sacco, led to tens of thousands of responses, including rape and murder threats against her and her family and friends, as well as to her immediate firing from her job. The *New York Times* titled its report on the incident, "Is the Internet a Mob Without Consequences?" Nick Bilton (2013), who wrote the *New York Times* piece, noted that "in the eyes of the mob," justice had been done, and yet those who engaged in issuing murderous threats suffered no consequences themselves.

As he pointed out, although mobs that begin with a small spark and then erupt into chaos are nothing new, in the past it was generally the poor who rose up against the rich and powerful. Today, however, "it is the powerful, specifically those with the largest followings online, that could help quell these eruptions, yet instead douse them with more anger and hate."

Bilton's comment reminds us that online mobs cannot be equated with the uneducated masses of Marx's *lumpenproletariat*. On the contrary, online swarming may often be induced, inspired, and manipulated by well-educated people who take part in the action in order to advance certain commercial, political, or other agendas, or simply to have some fun. As Wadhwa (2013) commented regarding the Justine Sacco case, "It was unsettling for me to watch my Twitter feed full of professionals I admire and respect join in on the fun. Their actions were largely harmless, but we're all setting the standard for how people will be treated when we don't like something they've said online."

Or, as the case may be, when we don't like something that we've heard they said. As Dominic Sandbrook (2009) points out in a *New Statesman* article titled "Trial by Fury," written in the wake of online shaming incidents in Great Britain, many of those who join in righteous mobs are reacting secondhand. They may not actually have read the comments deemed offensive: it is enough that others have pronounced them offensive. As Sandbrook (2009, 34) warns, we are closer today than we might think to ancient Roman crowds, whose blind hatred symbolized "all that is worst in human nature." In contrast to Hewitt, who celebrates the power of the mob to chastise those who voice unpopular positions, Sandbrook considers the swarming of online mobs a danger to freedom of speech, asking whether we now prefer to live "by the will of Twitter's loudest minority." As she puts it, "we tell ourselves that in a democratic society, the will of the people is what matters—except when the people have the wrong idea" (36).

In "Cyber Civil Rights," law professor Danielle Keats Citron (2009) goes a step further, claiming that the harm inflicted by online mobs ought to be regarded as civil rights violations and addressed in the same way that similar violations by offline thugs, bullies, and supremacists are handled by the legal system. "Because destructive online mobs are unlikely to correct themselves," she writes, "a comprehensive legal response is essential to deter and redress the harm they cause" (84). Citron reviews four dangers that social scientists associate with group behaviour: the tendency of groups united by homogeneous views to become more extreme when members of the group deliberate among themselves; the loss of a sense of personal responsibility on the part of individuals acting in groups; the tendency of groups to dehumanize their victims, thereby eliminating feelings of remorse; and the increase in aggressiveness when group members sense that authority figures support their efforts (81–82). She goes on to argue that "the Internet magnifies the dangerousness of group behavior in each of these respects":

> Web 2.0 platforms create a feeling of closeness among like-minded individuals. Online groups affirm each other's negative views, which become more extreme and destructive. Individuals say and do things online they would never consider saying or doing offline because they feel anonymous, even if they write under their real names. Because group members often shroud themselves in pseudonyms, they have little fear that victims will retaliate against them or that they will suffer social stigma for their abusive conduct. Online groups also perceive their victims as "images" and thus feel free to do anything they want to them.

In short, Rowland's hopes for "a civilization that promotes and values diversity" may have been premature. However self-righteous, online mobs that organize around affect feed on themselves, in an environment that promotes disinhibition and a sense of freedom from moral responsibility.

Conclusion: The Virtues of Restriction

It is perhaps impossible to predict whether the new global environment, in which much public discourse takes place online, will tend, in the main, to lead to extreme and destructive behaviour or rather will encourage constructive civil deliberations. The limited case study discussed here cannot provide an answer to this question, but it serves to highlight some of the challenges posed to democracy by disinhibition. Today's online discourse engages more individuals in group conversations than ever before, and personal concerns formerly banished from the public sphere now have an opportunity to be considered. However, all too frequently, the disinhibition associated with online behaviour leads to anything but meaningful civil discourse, a crucial precondition of democracy.

Judging by the hundreds of comments posted in January 2007 regarding my book—a book that few people had yet had a chance to read—the online discourse has in this case been, on the whole, dull, shallow, and repetitive, reminiscent of newspapers in totalitarian regimes or of lengthy speeches by leaders in those regimes, where many words are spilled over thin substance. I found very little contemplation in these texts, and few signs of intellectual exchange: once expressed, an opinion was rarely subjected to contradictory arguments. It is as if every commentator is entitled only to one view, which is to be asserted in full confidence, and then it is someone else's turn to speak. And, of course, some of the comments were simply abusive. As one commentator on the *Globe* article usefully observed: "I just don't understand why so many people champion the blogging community as some sort of noble undertaking when in most cases all they really accomplish is to provide an anonymous forum for abusive behaviour."

Among its many contributions, the Internet has provided an outlet for much of the shallow and vulgar behaviour that exists in any society. This, in itself, would be of no importance were it not for the fact that disinhibited discourse is spilling over into traditional intellectual enterprises. Today, many writers, journalists, scholars, and other persons of letters seem to feel that in order to compete in the market of ideas, they need to abandon the inhibitions that established that market in the first place. May the above case study, despite its limited scope, serve as a reminder of the need to maintain the time-honoured restraints on intellectual conduct, without which society may sacrifice its barriers against tyranny.

Notes

1 The comments I quote were originally posted at http://www. theglobeandmail.com/technology/author-laments-lonely-life-of-bloggers/ article1069859/. Aside from the occasional bracketed emendation, I have reproduced these comments exactly as they appeared. All errors (spelling, punctuation, and so on) are therefore in the originals.

References

"Bea." 2007. "Lonely Hearts Club." *Bub and Pie* (blog). 31 January. http:// bubandpie.blogspot.com/2007/01/lonely-hearts-club.html.

Bilton, Nick. 2013. "Is the Internet a Mob Without Consequence?" *New York Times*, 24 December.

Canetti, Elias. (1962) 1991. *Crowds and Power*. Translated by Carol Stewart. New York: Noonday Press. Originally published as *Masse und Macht* (1960).

Citron, Danielle Keats. 2009. "Cyber Civil Rights." *Boston University Law Review* 89: 61–125.

"CK." 2007. "Loser." *CK's (Innovation!) Blog*, 5 February. http://www.ck-blog.com/cks_blog/2007/02/lonely_girl.html.

Donovan, G. Murphy. 2012. "The Internet and the Agora." *American Thinker*, 27 February. http://www.americanthinker.com/2010/02/the_internet_and_the_agora.html.

Drezner, Daniel W. 2009. "Public Intellectuals 2.1." *Society* 46 (1): 49–54.

Elshtain, Jean Bethke. 2001. "Why Public Intellectuals?" *Wilson Quarterly* 25 (4): 43–50.

Etzioni, Amitai. 2006. "Are Public Intellectuals an Endangered Species?" In *Public Intellectuals: An Endangered Species?* edited by Amitai Etzioni and Alyssa Bowditch, 1–27. Lanham, MD: Rowman and Littlefield.

Gardels, Nathan. 2012. "Democracy and the Smart Mob." *NPQ: New Perspectives Quarterly* 29 (2): 13–17.

Graveland, Bill. 2007. "Author Laments Lonely Life of Bloggers." *Globe and Mail*, 31 January.

Habermas, Jürgen. 1994. "Three Normative Models of Democracy." *Constellations* 1 (1): 1–10.

Hewitt, Huge 2005. *Blog: Understanding The Information Reformation That's Changing Your World*. Nashville: Nelson Books.

Hurwitz, Roger. 2003. "Who Needs Politics? Who Needs People? The Ironies of Democracy in Cyberspace." In *Democracy and New Media*, edited by Henry Jenkins and David Thorburn, 101–12. Cambridge, MA: MIT Press.

Jacoby, Russell. 1987. *The Last Intellectuals: American Culture in the Age of Academe*. New York: Basic Books.

Jennings, Jeremy, and Tony Kemp-Welch. 1997. "The Century of the Intellectual: From the Dreyfus Affair to Salman Rushdie." In *Intellectuals in Politics*, edited by Jeremy Jennings and Anthony Kemp-Welch, 1–21. London: Routledge.

Keren, Michael. 2010. "Blogging and Mass Politics." *Biography* 33.1 (Winter 2010): 110–26.

———. 2006. *Blogosphere: The New Political Arena*. Lanham, MD: Lexington.

Larson, Magali Sarfatti. 1990. "In the Matter of Experts and Professionals, or How Impossible It Is to Leave Nothing Unsaid." In *The Formation of the Professions: Knowledge, State and Strategy*, edited by Rolf Torstendahl and Michael Burrage, 24–50. London: Sage.

Lasch, Scott. 2002. *Critique of Information*. London: Sage.

Mannheim, Karl. (1936) 1968. *Ideology and Utopia: An Introduction to the Sociology of Knowledge*. Translated by Louis Wirth and Edward Shils. New York: Harcourt, Brace and World. Originally published as *Ideologie und Utopie* (1929).

Ortega y Gasset, José. 1985. *The Revolt of the Masses*. Translated by Anthony Kerrigan. Notre Dame, IN: University of Notre Dame Press. Originally published as *La rebelión de las masas* (1930).

Papacharissi, Zizi A. 2012. *A Private Sphere: Democracy in a Digital Age*. Malden, MA: Polity Press.

Park, David W. 2006. "Public Intellectuals and the Media: Integrating Media Theory into a Stalled Debate." *International Journal of Media and Cultural Politics* 2 (2): 115–29.

———. 2009. "Blogging with Authority: Strategic Positioning in Political Blogs." *International Journal of Communication* 3: 250–73.

Peters, John Durham. 1999. *Speaking Into the Air: A History of the Idea of Communication*. Chicago: University of Chicago Press.

Posner, Richard A. 2001. *Public Intellectuals: A Study of Decline*. Cambridge, MA: Harvard University Press.

Price, Vincent. 2011. "Citizens Deliberating Online: Theory and Some Evidence." In *Approaching Deliberative Democracy: Theory and Practice*, edited by Robert Cavalier, 223–32. Pittsburgh: Carnegie Mellon University Press.

Rheingold, Howard. 2002. *Smart Mobs: The Next Social Revolution*. Cambridge, MA: Persesus.

Rowland, Wade. 1999. *Spirit of the Web: The Age of Information from Telegraph to Internet*. Toronto: Key Porter Books.

Sandbrook, Dominic. 2009. "Trial by Fury." *New Statesman* (November): 34–36.

Shils, Edward. 1973. "Intellectuals, Traditions, and the Traditions of Intellectuals: Some Preliminary Considerations." In *Intellectuals and Tradition*, edited by Shmuel Noah Eisenstadt and Stephen Richards Graubard, 21–35. New York: Humanities Press.

Sreberny, Annabelle, and Gholam Khiabany. 2007. "Becoming Intellectual: The Blogestan and Public Political Space in the Islamic Republic." *British Journal of Middle Eastern Studies* 34 (3): 267–86.

Suler, John. 2004. "The Online Disinhibition Effect." *CyberPsychology and Behavior* 7 (3): 321–26.

Talmon, Jacob L. (1952) 1970. *The Origins of Totalitarian Democracy*. New York: W. W. Norton.

Wadhwa, Tarun. 2013. "Justine Sacco, Internet Justice, and the Dangers of a Righteous Mob." *Forbes*, 23 December.

Contributors

Barry Cooper, a fourth-generation Albertan, was educated at Shawnigan Lake School, the University of British Columbia, and Duke University, where he received his doctorate in 1969. He taught at Bishop's University, at McGill, and at York University before coming to the University of Calgary in 1981. Much of his teaching has focused on Greek political philosophy, whereas his publications have been chiefly in the area of contemporary French and German political philosophy. Cooper's other area of continuing interest has been Canadian politics and public policy. Here he has brought the insights of political philosophers to bear on contemporary issues, including the place of technology and the media in Canada, the ongoing debate over the constitutional status of Québec, and Canadian defence and security policy. He is the author, editor, or translator of thirty books and has published over 150 papers and book chapters. He writes a regular column for the *Calgary Herald*.

Jacob G. Foster is an assistant professor in the Department of Sociology at UCLA. He studies the birth, life, and death of ideas. After studying mathematical physics at Oxford as a Rhodes Scholar, he received his PhD in physics from the University of Calgary in 2010 and was a postdoctoral scholar in the Department of Sociology at the University of Chicago from 2010–2013. He blends network analysis, complex systems thinking, and computational modeling with the qualitative insights of the science studies literature to probe the strategies, dispositions, and social processes that shape the production and persistence of scientific ideas. He also develops formal models of the evolutionary dynamics of ideas and institutions.

Fundamentally, he aims to understand the social world as constituted by, and constitutive of, ideas, beliefs, and practices. His approach is strongly informed by research on complex systems and biological and cultural evolution. His work has appeared in journals like *Science, Proceedings of the National Academy of Sciences, Sociological Science, Social Networks*, and *American Sociological Review*.

Richard Hawkins is a political economist specializing in information and communication technology policy. He holds BA and MA degrees from Simon Fraser University and a DPhil from the University of Sussex (UK). Before coming to the University of Calgary, Hawkins was leader of the Network Economy Programme at the Netherlands Organisation for Applied Scientific Research (TNO) and senior consultant to the TNO Society, Technology and Innovation Programme. In addition to academic work, Hawkins has extensive international experience as a policy consultant and advisor. Clients have included the European Commission, the OECD, the World Bank, the UK Department of Trade and Industry, the Dutch Ministry of Economic Affairs, the European Science and Technology Observatory, the European Committee for Standardisation (CEN), the UK Office of Science and Technology, the International Labour Organisation, the Italian Communications Regulatory Authority, the London Metropolitan Police Service, and the British Standards Institution.

Karim-Aly Kassam is international associate professor of environmental and indigenous studies at Cornell University. He is also associate editor of the journal *Action Research* and a member of the board of the International Society of Ethnobiology. He holds a PhD in natural resource policy and management from Cornell University, an MSc in social policy and planning in developing countries from the London School of Economics, an MPhil in Islamic studies from the University of Cambridge, and a BA in economics from the University of Calgary. Kassam's objective is to seamlessly merge teaching with applied research in the service of communities. His research focuses on the complex connectivity of human and environmental relations, addressing indigenous ways of knowing, food sovereignty, sustainable livelihoods, and climate change. This research is conducted in partnership with indigenous communities.

Michael Keren is a professor and Canada Research Chair in the Department of Political Science and the Department of Communication, Media, and Film at the University of Calgary. He is the author of several books on public intellectuals, including *Ben-Gurion and the Intellectuals: Power, Knowledge and Charisma*, *The Pen and the Sword: Israeli Intellectuals and the Making of the Nation State*, and *Professionals Against Populism: The Peres Government and Democracy*.

Boaz Miller is a Postdoctoral Fellow at the Hebrew University of Jerusalem Sidney M. Edelstein Center for History and Philosophy of Science, Technology and Medicine, and a Teaching Fellow at the Bar Ilan University Graduate Program in Science, Technology and Society. He works in social epistemology. His most recent paper, forthcoming in *The Philosophical Quarterly*, is "Why (Some) Knowledge is The Property of a Community and Possibly None of its Members."

Liz Pirnie is a doctoral candidate in the Department of Communication, Media, and Film at the University of Calgary. Her current research examines the securitization of citizenship in Canada and its relationship to discourses on Canadian identity and foreign policy. She is particularly interested in the contingent and transformative conditions under which the allocation and rights of citizenship become the object of state and public scrutiny.

Eleanor Townsley is professor in the Department of Sociology, and serves as the associate dean of Faculty at Mount Holyoke College. She is interested in the role of intellectuals and ideas in social change. Her current research examines the nature and influence of media intellectuals in the contemporary United States, most recently in her book with Ron Jacobs, *The Space of Opinion: Media Intellectuals and the Public Sphere* (2011).

Index

Gore, Al, 49–50, 113, 168, 170
Grant, George, 171
Gzowski, Peter, 164

Habermas, Jürgen, 5, 64, 158, 186
hacktivism, 10, 92, 97, 99–100, 103, 108
Hannity, Sean, 45
Hanrahan, Nancy W., 87n8
Harding, Sandra, 122, 127
Harper, Stephen, 114, 123, 167–68, 170, 172n2, 174–76
Havel, Václav, 2, 176
Hawking, Stephen, 29, 37n2
Hayek, Friedrich, 74, 172n1
hegemony of ideas, 12, 92–94, 108, 119–20
Heidegger, Martin, 157
Heilbroner, Robert L., 4
Helbing, Dirk, 77
Hemingway, Ernest, 161
Hewitt, Hugh, 190, 192
hierarchy, 32, 80, 85, 158
Hindman, Matthew, 79
Hitchens, Christopher, 161–62, 169
Hitler, Adolf, 157
hive mind, 70, 72, 103
Holton, Gerald J., 24
Horkheimer, Max, 5
Hudson, Alan, 92
human ecology, 10, 134, 153
Huizinga, Johan, 162

Illouz, Eva, 97
indigenous communities, 134, 143–44, 149
indigenous knowledge, 9, 73, 100, 138, 140, 143
inhibition, 176, 181, 186–88, 193–94
Institute for Sustainable Energy, Environment, and Economy (ISEEE), 170, 172

intellectual(s). See public intellectual(s)
intelligence, 9, 69–75, 77–84, 86, 89, 140–42, 151–52
Intergovernmental Panel on Climate Change (IPCC), 115, 117, 123, 125–26, 168–70
Internet Relay Chat. See Anonymous
IPCC. See Intergovernmental Panel on Climate Change
ISEEE. See Institute for Sustainable Energy, Environment, and Economy

Jacoby, Russell, 161, 175–76
Jacobs, Ron, 43, 51
James, William, 80, 82–84, 86n5, 87n9
Jennings, Jeremy, 176
Jervis, Robert, 141
Jobs, Steve, 28–29
Jordan, Tim, 99
Juneau, Pierre, 164–65

Kahn, Herman, 163
Kahneman, Daniel, 75
Kant, Immanuel, 161
Kasparov, Garry, 72
Kellner, Douglas, 94
Kemp-Welch, Tony, 176
Khiabany, Gholam, 178
Kierkegaard, Søren, 10, 94–95, 106–7, 109–10
Klein, Naomi, 50
Knopff, Rainer, 172n2
Kojève, Alexandre, 157
Krugman, Paul, 29, 36n2, 70
Krush, Irina, 83
Kuhn, Thomas, 122, 139
Kyoto Protocol, 114, 165–66, 169

A SOCIAL HISTORY OF
THE EARLY CHURCH